Praise for *Can Two Rights Make a Wrong?*

"This is the book for people who never get past page two of a management book—it is as close as the genre comes to being a compulsive page turner. Its main thesis is built on at least three big ideas that are individually persuasive and cumulatively compelling. They naturally fit into an alignment tool that is applied to the range of day-to-day and exceptional challenges all enterprises face, including the Holy Grail of transformational change."

—Donald Macrae, general counsel and chief knowledge officer, Department for Environment, Food and Rural Affairs, England

"Having been in the business of cultural transformation and alignment for many years, I've carefully looked for a thoughtful strategy and an intentional approach to bringing about healthy and thriving cultures. *Can Two Rights Make a Wrong?* is simply the best—it is the most thoughtful and practical work I've seen in this growing and critical area. This is a must buy!"

—Dr. Ron Jenson, Future Achievement International, international author, speaker, and consulting and executive coach

"*Can Two Rights Make a Wrong?* is a superb account of how to manage the 'soft side' of mergers and acquisitions, but it has great value for managing many other new business practices as well, such as Open Innovation. It provides a powerful, practical method to identify conflicts, develop alignment, and achieve effective coordination between two parties that would be tremendously helpful in a variety of collaborative contexts, such as alliances, research partnerships, or joint ventures. Moulton Reger and her colleagues at IBM should be congratulated for a thoughtful, insightful book."

—Henry Chesbrough, professor at University of California Berkeley's Haas School of Business, author of Open Innovation

"Numbers are neat and clean. Human beings are often messy and complex. If everyone in your organization knew what to do and when, how, where, and—most importantly—why to do it, how would your organizational culture be defined? The authors of *Can Two Rights Make a Wrong?* have introduced new ways to proactively address culture and, most importantly, tie it to bottom-line benefits."

—James H. Amos, Jr., chairman emeritus, MBE/The UPS Store

"This book is a must read for leaders hoping to change their organization's culture as well as those attempting to merge firms with uniquely different cultures. Moulton Reger's insights are grounded in theory and real-world experience. In this unique book, culture change is a complex concept broken down into bite-sized pieces and presented in a way that any leadership team can embrace at its own pace."

—Merrill J. Oster, author of Vision Driven Leadership,
founder Oster Communications, Inc.

"Here at last is a business book that takes culture seriously and isn't intimidated by it. The method described can be used with practically any type of business problem in any industry, and the book does an excellent job of drawing on research and theory while keeping the focus practical. The three elements of Outcome Narratives, Right vs. Right, and Business Practices are significant ideas in their own right—each is a unique insight. All three ideas have been around in various guises for several years, but have not been as well crystallized or as focused on complex business problems as they are in this book. The authors' achievement is extraordinary and goes a long way toward making the juicy idea of culture something to be built on and worked with."

—Peter Vaill, professor, Antioch University

"The Achilles heel for any major organizational change is that organization's culture. In every change, consultants talk about culture, but few provide specific sequential steps designed to actually do anything about it. This book provides such steps, and provides them in ways that makes sense. 'Makes sense' is the key because the steps provided can be easily adapted to virtually any organization, large or small."

—George Falldine, Air Force civil servant,
Air Force Materiel Command

"Sara Moulton Reger is one of the premier organizational design consultants in the country, and this book reflects her in-depth knowledge of and experience with the subject matter. This book is essential reading for those striving to achieve greater results from ongoing change initiatives. *Can Two Rights Make a Wrong?* contains a broad range of concepts, examples, and specific steps culled from Moulton Reger's direct experience. Such a complete presentation of strategic and tactical advice makes *Can Two Rights Make a Wrong?* a mandatory addition to every manager's bookshelf."

—Steven Bragg, CPA, author of twenty-eight business
books, CFO of Premier Data Services

"This is a serious book that gives intelligent guidance to anyone who leads an organization and takes creating and managing culture seriously. The section on Outcome Narratives is the best 'how to' on casting a unifying vision that I have seen. If you're a leader and take your role in creating and managing corporate culture seriously, then you should read this book."

−Regi Campbell, principal, Seedsower Investments,
author of About my Father's Business

"I don't read most 'culture change' books—waste of time. This book is different. *Can Two Rights Make a Wrong?* combines both soft and hard approaches, with a continuous focus on how-to and results. Buy it. But, more importantly, read it."

−Jack Grayson, founder and chairman, American
Productivity and Quality Center (APQC)

"We used Right vs. Right to help integrate an important acquisition—one that brought many differences we needed to carefully leverage to achieve IBM's business objectives. I found it to be a powerful technique for quickly reconciling strategic views of the business model and different operating preferences. Now, a few months later, we have the business results—and employee satisfaction—to prove Right vs. Right works."

−Jim Corgel, general manager, Small and Medium
Business Services, IBM

"Leaders wouldn't think about doing a major project without a plan and a project manager, but how many consider the cultural implications? This book fills a key void because it clarifies the topic of culture so that it is easier to understand, and includes examples for applying the framework to many types of situations, including business-to-business alliances and cross-geography teams."

−Cindy Berger, vice president, American Express

"There is no question that the biggest hurdle to achieving a successful merger is culture. Market opportunities may be staggering and synergies may seem perfect, but, without a cultural match, odds are the merged company will struggle. *Can Two Rights Make a Wrong?* can help you avoid the problems. Even if you are not contemplating a merger, Moulton Reger's deep insight provides an excellent management primer and interesting historical perspective. A worthwhile read."

−John R. Patrick, author of Net Attitude,
president of Attitude LLC

"This is an excellent book that provides a pragmatic approach to identifying and alleviating cultural issues created when two groups of people must work together. Effectively blending business cultures is a key requirement for successful outsourcing, and most companies lack the tools necessary to do this. Companies looking to reduce outsourcing risk should follow IBM's *Tangible Culture* approach."

—*Lance Travis, vice president, Outsourcing Strategies, AMR Research*

"This book will help leaders and cultural-change practitioners take a practical, well-architected approach to creating the culture they need to support their strategies. Thanks, IBM, for sharing what you have learned from your own transformation."

—*Valerie Norton, vice president, Talent Management and Organizational Effectiveness, Merck & Co., Inc.*

"Based on IBM's own experience with organizational transformation and mergers, this book belongs on the reading list of any executive contemplating major changes to their business."

— *Peter Richerson, professor, University of California Davis*

"Finally, a book that goes beyond just declaring 'it's the culture change' and gets to a real recount of why and *how* to move on that need. This is a practical approach for senior leaders in large corporations and government to address the most pressing issues in modern business life!"

—*Kenneth I. Percell, executive director, Warner Robins Air Logistic Center*

"I like the way the authors move the idea of organization culture from intangible (values) to tangible and practical. They offer that culture can be viewed and changed by examining and discussing what people *do*. Using the techniques described in *Can Two Rights Make a Wrong?* will demystify culture clash."

—*Lynda Aiman-Smith, Ph.D., North Carolina State University*

"A must read for leaders charged with planning and executing major change initiatives involving a single organization or multiple organizations. The book is original, thoughtful, thorough, and pragmatic. The elements of *Can Two Rights Make a Wrong?* and their interrelationships that work to drive successful change are particularly beneficial. The authors demonstrate a hands-on grasp of this important subject and the related literature. The material is presented in a concise, easy-to-understand format, with lots of tables, charts, and illustrations to help guide the reader."

—*Stephen W. Brown, Edward M. Carson chair in services marketing, professor and executive director, Center for Services Leadership, W. P. Carey School of Business, Arizona State University*

"Many have observed that mergers and acquisitions will fail to achieve their goals without proper attention to human and cultural factors, but few have shown us the way to manage these factors in any meaningful way. This book takes up that challenge and delivers a real solution by identifying business practices as the crucial element of 'culture' that can make or break a merger or acquisition, and by providing a hands-on methodology for managing and aligning differences across cultures."

—*Marietta Baba, dean of the College of Social Science, professor of Anthropology, Michigan State University*

"Sara Moulton Reger's application of Business Practices, Right-vs. Right, and Outcome Narratives to business transformation spoke directly to my own business experience. I found the book's comprehensive approach very appealing. It brought together the story of a historic merger; a review of traditional approaches to culture transformation in business organizations; the powerful new techniques of Outcome Narratives, Right vs. Right, and Business Practices Alignment; and useful examples of the way to apply these techniques."

—*Dwight E. Collins, Ph.D., adjunct professor, Presidio School of Management, sustainable business and supply chain optimization consultant, president, Collins Family Foundation*

"We know unsuccessful mergers and acquisitions are often the result of underestimating the people and the cultural issues. Derived from experience, here is practical help in improving your chances of being one of the success stories."

—*David Hope, human resources director, Norwich Union Insurance*

"This is state-of the-art. This practical approach is extremely useful for anyone involved in integrating two large organizations, especially professional organizations. I found the book *Can Two Rights Make a Wrong?* fascinating—excellently describing the preparation and process that is required in integrating culturally different organizations."

—*Fred WI Lachotzki, professor of business policy, Nyenrode University, coauthor of Beyond Control: Managing Strategic Alignment through Corporate Dialogue*

Register Your Book
at www.ibmpressbooks.com/ibmregister

Upon registration, we will send you electronic sample chapters from two of our popular IBM Press books. In addition, you will be automatically entered into a monthly drawing for a free IBM Press book.

Registration also entitles you to:

- Notices and reminders about author appearances, conferences, and online chats with special guests
- Access to supplemental material that may be available
- Advance notice of forthcoming editions
- Related book recommendations
- Information about special contests and promotions throughout the year
- Chapter excerpts and supplements of forthcoming books

Contact us

If you are interested in writing a book or reviewing manuscripts prior to publication, please write to us at:

Editorial Director, IBM Press
c/o Pearson Education
One Lake Street
Upper Saddle River, New Jersey 07458

e-mail: IBMPress@pearsoned.com

Visit us on the Web: www.ibmpressbooks.com

Can Two Rights Make a Wrong?

Can Two Rights Make a Wrong?

Insights from IBM's Tangible Culture Approach

Sara J. Moulton Reger

With Contributors from IBM Business Consulting
Services, Research, and Institute for Business Value

IBM Press
Pearson plc

Upper Saddle River, NJ • New York • San Francisco
Toronto • London • Munich • Paris • Madrid
Cape Town • Sydney • Tokyo • Singapore • Mexico City

www.ibmpressbooks.com

IBM Press Program Manager: Tara Woodman, Ellice Uffer
IBM Press Consulting Editor: Jennifer Kemp
Cover design: IBM Corporation
Published by Pearson plc
Publishing as IBM Press

IBM Press offers excellent discounts on this book when ordered in quantity for bulk purchases or special sales, which may include electronic versions and/or custom covers and content particular to your business, training goals, marketing focus, and branding interests. For more information, please contact:

U. S. Corporate and Government Sales
1-800-382-3419
corpsales@pearsontechgroup.com.
For sales outside the U. S., please contact:
International Sales
international@pearsoned.com.

 This Book Is Safari Enabled

The Safari Enabled icon on the cover of your favorite technology book means the book is available through Safari Bookshelf. When you buy this book, you get free access to the online edition for 45 days. Safari Bookshelf is an electronic reference library that lets you easily search thousands of technical books, find code samples, download chapters, and access technical information whenever and wherever you need it.

To gain 45-day Safari Enabled access to this book:

- Go to http://www.awprofessional.com/safarienabled
- Complete the brief registration form
- Enter the coupon code J9L7-GTIM-TXDB-NHM5-XKRX

If you have difficulty registering on Safari Bookshelf or accessing the online edition, please e-mail customer-service@safaribooksonline.com.

Pearson Education, Inc.
Rights and Contracts Department
One Lake Street
Upper Saddle River, NJ 07458
Published in association with the literary agency of Sanford Communications, Inc., 6406 NE Pacific St., Portland, OR 97213.

ISBN 0-13-173294-3
Text printed in the United States on recycled paper at R.R. Donnelley and Sons in Crawfordsville, Indiana.
First printing, March 2006

Library of Congress Cataloging-in-Publication Data

Moulton Reger, Sara J.
    Can two rights make a wrong? : insights from IBM's tangible culture approach / Sara J. Moulton Reger ; with contributors from IBM Research, Business Consulting Services, and Institute for Business Value.
        p. cm.
    ISBN 0-13-173294-3 (hardback : alk. paper) 1. International Business Machines Corporation. 2. Corporate culture. 3. Consolidation and merger of corporations. I. IBM Research. II. IBM Business Consulting Services. III. Institute for Business Value. IV. Title.
    HD58.7.M688 2005
    658.4'06—dc22

                            2005034820

To Hal and Ora Moulton for giving me a lifetime of encouragement.

Contents

xviii

Can Two Rights Make a Wrong?
Insights from IBM's Tangible Culture Approach

xx

Can Two Rights Make a Wrong?
Insights from IBM's Tangible Culture Approach

Foreword

Pardon my cynicism, but at this point in my life, the last thing I expect from a publication on organizational culture is to be impressed. Sure, I anticipate a few nuggets of useful information or I wouldn't bother to open a book at all, but I've learned it is best to keep my expectations low when browsing this genre. My skepticism is not so much an indictment of the authors who brave these deep waters as much as a recognition that this stone has been turned many times with little new to show for it in recent years, aside from a few notable exceptions.

Also, when I first received this particular manuscript for review, I thought the authors were asking for trouble because of the title they had chosen. With *Tangible Culture* on the cover, I was sure their collective necks were stuck out dangerously far. First, there is a claim associated with a tag like this. It implies a promise to help the reader grasp organizational culture as something other than the amorphous, nebulous enigma it has been throughout most leaders' careers. In addition, to live up to the headline hype, not only must the concept of culture come across as grounded and concrete, but the writing must also be relevant to the real world. To stand up against the title's portend, the book must come across to the reader as accessible, explicit, and substantive; but beyond that, it must be germane to the accelerated pace and advanced sophistication leaders contend with every day.

I thought the topic and the choice of title put the authors at risk, but, on the other hand, I knew that if they could carry through on their assertion, there was an eager readership waiting for the next meaningful advance in understanding this convoluted subject. Meeting either of the implied undertakings the title suggests (making culture discernible and

xxii

Can Two Rights Make a Wrong?
Insights from IBM's Tangible Culture Approach

making the reading of it palpable) would justify the reader's investment, but accomplishing them together would make this book a welcome relief from the many others on the same subject that have more insight and significance in their dust jacket's description than in their actual contents. I'm happy to declare that the authors have delivered on both.

Sara Moulton Reger and her associates have taken some important steps toward uncloaking the mystery that has surrounded corporate culture since it was first recognized as a key variable in organizational transformation. *Tangible Culture* offers the following:

- Solid conceptual support for the positions it advocates
- Easy-to-understand approaches, techniques, and application stories

The combination is what brings the title's promise of something "tangible" into focus.

Assuming that changing corporate culture is of more than a passing interest to you and that you are or soon will be involved in orchestrating a significant cultural shift for your organization (or one you are serving), I predict you will want to keep this book close by when it's time to produce measurable results.

Daryl Conner
Author of the best-selling books *Managing at the Speed of Change* and *Leading at the Edge of Chaos*

Preface

All of us experience them—those significant opportunities disguised as "what do we do now?" moments. They're the chance to push the envelope, learn new lessons, and (for those of us who like to talk), gather great stories to tell and retell. This book is about one such moment—IBM's $3.5 billion acquisition of PricewaterhouseCoopers Consulting. But more important, it is about what we learned and how it expanded our capabilities in handling business culture challenges. We call these capabilities, and this book *Tangible Culture*.

Tangible Culture is written for business people. It is a step forward in demystifying the topic of business culture—making it more workable. It also provides new ways to think about culture and act on it.

We tell you what we did and what happened, and then give you examples and work steps of how to apply this learning to your own situations. Whether you are facing a merger or acquisition—like we were—an alliance, major transformation, or restructuring—or if you just want to know whether you are hiring the right people, making the best strategy decision, or ready to launch your vision or project—you will find some new thinking and new techniques here.

Specifically, you will find an actionable surrogate for the vast topic of culture—one that business people readily identify with, and agree is important and not simply "soft and squishy." You will also find out how two rights *can* make a wrong—often the basis for culture clash—and what you can do about it. And you will learn a technique for clarifying expectations in a way that people will really "get" it—and do it. And best of all, each of these insights and techniques can be added to what you are already doing. You do not need to unlearn anything you already know about dealing with culture requirements.

And, because business people have limited time, we have organized the materials so that you will not have to read the entire book to get benefit. There are signposts to help you choose how to read it and gain exactly the help you need.

Tangible Culture is written in three sections. The first details our learning—every step along the way of developing this new approach to culture transformation and integration. The second section shows you how to apply the approach to a series of initiatives where culture is important. Finally, you will see how some have applied the concepts creatively to their own efforts.

All in all, we truly hope that you find new ways to address culture proactively—taking it from a risk to competitive advantage.

Acknowledgments

As with any effort of this kind, there are so many people whose help has been invaluable. All of the authors are especially indebted to the following people, and we want to recognize them specifically and express our sincere gratitude:

Kathleen Addis	Loretta Dunn	Abby Lewis
Matt Berry	Erika Flint	Hal Moulton
Ed Bevan	Heather Fox	David Sanford
Doug Cameron	Carol Graser	Chris Steel
Andrew Carlyle	Bernard Goodwin	Ellice Uffer
Johnny Colino	Christy Hackerd	Robin Williams
Louis Columbus	Mark Harris	Tara Woodman
Jay Comi	Jenny Hunter	Karen Young
Lisa Costantino	Jennifer Kemp	
Mark Dean	Toby Lehman	

And I (Sara Moulton Reger) am especially grateful to each of the contributing authors, sidebar contributors, Daryl Conner, and those who provided quotes and testimonials for lending their expertise. I also want to thank my wonderful husband, Stephen Reger, for all the support and prayers he provided throughout this project.

And we are thankful to you, too, for reading this book. We truly hope that *Tangible Culture* brings great value to you in your business endeavors.

About the Author

Sara Moulton Reger began the journey of writing *Can Two Rights Make a Wrong?* as the practice executive responsible for IBM's Organization Design and Change Management practice. From this leadership position in Strategy and Change Consulting, she was asked to help lead the "people" workstreams for integrating the Pricewaterhouse-Coopers Consulting acquisition beginning in mid-2002. After completing the integration work, she was asked to join IBM's Almaden Services Research group as one of the first consulting subject matter experts to do a rotation within IBM Research. Her charter has been to hone the integration experiences, develop and publish other thought leadership (her secondary area of focus is the concept of Needless Complexity), and help initiate IBM's new services sciences management and engineering research area. During her time in Research, she has helped a number of IBM clients and internal organizations adopt the learnings reflected in this book.

Sara has been a management consultant since 1988, specializing in business transformation, organizational change, culture transformation, and governance both at IBM and other leading consulting firms. Sara is a Certified Management Accountant, and before becoming a consultant, she held financial leadership roles. Sara has a bachelor's degree in business administration and an MBA concentrated in finance and management. She also received the Certified Level III Organizational Change Management expert designation from Ernst & Young in 1993. Sara is the primary inventor on the IBM method patent application "Business Practices Alignment Methods," upon which *Tangible Culture* is based. Sara has published on a variety of topics, including business culture, business complexity, On Demand Business, governance, e-business, communications, project risk management, change management, quality, and financial management.

Sara lives in Scottsdale, Arizona with her husband Stephen and their two Keeshond dogs, Doodle and Racee. She is active in her Christian church, and enjoys exploring and photographing the southwest landscape and ancient Native American dwelling sites. You may contact her at www.tangibleculture.com.

Contributing Authors

IBM Business Consulting Services

Michael Armano
Barbarajo Bliss
Susan Blum
Andrew Duncan
Ron Frank
Cheryl Grise
Anthony W. Harris
Dave Lubowe
Michael Lueck
Patrick N. McDonnell
Len Nanjad
Kristin Pederson
Mary Sue Rogers
Lynn Schuster
Kristin von Donop

IBM Research

Jeanette Blomberg
Melissa Cefkin
Lisa D. Kreeger
Jeff Kreulen
Paul Maglio
Doug McDavid
Dean Spitzer
Jim Spohrer
Ray Strong
Jennifer Q. Trelewicz

IBM Institute for Business Value

Eric Lesser
George Pohle

For more about each contributing author, please see "About the Contributors" in the back of this book.

The Basics

S ection I, "The Basics," gives you an opportunity to learn the concepts and techniques of *Tangible Culture*. It provides core understanding for applying the concepts in Section II, "The Application," and Section III, "The Projects."

I

Introduction— An Overview of *Tangible Culture*

By Sara Moulton Reger, Barbarajo Bliss,
Jeanette Blomberg, Sue Blum, Lisa Kreeger
and Kris Pederson

Chapter Contents

4

Can Two Rights Make a Wrong?
Insights from IBM's Tangible Culture Approach

Overview

This chapter provides an overview of the book, which we refer to as *Tangible Culture*. It describes the importance of culture to business, and briefly covers the key topic areas of *Tangible Culture* and the structure of the book. Readers familiar with the topic of culture may want to skim through the general materials in the middle of the chapter.

Will You Find Value in This Book?

Rather than risk wasting your time, we are going to be really candid: If you are looking for a silver bullet for fixing your organization's culture issues, you will be disappointed with this book. However, if you are open to some new ways of thinking about culture, and some new approaches to dealing with it, we have something for you.

If you nod as you read these questions, we believe you will find value in *Tangible Culture*:

- Have you ever made changes to processes, procedures, measures, incentives, and so on, but failed to see the desired improvement in performance?
- Have you ever taken action to address some cultural issues, but felt disappointed with the results—or perceived the actions as "soft and squishy, feel good"?
- Are you looking for practical business approaches to address your cultural issues—ones you can do without being reliant on culture experts?

Tangible Culture is written for business people, not for consultants or experts in the topic of culture. Of course, we hope the experts find value, too, but our purpose is to help business leaders and members of their organizations. We believe that you will find value because we have found value—and are continuing to find even more by using the concepts and techniques in this book.

Please do not let the size of this book deter you. We suggest you *not* read it straight through. Instead, we guide you through it, beginning with an understanding of the overall concepts. Then we help you use this book as a reference to address situations where culture is relevant. Our hope is that you will come back to this book again and again, and that our conversational style will feel like we are chatting with you about your business requirements and how *Tangible Culture* can help you with them.

Why Did IBM Decide to Write This Book?

Tangible Culture represents some new thinking and approaches IBM developed while integrating its $3.5 billion PricewaterhouseCoopers Consulting (PwCC) acquisition. We used the approaches on that effort, and later honed them in IBM Research into what you see today. The underlying concepts and method were filed for patent protection in 2004 by co-inventors Sara Moulton Reger and Mike Armano; however, we think more can be gained by sharing these concepts than by jealously guarding them.

Tangible Culture is new, yet ready to use. We say it is "proving" rather than "proven," and we call this stage of development "launch and learn." We are launching our current knowledge—and we know from experience that we will learn even more by doing so.

Since 2002, we have used these techniques in IBM and have gained benefits. First, we have new terminology to communicate more effectively. Second, we have new lenses to better understand our cultural challenges and how to address them. Third, we are better able to clarify expectations (important with our large, global employee population and with the increasingly complex business environment). Fourth, we can now go beyond the obvious and see the subtle misalignments that will impede progress if not addressed. Finally, we can now objectively evaluate progress on our culture-change efforts despite the fact that it is a highly intangible area. This has been valuable for IBM—and we want to share it.

In sharing this new knowledge, we expect mutual benefits. Certainly, we believe that readers will benefit from new approaches to difficult culture challenges. And IBM hopes that *Tangible Culture* demonstrates that IBM is much more than a technology expert. We understand business issues well—in fact, we need to navigate complex, global ones ourselves as well as help clients with them. Finally, we hope that readers will share their insights and experiences in using these materials so that we can learn from them.

Is Culture Really *That* Important?

Culture is frequently mentioned in business settings and, in our experience, it comes up most readily when it is viewed as a hindrance rather than a help. The authors believe that culture is an important business topic, but we are admittedly biased. So let's look at what other business and thought leaders say about it.

John Kotter, Konosuke Matsushita professor of leadership at Harvard Business School:

> *Culture is powerful for three primary reasons: 1) Because individuals are selected and indoctrinated so well. 2) Because the culture exerts itself through the actions of hundreds or thousands of people. 3) Because all of this happens without much conscious intent and thus is difficult to challenge or even discuss. Consultants, industrial salespeople, and others who regularly see firms up close without being employees know well how much culture operates outside of people's awareness, even rather visibly unusual aspects of a culture.*

Tom Davenport, academic director of the process management research at Babson College and Accenture fellow (formerly with Towers Perrin):

> *Think of culture as the DNA of an organization—invisible to the naked eye, but critical in shaping the character of the workplace.*

Larry Bossidy, retired chairman and CEO of Honeywell International, and Ram Charan, business advisor, speaker, and author:

> *When a business isn't going well, its leaders often think about how to change the corporate culture. They're right to recognize that the "soft" stuff—people's beliefs and behaviors—is at least as important as hard stuff, such as organizational structure, if not more so. Making changes in strategy or structure by itself takes a company only so far. The hardware of a computer is useless without the right software. Similarly, in an organization the hardware (strategy and structure) is inert without the software (beliefs and behaviors).*

Kim Cameron, professor of management and organizations, Michigan Business School (formerly with Brigham Young University), and Robert Quinn, Margaret Elliott Tracy collegiate professor in business administration and professor of management and organizations, Michigan School of Business:

> ... *successful companies have developed something special that supersedes corporate strategy, market presence, or technological advantages. Although strategy, market presence, and technology are clearly important, highly successful firms have capitalized on the power that resides in developing and managing a unique corporate culture.*

Terrence Deal, Irving R. Melbo professor at the University of Southern California, and Allan Kennedy, writer and management consultant:

> *Understanding the culture can help senior executives pinpoint why their company is succeeding or failing. Understanding how to build and manage the culture can help the same executives make a mark on their company that lasts for decades.*

Dave Ulrich, professor of business administration at University of Michigan, Steve Kerr, chief learning officer and managing director at Goldman Sachs, and Ron Ashkenas, managing partner of Robert H. Schaffer & Associates:

> *Investors have recently recognized the importance of intangibles that reflect the market value of a firm above or beyond its expected market value given cash flows or earnings. Culture and its derivatives (employee commitment and competence) become intangibles when they lead to investor confidence in the firm's future growth. Cultures can also become negative intangibles when the investor perception shifts....*

Jack Welch, former CEO of General Electric (describing GE when he took the CEO position in 1981):

> *To be a winner, we had to couple the "hard" central idea of being No. 1 or No. 2 in growth markets with intangible "soft" values to get the "feel" that would define our new culture.*

8

Can Two Rights Make a Wrong?
Insights from IBM's Tangible Culture Approach

Sam Palmisano, CEO, IBM:

In the long term, I think, whether or not you have a value-driven culture is what makes you a winner or a loser.

Lou Gerstner, Former CEO, IBM:

Until I came to IBM, I probably would have told you that culture was just one among several important elements in any organization's makeup and success—along with vision, strategy, marketing, financials, and the like.... I came to see, in my time at IBM, that culture isn't just one aspect of the game—it is the game.... You've probably found, as I have, that most companies say their cultures are about the same things—outstanding customer service, excellence, teamwork, shareholder value, responsible corporate behavior, and integrity. But, of course, these kinds of values don't necessarily translate into the same kind of behavior in all companies—how people actually go about their work, how they interact with one another, what motivates them. That's because, as with national cultures, most of the really important rules aren't written down anywhere.

This last quote describes what this book is about: how people perform their work in response to the unwritten rules—which are often informal, tacit, and difficult to articulate. *Tangible Culture* provides ways to make these rules visible and workable—and, well, tangible. And we offer up the concept of Business Practices as a respectable surrogate definition for culture, as you will see later in this chapter.

To bolster the importance of culture identified above, there are many studies that point to culture as a frequent barrier to business efforts. Here are a few:

- A study of 156 bank mergers and acquisitions cited overlooking cultural differences as the first reason for failure. "If banks spent half as much time on 'organizational' due diligence as they do on the traditional kind, the number of deals would probably drop, but the success rate would rise." (Wall)
- In an ATKearney study of 115 mergers from 1993 to 1996, 58 percent destroyed business value, and culture was cited as a top barrier to integration.

- In a survey of reasons for alliance failure, 69 percent of respondents listed clashes of corporate culture as one of the leading causes. (Corporate Executive Board)

- A cross-industry study of companies engaged in multiple alliances reported that the most common cause for alliance failure was "inability of partner organizations to work together." (Ertel, Weiss, and Visioni)

- The GLOBE (Global Leadership & Organizational Behavior Effectiveness) Study of 62 societies, with more than 17,000 participants, confirmed that cultural barriers—or more specifically, the lack of cultural literacy—are impediments to global leadership. (House, Hanges, Javidan, Dorman, and Gupta)

After reviewing a number of relevant studies, Carleton and Lineberry dubbed culture clash as "undeniably the primary causal factor in the failure of mergers and acquisitions and strategic alliances."

Given these studies, culture is an easy target to blame when things are not going well. In fact, the Corporate Executive Board states in their list of alliance myths, "Executives attribute the majority of alliance failures to unavoidable cultural mismatch between partners, believing that the alliance was 'doomed from the start.'"

We agree with the Board that culture is sometimes unduly blamed. We also agree that the issue is not whether cultural gaps exist, but rather what should be done to address them. *Tangible Culture* helps business leaders take this kind of proactive approach: Because culture is likely to be an issue, what can be done and when should we start?

What Happens If Culture Is Not Addressed?

Companies face a number of issues when culture challenges are not addressed:

- **Increased costs and decreased productivity**—From a variety of sources, including delays, strife, rework, overturned decisions, and the duplication often allowed to exist in response to unresolved disagreements

- **Lost revenues and competitive risks**—From inconsistencies and increased internal focus

Can Two Rights Make a Wrong?
Insights from IBM's Tangible Culture Approach

10

- **Staff issues**—From increased resistance, decreased morale, and potential loss of key personnel ("This is really frustrating, and that grass sure looks greener....")
- **ROI shortfalls**—From slower results, higher costs, and/or lower productivity and revenues

In short: more risk and fewer results. Certainly, these issues erode business value, and this is what we want to address with *Tangible Culture*. We hope to help you avoid some costly problems, and give you techniques for dealing with ones you cannot avoid.

What Makes This Approach to Culture Tangible?

Edgar Schein produced a robust set of culture categories in his book *Organizational Culture and Leadership*. It is terrific, so we got permission to reproduce it in Table 1-1.

Table 1-1 Various Categories Used to Describe Culture from Schein's *Organizational Culture and Leadership*[1]

Observed behavioral regularities when people interact: the language they use, the customs and traditions that evolve, and the rituals they employ in a wide variety of situations (Goffman, 1959, 1967; Jones, Moore, and Snyder, 1988; Trice and Beyer, 1993, 1985; Van Maanen, 1979b).
Group norms: the implicit standards and values that evolve in working groups, such as the particular norm of "a fair day's work for a fair day's pay" that evolved among workers in the Bank Wiring Room in the Hawthorne studies (Homans, 1950; Kilmann and Saxton, 1983).
Espoused values: the articulated, publicly announced principles and values that the group claims to be trying to achieve, such as "product quality" or "price leadership" (Deal and Kennedy, 1982, 1999).
Formal philosophy: the broad policies and ideological principles that guide a group's actions toward stockholders, employees, customers, and other stakeholders, such as the highly publicized "HP Way" of Hewlett-Packard (Ouchi, 1981; Pascale and Athos, 1981; Packard, 1995).

[1]. *Organizational Culture and Leadership*, Third Edition; Schein, E. H.; Copyright © 2004, Jossey-Bass. Reprinted with permission of John Wiley & Sons, Inc.

Rules of the game: the implicit, unwritten rules for getting along in the organization; "the ropes" that a newcomer must learn in order to become an accepted member; "the way we do things around here" (Schein, 1968, 1978; Van Maanen, 1979a, 1979b; Ritti and Funkhouser, 1987).

Climate: the feeling that is conveyed in a group by the physical layout and the way in which members of the organization interact with each other, with customers, or other outsiders (Ashkanasy, Wilderom, and Peterson, 2000; Schneider, 1990; Tagiuri and Litwin, 1968).

Embedded skills: the special competencies displayed by group members in accomplishing certain tasks, the ability to make certain things that gets passed on from generation to generation without necessarily being articulated in writing (Argyris and Schön, 1978; Cook and Yanow, 1993; Henderson and Clark, 1990; Peters and Waterman, 1982).

Habits of thinking, mental models, and linguistic paradigms: the shared cognitive frames that guide the perceptions, thought, and language used by the members of a group and taught to new members in the early socialization process (Douglas, 1986; Hofstede, 2001; Van Maanen, 1979b; Senge and others, 1994).

Shared meanings: the emergent understandings created by group members as they interact with each other (as in Geertz, 1973; Smircich, 1983; Van Maanen and Barley, 1984; Weick, 1995).

"Root metaphors" or integrating symbols: the ways in which groups evolve to characterize themselves, which may or may not be appreciated consciously but become embodied in buildings, office layout, and other material artifacts of the group. This level of the culture reflects the emotional and aesthetic response of members as contrasted with the cognitive or evaluative response (as in Gagliardi, 1990; Hatch, 1990; Pondy, Frost, Morgan, and Dandridge, 1983; Schultz, 1995).

Formal rituals and celebrations; the ways in which a group celebrates key events that reflect important values or important "passages" by members, such as promotion, completion of important projects, and milestones (as in Deal and Kennedy, 1982, 1999; Trice and Beyer, 1993).

Many of the categories in Table 1-1 are hard to see directly, such as habits of thinking and shared meanings. Others may be easy to see but may not be as easy to equate with the "real" culture, such as espoused values and formal philosophy. Schein's list helps to demonstrate the complexity of culture, and this makes it difficult to describe and act on directly. And these same characteristics make culture intangible and vague.

Tangible Culture helps to make culture efforts more understandable and objective. First, it defines a proxy for culture—one that business leaders agree is relevant and under their influence. Second, it provides a way to constructively resolve conflicts that arise. Finally, it provides a technique to define a contextually relevant future state, which helps people understand expectations and enables an objective evaluation of progress on culture efforts. All of these help to make culture more tangible.

What's in *Tangible Culture?*

Tangible Culture is divided into three sections:

- **Section I, "The Basics,"** tells the story of our journey in developing *Tangible Culture*. It begins with IBM's acquisition of PwCC and the need to integrate it into an existing consulting unit. We used some traditional approaches and developed some new ones. Our evolving thought processes are laid out to help you understand and apply them easily.

- **Section II, "The Application,"** moves beyond the IBM acquisition story and presents a menu of initiatives where culture is important. From mergers to alliances to transformation and beyond, we discuss some ways to apply *Tangible Culture* concepts by adding them to efforts planned or already underway. You may want to scan the topics available, read those most relevant to your current needs, and return to other chapters to meet your future needs.

- **Section III, "The Projects,"** briefly presents situations where the concepts have been applied creatively. It demonstrates how others are using them and assures you that *Tangible Culture* is worthy of consideration even though it is still "proving."

To help *Tangible Culture* be a ready reference, there is a short overview for each section and chapter. Also, to keep the content brief and make it easier to apply as a reference, we often communicate in bulleted lists and tables.

Have limited time and want to target your reading? See Table 1-2 for some ideas.

Table 1-2 Targeting Chapters

Are you thinking...?	Target Chapters
I just want the basics.	Chapters 4–7 (plus Chapter 3 for traditional approaches to culture)
Tell me what IBM learned when it integrated PricewaterhouseCoopers Consulting.	Chapters 2, 4–7
I've got a culture challenge today. Can you help me?	Chapters 8–12 (plus Chapters 4–7 for explanation of the basics)
How have others applied these concepts? Is there only one way to use them?	Chapters 13–14

The foundational concepts within *Tangible Culture* are Business Practices, Right vs. Right, and Outcome Narratives. Let's spend a little time on each one of them:

- **Business Practices**—The unseen hand (or autopilot) that propels organizational action.

  Business Practices are the informal rules that tell people how to execute their work. They are patterns of action that members of the same organization exhibit. They are powerful because they make organizations distinct, even if they use the same processes, policies, measures, and technologies that other organizations use.

  Business Practices exist for every area of the organization, including processes, policies, leadership, measures, technology, strategy, rewards, and recognition. They establish specific expectations for each of those areas; they are important drivers of action yet they are not discussed regularly.

  Business Practices are a sufficient surrogate for the complex topic of culture in business settings. They are easier to see and describe than other culture definitions, and can be acted on directly if necessary to meet the organization's requirements. They are also complementary to other techniques, such as values, principles, and behavior statements.

Can Two Rights Make a Wrong?
Insights from IBM's Tangible Culture Approach

14

■ **Right vs. Right**—The good thing that can cause big trouble.

Having lots of good options is a good thing, isn't it? Well, not always—and definitely not when the options conflict and are currently in practice. In most situations where previously separate internal or external groups must work together—such as a merger, acquisition, alliance, or major reorganization—there is a clash of Right vs. Right: options that are correct for achieving the objective yet in conflict with each other. In some types of situations, the conflict is Right vs. Right Business Practices, and in others, Right vs. Right mindsets are the issue.

Right vs. Right tends to crop up at the operational level—when executing the strategy or design. Most often, top leaders delegate these details to middle and lower levels, and here is where history and preferences come into play, and the conflicts begin.

Right vs. Right facilitates candid discussions of areas hampering current results, or that are likely to hamper future results. Right vs. Right is a constructive way to look at these common issues. The approach helps to overcome culture clash and helps companies to achieve targeted results more quickly.

■ **Outcome Narratives**—How to get to the right place the right way.

Due to continual change and more multi-enterprise situations, business complexity is an ever-increasing issue. More frequently, multiple people are required to make difficult decisions and take action together. Unfortunately, many of these situations are unclear and reasonable people will disagree about how to handle them. Outcome Narratives are a new format, based on structured storytelling, which clarifies these situations. They are also an effective way to communicate Right vs. Right decisions.

The key to Outcome Narratives is their structuring. A likely problem is identified, along with the desired outcome, the roles needed to achieve that outcome and how people are expected to fulfill their roles. They are an effective communication tool, and spotlight the subtle changes that need to be made. And they provide an objective foundation to evaluate progress—a difficult challenge that has hampered culture work—and help to pinpoint additional actions needed to overcome remaining barriers.

These three concepts—Business Practices, Right vs. Right, and Outcome Narratives—are separate, but interrelated. We like to think of them as three bags of "Legos" or building blocks. You can select one or more of the bags and use the contents to configure many different solutions to culture needs. This is helpful because no situation involving culture is completely like another one.

The concepts may also be combined with other traditional approaches. It is like buying a new lens and filter for a camera: The camera is now more capable, yet none of the previous capabilities have been lost and may be used as desired.

Conclusion

Culture is an important and difficult business topic. *Tangible Culture* is IBM's open sharing of its thought leadership for culture transformation and integration. It includes some new concepts, how they were developed, and how they can be applied to a variety of business situations. We hope *Tangible Culture* gives you some new ways to think about culture, and new terminology and approaches to address it. We also hope that this book becomes a reference manual for helping with your business initiatives.

References

ATKearney. "Corporate Marriage: Blight or Bliss? A Monograph on Post-Merger Integration." 2000.

Bossidy, L., and R. Charan. *Execution: The Discipline of Getting Things Done.* New York: Crown Business, 2002, p. 85.

Cameron, K. S., and R. E. Quinn. *Diagnosing and Changing Organizational Culture.* Reading, MA: Addison-Wesley Publishing Company, Inc., 1999, p. 4.

Carlton, J. R., and C. S. Lineberry. *Achieving Post-Merger Success: A Stakeholder's Guide to Cultural Due Diligence, Assessment, and Integration.* San Francisco: John Wiley & Sons, Inc., 2004, p. 13.

Corporate Executive Board. "Institutionalizing Alliance Capabilities." Corporate Strategy Board, 2000.

———. "Beyond Good Intentions: Closing the Strategy-Execution Gap in Strategic Alliances." 2001, p. 6.

Davenport, T. "The Integration Challenge." *American Management Association International*, January 1998, p. 25.

Deal, T. E., and A. A. Kennedy. *Corporate Cultures: The Rites and Rituals of Corporate Life*. New York: Perseus Books Publishing, 2000, p. 18.

Ertel, D., J. Weiss, and L. J. Visioni. "Managing Alliance Relationships: Ten Corporate Capabilities." Vantage Partners, 2001, p. 16.

Gerstner, L. V. *Who Says Elephants Can't Dance? Inside IBM's Historic Turnaround*. New York: HarperCollins Publishers, 2002, pp. 181–182.

Grossman, R. L. "Irreconcilable Differences." *HR Magazine*, April 1999.

House, R. J., P. J. Hanges, M. Javidan, P. W. Dorfman, and V. Gupta (Eds). *Culture, Leadership, and Organizations: The GLOBE Study of 62 Societies*. Thousand Oaks, CA: Sage Publications, 2004, p. 5.

Kotter, J. P. *Leading Change*. Boston: Harvard Business School Press, 1996, pp. 150–151.

Palmisano, S. J., P. Hemp, and T. A. Stewart. "Leading Change When Business Is Good." *Harvard Business Review*, December 2004, p. 70.

Schein, E. H. *Organizational Culture and Leadership*. San Francisco: Jossey-Bass, 2004 (Third Edition; First Edition 1985), pp. 12–13, [pp. 419–428 for complete listing of references cited in Table 1-1].

Ulrich, D., S. Kerr, and R. Ashkenas. *The GE Work-out: How to implement GE's revolutionary method for busting bureaucracy and attacking organizational problems—fast!* New York: McGraw-Hill, 2002, pp. 264–265.

Wall, S. "How to Achieve Growth via M&A." *American Banker*, March 2004, p. 10.

Welch, J. F. *Jack: Straight from the Gut*. New York: Warner Business Books, 2001, p. 106.

2

We Can't Do This the Traditional Way— IBM's Acquisition of PricewaterhouseCoopers Consulting

By Sara Moulton Reger, Michael Armano, Anthony Harris, Michael Lueck, and Lynn Schuster

Chapter Contents

Can Two Rights Make a Wrong?
Insights from IBM's Tangible Culture Approach

18

Overview

This chapter briefly describes IBM's purchase of Pricewaterhouse-Coopers Consulting (PwCC). Given the size and complexity of the deal, volumes could be written on the integration effort. This chapter focuses on the cultural integration. We discuss key steps in the "people" work-streams, and provide a candid description of our challenges and learning, and how they led to *Tangible Culture*.

The Acquisition

In mid 2002, IBM announced its intent to purchase PwCC. It was an interesting time. The dot-com bust was greatly impacting the economy—and especially the consulting and services industry. PwCC had announced its intent to go public under the name Monday.

At the time, IBM was well recognized for technology expertise. PwCC had high brand awareness for industry and business expertise. The combined value proposition would put IBM Global Services (IGS) in a dominating position from consulting to delivery to outsourcing, from strategy to business operations to technology. And it would enable IBM's clients to simplify their decisions and implementations.

Now IBM just needed to realize this potential by effectively integrating PwCC into IGS.

PwCC was a partnership of 30,000 partners and consultants globally. IBM had its own consulting organization—Business Innovation Services (BIS)—which had 30,000 executives and employees globally.[1]

Several key decisions were made early:

- The two groups would be merged into one organization of 60,000 people globally.

---

1. We use these organizational initials throughout Section I, "The Basics," and do not want you to get lost in them! PwCC is the consulting organization IBM purchased. BIS is the consulting business unit that existed within IBM before the PwCC acquisition. BCS—Business Consulting Services—is the current integrated consulting business unit.

- The new business unit—Business Consulting Services (BCS)— would leverage the best aspects of both and not simply adopt one or the other.

- The deal would close in 60 days, on October 1, 2002, yet the two organizations would operate somewhat separately until January 1, 2003.

IBM wanted BCS to be more than a collection of previous capabilities. It truly wanted transformed consulting—a tight, two-way integration of deep business insights with well-established technical capabilities that could carry client value to a whole new level. And this would require change for everyone. Figure 2-1 shows some fundamental decisions made to guide the integration effort.

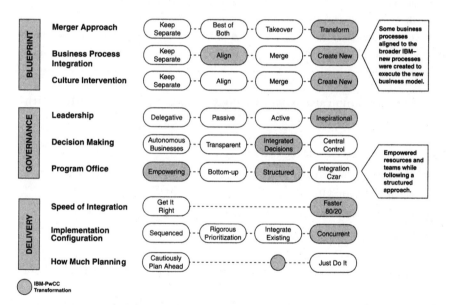

Figure 2-1 Integration decisions.

Among these key decisions, a new culture was targeted—one combining the best of both yet capitalizing on the opportunity to do something new in the marketplace.

Getting Started

"Yes, I want to help. How quickly can we get started?"

"Let's meet in Cambridge on Monday and put some thoughts together. We'll be meeting up with the PwCC 'people' team on Tuesday in Greenwich."

In August of 2002, an integration team of experienced merger and acquisition consultants and subject matter experts from BIS and PwCC assembled to begin the task of merging the two organizations. Table 2-1 shows the workstreams for this effort.

Table 2-1 Integration Workstreams

■ Operating Model	■ Business Process and IT
■ Clients and Alliance Partners	■ Partner Sell and Vote
■ Human Capital	■ Subsidiaries, Affiliates, and Joint Ventures
■ Finance and Operations	■ Communications and Change Management

The Communications and Change Management team started with a few basic beliefs:

- Two cultures are never the same.
- Merging two cultures, or creating a new one, is painful whatever actions are taken.
- Communications are vital to success.
- Change is always personal.

From the outset, the "people" team pondered how to handle the issues:

- Different business models: IBM's corporate, public structure compared to PwCC's private partnership structure.
- Need to leverage the best of both, using the chosen "adopt and go" strategy.
  - ◆ "Adopt and go" meant that both companies' current approaches would be evaluated, and the best would be adopted.

- "Merger of equals" (both had 30,000 employees)—a tougher proposition.
- Need to integrate and operate globally—and quickly.

On the ride into Greenwich, two members of BIS, Mike Armano and Sara Moulton Reger, chatted about the approach that would be needed.

"We can't do the culture work the traditional way. Behavior definitions just won't do it. Neither will values or principles. We need a new way to address the culture. It's just going to be too easy for people *not* to get it—but think that they *do* get it."

"I agree. Nothing would be worse than a bunch of platitudes communicated via e-mail. We've got to make sure it's clear how things will change—for *everybody*."

"Do you think we could use stories to communicate the new expectations—vignettes or something like that?"

"Yes. Stories are a good idea—vignettes or scenarios—anything to explain how we want people to act in this new organization."

The seeds for *Tangible Culture* were born during that conversation.

And PwCC members, Anthony Harris and Michael Lueck, also on their way to Greenwich, expressed similar concerns. "These two cultures are really different. We're going to need something we've never tried before."

In Greenwich, the leaders for the Communications and Change Management workstream designed a work plan—and, eventually an analogy for the challenge. "We have an 'arranged' marriage between people who both have children. They don't really know each other, let alone love each other. And their children, well, let's admit that they have mixed feelings about this 'blended family' thing." The Change and Culture team needed to help make this a family—and a happy, effective one at that!

During the first few days of planning, a decision was made to separate the "people" work into two workstreams: (1) Communications and (2) Change and Culture. The reasons were as follows:

- Communications are urgent and immediate, and could cause neglect of the longer-term Change and Culture work if combined together.
- Change and Culture needed to adopt a longer-term view and focus on different elements of the integration effort.

22

Can Two Rights Make a Wrong?
Insights from IBM's Tangible Culture Approach

> *"With the PwCC integration, communication was a foundation for success, and a way to help overcome uncertainty and confusion. We needed to tell people what was happening, or risk that they'd fill in the blanks on their own—usually incorrectly. Frequent and frank contact with those most affected helped to provide the information needed to understand the mission, goals, objectives, and impacts of the acquisition."*

Larry Hupka
Retired Partner
IBM Business Consulting Services

Change and Culture Workstream

The first phase of Change and Culture work began in August 2002 and was completed by the end of September. Later phases, which consisted of periodical evaluations, carried through the rest of 2002 and into 2003. The initial focus was on effective transition, with building the desired BCS culture increasingly important as time went on.

Some of the key actions undertaken were as follows:

- Risk assessment
- Stakeholder assessment
- As-is culture assessment
- High-level to-be culture dimensions
- Vision and operating principles
- To-be culture blueprint and transition approach
- Geography and workstream interlocks
- Climate checks

We briefly describe each of them and emphasize the connection to the culture work in the following subsections.

Risk Assessment

The Change and Culture team knew it was important to focus on the most significant "people" risks. A risk assessment was conducted and communicated to other members of the integration effort. Of the top five risks surfaced, one indicated the two cultures were not the same and would not integrate quickly or easily.

Stakeholder Assessment

With an organization of 60,000 people in 160 countries, understanding who would be impacted by what was a big task. We needed to understand the stakeholders for communications and for designing change strategies for regional deployment. We also needed to select a cross-section of the stakeholders for the as-is culture assessment.

As-Is Culture Assessment

To get broad-based involvement, information was collected about the existing cultures. Interviews were conducted with approximately 100 senior leaders, and facilitated discussions were conducted with more than 1,000 participants globally.

Information was collected for both culture and change management purposes. A quantitative survey was administered to measure the distance between BIS and PwCC on certain cultural aspects. Qualitative questions were discussed to gather depth and to provide quotes to validate the findings and communicate what people were thinking.

The two companies were assessed separately so that the participants could speak freely and ask questions relevant to them. The facilitated discussions were held around the globe, enabling broad participation. A senior leader attended each session to answer questions.

The data was compiled by country, region, geography (that is, Americas, Europe/Middle East/Africa, Asia Pacific), and globally. It validated the risk assessment: We indeed had cultural differences to address—and also some important similarities to build on—as shown in Table 2-2.

This was important information to understand the challenge, yet not enough to begin work. To move forward, we needed to define key aspects of the to-be culture.

24

Can Two Rights Make a Wrong?
Insights from IBM's Tangible Culture Approach

Table 2-2 As-Is Culture Assessment

Example Areas Where BIS and PwCC Answers Were Similar	Example Areas Where BIS and PwCC Answers Showed Noticeable Differences
■ Career opportunities were perceived as a balance between promotions and developing depth and breadth of capability.	■ Degree to which procedures were standardized and followed consistently versus treated as guidelines.
■ Both team and individual effectiveness were necessary for success, with a discernible lean toward teaming.	■ Proportions of leader time devoted to people management and growth responsibilities versus administrative business requirements.
■ Professionals viewed it as their own responsibility to learn rather than relying solely on the company to train them.	■ Degree to which employees were mobile and operated virtually.

High-Level To-Be Culture Dimensions

In parallel with the as-is culture assessment, work on a high-level definition of the to-be culture attributes began. It started with an informal list of differences between the two companies on aspects such as decision making, leadership style, approaches to professional development, and communication styles.

The list was socialized across the integration team and refined. Eventually, the attributes shown in Figure 2-2 became part of the BCS to-be culture.

Vision and Operating Principles

In parallel, the Management Committee was deciding priorities for BCS. These top leaders were Ginni Rometty (IBM legacy), the Global Managing Partner for BCS, and her direct reports, Mike Collins, David Dockray and Hideki Kurashige, the Managing Partners for Americas, Europe/Middle East/Africa, and Asia Pacific (PwCC legacy). These leaders crafted a vision and series of operating principles to guide BCS as shown in Table 2-3.

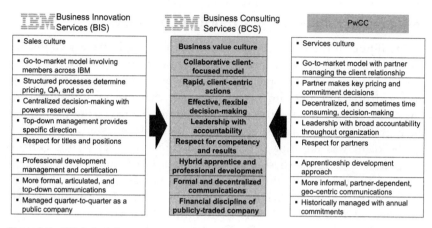

Figure 2-2 BCS to-be culture.

Table 2-3 BCS Vision and Operating Principles

Vision		The world's leading business partner trusted to unlock economic advantage by delivering innovative business and technology solutions
Operating principles	Focus:	■ On the Client ■ On the Value to all stakeholders ■ On the global framework
	Speed:	■ Ruthless prioritization ■ Make decisions once ■ Adopt and go
	Team:	■ Get the "right" people ■ Straight talk ■ Aggressively manage the politics ■ "Grab a shovel"

These priorities became important foundation for the to-be culture.

To-Be Culture Blueprint and Transition Approach

The input on the to-be culture was helpful, yet admittedly confusing and difficult, especially with the compressed timelines. It was five weeks into the integration work and the team was being pressed to identify the to-be culture, and more important, the gaps that needed to be bridged. The to-be culture needed to take into account the operating principles, the high-level to-be dimensions, and the as-is culture assessment gaps.

The team was familiar with the traditional approaches for culture integration and knew these approaches would fall short. So, the team developed a new one—which became the foundation for the Business Practices Alignment method covered in Chapter 7, "Putting It All Together—The Business Practices Alignment Method."

Several steps were used for the culture blueprint and transition approach:

1. For each to-be culture dimension, the desired end state was defined. The key question: Should BCS be more like BIS or PwCC in this area? A combination was eventually crafted—along with some areas where both needed to change.

2. The high-level gaps were identified for each dimension:
   - The magnitude of change for BIS
   - The magnitude of change for PwCC
   - The current gap between BIS and PwCC

3. Each of the to-be culture dimensions was further clarified by a series of design principles in the form of continuum choices. For instance:
   - For decision processes, should decisions be more centralized or decentralized? Rule-based or judgment-based?

4. The results of the design principles were used to craft summary statements for each to-be culture dimension, as shown in Figure 2-3.

5. The implications of implementing the actions and behaviors identified for each dimension were then identified for BIS and PwCC:
   - What specifically needed to change?
   - What new mindsets would be needed?
   - What new capabilities were necessary?

6. A series of structured stories were developed to bring these decisions to life by identifying likely problems and desired outcomes, along with the changes necessary to enable BCS to function that way.

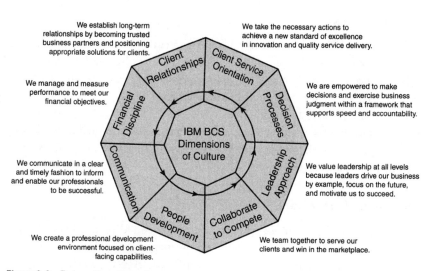

Figure 2-3   To-be culture dimensions.

Leadership Model

To emphasize and support the leadership of BCS, a new leadership model was developed. The design principles were one of the inputs used to craft a Leadership Competency model, along with the identified behavioral implications to those design principles. This information was woven together with IBM's overall leadership competencies, and the resulting Leadership model was disseminated to the BCS partners to clarify expectations.

Geography and Workstream Interlock

Much of the work needed to be deployed locally. With a high-level global design complete, the work turned to clarifying expectations for people in each country. Geography teams coordinated with the global team and balanced the need to keep decisions consistent worldwide yet appropriate for local customs and requirements.

In addition, much of the Change and Culture work needed to be enacted through the other workstreams. Members of the Change and Culture team were assigned to each of the other integration workstreams to coordinate bidirectional information sharing.

Climate Checks

Early in BCS' life, ongoing climate checks were performed every three months to evaluate progress. Each geography leader received a "visit" from the then part-time members of the Change and Culture team to discuss progress and additional actions.

The first of these climate checks occurred in December; 80 leaders and 700 employees were included in interviews and facilitated discussions, similar to the as-is culture assessment. Each geography was responsible to act on the identified issues.

Combined Work Effort

The work was completed quickly—and it needed to be. People were waiting for information they needed to perform appropriately. If we did not get it to them—or did not get it right—we risked negative impacts on many stakeholders, including our clients.

Figure 2-4 shows the activity overlap, which meant that different people performed different tasks. We coordinated efforts—and admit that we could have done better on it.

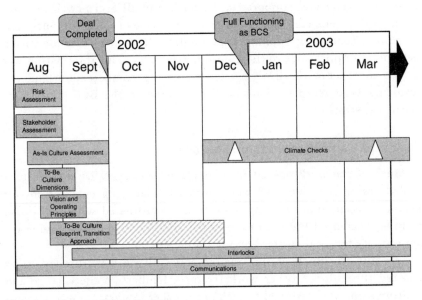

Figure 2-4 Change and Culture activities.

The Debate

Shortly after the risk assessment was completed and communicated, a pivotal debate arose. It centered on how significant the culture challenge would actually be.

There was important evidence of the previous cultures, and there was a lot of commonality between BIS and PwCC in these areas. First, the organization structures were similar, which indicated that the companies perceived the market consistently. And the stated values were also simi-lar—an important indicator of culture. Finally, creating the operating principles had gone more smoothly than some expected. Together these factors indicated that culture was not going to be that big of a concern, right?

Well, let's just say there were strong advocates of both views—that culture would be a challenge and that it would not be *too* much of a challenge.

As explained in Chapter 6, "The Unseen Hand That Propels Organizational Action—Business Practices," we eventually understood this debate to be based on different definitions of "culture." But until we understood it, the debate persisted.

> *"At first, PwCC and IBM seemed like different life forms. We couldn't understand each other—and each tried to convince the other that its language and beliefs were correct. PwCCers wanted a professional services culture and IBMers believed in operational excellence. Through it all, we discovered the starting point for our new culture—shared dedication to clients. Focusing on it helped the rest to follow."*
>
> **George Bailey**
> **Partner and Former BCS Integration Executive**
> **IBM Business Consulting Services**

Our Results

You are probably wondering how well this work addressed our culture challenges. As you might suspect, we did some things well, and would do others differently if given the chance. Some aspects of our assessment appear in Table 2-4.

Table 2-4 Assessment of Culture Work

What We Would Do Again	But We Would...
Separate Change and Culture from Communications, because that enabled a dual focus on the immediate and long-term nature of the people issues.	Improve the connections between the teams. Although the teams were co-located and often worked together, enhanced connections could have helped us to use Communications to propel more Change requirements.
Establish and maintain linkages between the Change and Culture team and the other integration workstreams.	Make these connections earlier and stronger, especially focusing attention on the Operating Model, which would have helped us embed the to-be culture while it was being developed.
Involve the local geography and regional teams in refining the integration design and execution guidelines, including the Change and Culture work.	Involve them earlier and in a stronger way to ensure good understanding, reduce rework, and accelerate local implementations.
Gather broad-based leader and employee feedback, both structured and unstructured.	Share the feedback more broadly across the full integration team, and provide responses—even if those responses were less than what we would like them to be (for example, "we don't know," "not now," or "we cannot do that because...").
Focus Communications attention on Day One (October 1, 2002).	Resist the temptation to let our focus on Communications wane after Day One, believing that we were "almost done."
Involve other members of the full integration team in defining and clarifying the to-be culture definition.	Focus our discussions more specifically on what we meant by the words we were discussing, thus making the discussions more practical and valuable.
Maintain a separate team dedicated to culture.	Work to ensure that all of BCS' leadership and the full integration team together understood they "co-owned" the work along with this team.
Continue the culture work, particularly evaluations of progress, well after BCS was operating in fully integrated mode.	Provide more tangible information to help the leaders to understand the progress and what else needed to be done.

The last three points told us that we had work to do.

- How could we get to a common definition of culture so that we could start at the same place as we worked with a diverse, global team of leaders? Without this, we ran the risk of getting into the debate we mentioned earlier.

- How could we make culture even more practical and valuable in the discussions? Without this, leaders could feel that the effort was simply "feel good stuff."

- How could we get all the business leaders to understand that culture was their responsibility—as much as, and even more than, the people who were assigned to work on it? Without this, it was too easy for leaders to expect others to perform the needed actions.

- How could we really measure results while we were on the journey? Without this, it would be easy to declare success—or failure— too early.

- How could we determine what actions were needed if it became clear along the journey that we had not yet reached the to-be culture? Without this, lack of clarity on what to do could frustrate people and delay energy to take action.

The last few "do-betters" were not simply an issue of improving on what we knew to do—we did not know how to do them, or at least how to do them well. So our new approach to culture integration was only okay, but we believed that the idea had merit and that we could turn it into something truly powerful with more work.

This assessment led BCS to ask IBM Research, specifically the Almaden Services Research team, to work on answering those questions and hone the approach. The results of this process, along with how we developed *Tangible Culture*, are included in Chapters 4 through 6 ("How to Get to the Right Place the Right Way—Outcome Narratives," "The Good Thing That Can Cause Big Trouble—Right vs. Right," and "The Unseen Hand That Propels Organizational Action—Business Practices," respectively). But before we go there, let's discuss traditional approaches to culture change.

Conclusion

Shortly after IBM announced its intent to acquire PwCC, the "people"-integration effort began. A new approach was needed to deal with the complexities of the large-scale global merger, and one was developed and used—one that included structured stories to clarify expectations. The results indicated some successes, but more work was needed—specifically on ways to make culture more tangible and workable, and to help evaluate progress toward the to-be culture.

3

Traditional Approaches to Culture Transformation— How Others Have Dealt with the Challenge

By Sara Moulton Reger, Barbara Jo Bliss, Sue Blum, and Anthony Harris

---

Chapter Contents

Can Two Rights Make a Wrong?
Insights from IBM's Tangible Culture Approach

34

Overview

This chapter gives a brief overview of traditional culture change approaches along with associated pros and cons. It will help you to understand the advantages that *Tangible Culture* provides, as detailed in Chapters 4 through 6 ("How to Get to the Right Place the Right Way—Outcome Narratives," "The Good Thing That Can Cause Big Trouble—Right vs. Right," and "The Unseen Hand That Propels Organizational Action—Business Practices," respectively).

Introduction

The Change and Culture team mentioned in Chapter 2, "We Can't Do This the Traditional Way—IBM's Acquisition of Pricewaterhouse-Coopers Consulting," brought more than six decades of collective experience in culture change using the techniques in this chapter. We do not exhaustively cover culture approaches, but rather discuss some popular ones. Although they have shortcomings, IBM endorses and uses these traditional approaches, increasingly so by augmenting with Tangible Culture.

Culture is important to every aspect of business, so many people have developed ways to deal with it—from business leaders to human resources professionals to consultants. Four basic approaches have emerged as predominant:

- Values
- Principles
- Behaviors
- Attributes or characteristics

We cover each of these approaches briefly.

Values Approach

A short list of cultural components includes beliefs, behaviors, norms, assumptions, and values. Because values are a cultural component, it makes sense that business leaders would want to work on them directly.

IBM's CEO, Sam Palmisano, initiated a values-based transformation in 2003 to deal with our complex, global business requirements.

> *"Organizational culture is like red wine—the quality is determined by what goes into it, how it is treated, and how long it ages. Founders' personalities, values, and beliefs, the strategies and structures they enact, and the behaviors they reward, support, and expect determine culture. Effective cultures age well up to a point but they can turn bad; cultures must be monitored for their fit to the competitive environment."*
>
> Benjamin Schneider, Ph.D.
> Senior Research Fellow, VALTERA
> Professor Emeritus, University of Maryland

A values-based effort starts by defining the organization's key priorities, focus areas, and approaches to work. Often, this work is done by a single individual or a small group of senior leaders, as it was in 1914, when Thomas Watson, Sr. established IBM's basic beliefs:

- Respect for the individual
- The best customer service
- The pursuit of excellence

Nowadays, this top-down approach may be viewed as something imposed on a workforce. Consequently, many companies, including IBM, are taking a different approach. We will expand a little on IBM's approach to give you some ideas.

When IBM decided to revisit its core ideals, it used new technologies to create a live, multi-day online "jam." This gave the entire employee population the chance to engage in open discussion of what defined IBM—those things that would not change in the face of economic cycles, technology trends, or even geopolitical situations. The result was a restatement of the existing core beliefs in contemporary terms. (See the Palmisano, Hemp, and Stewart article in the *Harvard Business Review* for details on the jam approach.)

IBM's current values, crafted through the values jam, are as follows:

- Dedication to every client's success
- Innovation that matters—for our company and for the world
- Trust and personal responsibility in all relationships

In values-based approaches, the values themselves are often brief and clarified through detailed explanations. Value lists are often relatively short, with three to seven statements being common. Values often cover the topics included in Table 3-1.

Table 3-1   Common Value Topics

■ Customer commitment	■ Quality
■ Trust	■ Respect
■ Integrity	■ Excellence
■ Personal commitment	■ Diversity
■ Teamwork	■ Responsiveness

Once created, the values are communicated, and companies use a variety of approaches, from creative media to training and education courses. Beyond communications, the next step for values-based culture transformations varies. Companies may identify a list of changes needed to embed them, recraft their competency definitions to incorporate them, or incorporate them into measures, just to name a few.

Values-based approaches have some distinct advantages:

- Values are easy to define and understand.
- Values enable dialogue and give the organization common terminology and meaning.
- Values can be relevant to the organization for a long time.

Unfortunately, they are not perfect. Here are some concerns:

- Values may become words on paper unless actively integrated into the business fabric. Communications and training are often not enough.

- Value statements and their associated explanations typically fail to provide much, if any, clarification on *how* people are expected to enact the values.

- Values may lead to confusion, such as when parties to a merger or partnership compare their stated values and find commonality, yet later experience tells them they do not act them out in the same ways.

The first concern—making the values more than just words—takes work, but it can be done. IBM used the "jam" approach to extract, and then prioritize, great ideas to foster the new values (and build employee commitment to the values at the same time). The other two concerns are more difficult and have caused culture clash at times.

For example, we know two companies that agreed to an alliance and compared their value statements to better understand each other and gauge their culture risk. Because both had a stated value of "keeping commitments" and other similarities, they were confident things would go well. Soon, however, members of both companies were frustrated. What was behind the trouble? Table 3-2 shows some of the reasons.

Table 3-2 Differing Meanings of "Keeping Commitments"

Company A's Meaning	Company B's Meaning
People from Company B will understand that we often have to establish aggressive deadlines for them, and they will agree.	We will agree together on deadlines before they are established.
People from Company B will keep us informed every step along the way, even if everything is on track.	People from Company A will trust we will let them know when issues arise, but we will not waste anyone's time when things are on track.
We expect people from Company B to do whatever it takes to meet agreed-to deadlines and outputs.	If we tell people from Company A about unexpected issues, we will work together to determine what to do, including modifying agreements.

The value statement of "keeping commitments" became the source of miscommunication because of assumed meanings based in each company's experience. And, in this case, it led to strife and hard feelings, and eventually to mistrust that required personnel changes on both sides. This situation is not unique; people will bring their assumed meanings into new situations—assumptions that come from their experience at the company, within their profession, and within their national cultures, just to name a few.

Principles Approach

Like values, business leaders often select principles to clarify their culture expectations. They may take the form of guiding principles, operating principles, or even targeted topics, such as leadership or teaming principles.

Principles tend to be developed by leaders, often with little input from lower levels. Indeed, principles are one way for leaders to communicate expectations and priorities.

Because principles can be targeted at many different areas, they take on a broad range of characteristics. Table 3-3 shows a couple examples from different contexts.

Table 3-3 Example Principles

We will create and sustain trust by...	■ Honoring our commitments. ■ Holding open and honest discussions. ■ Supporting each other. ■ Admitting our mistakes. ■ Apologizing when necessary. ■ Avoiding blame. ■ Valuing diversity.
Speed is a top priority, and to achieve it, we will...	■ Prioritize ruthlessly. ■ Make decisions once. ■ Adopt and go.
We must focus both on people and business results.	■ We cannot achieve results without full engagement of our people. ■ Our people need to know where we are going—and why. ■ We grow employees' capabilities to serve customers and drive results. ■ Success requires balanced results for customers, shareholders and employees.

After the principles are defined, they are communicated. Many organizations also integrate them into the regular work context through regular reviews and education.

Principles have several advantages:

- Principles are easy to define and understand.
- Principles focus attention where leaders want it.
- Principles are flexible (for example, for a specific transition or project).
- Principles can be used to reinforce other approaches, such as value statements.

However, principles suffer from many of the same issues as the values approach:

- Principles can be seen as "flavor of the month," especially if they are changed too frequently and/or not woven into "real work."
- Principles can cause confusion if the words have different meanings for people who need to apply them (for instance, merger and acquisition or alliance context).
- Principles focus on *what* and provide little on *how* to perform them.

In creating BCS,[1] we saw some of these issues first hand. The leaders developed operating principles, but the words did not mean the same thing to everyone, and most of the differences were in *how* those principles were to be carried out.

Behaviors Approach

Now to the approach culture experts have been waiting for—behaviors. Remember the short list of culture components—beliefs, behaviors, norms, assumptions, values? It makes sense to work on behaviors directly—they are observable, whereas many other culture components are not.

---

1. BCS—Business Consulting Services—is IBM's current integrated consulting business unit.

"Too often, leaders try to delegate culture change to HR and integration specialists. In my experience, the single most critical lever for successful cultural change is active, engaged leadership. Without top leaders engaged in culture definition and change leadership, you tend to have multiple cultures which can conflict with each other and suboptimize overall organization performance."

Mike Markovits
Vice President
IBM Global Executive and Organizational Capability

Behavior statements are developed in various ways, often with input from several levels. They are used to clarify what people should do to support targeted business requirements.

For example, leaders of an organization may be concerned about customer satisfaction. They may develop value or principle statements, such as "We are responsive to our customers and prioritize their requests." Then, specific behavior expectations may be identified, such as the following:

■ We return phone calls within two business hours.

■ We ask questions and listen before responding to ensure we understand requests.

■ We seek feedback and modify our approach if appropriate.

These behavior statements go one important step further in helping to clarify the desired culture because they are expectations that can be seen, and thus measured.

When the behaviors are crafted, gaps are often identified. Because the basis is behaviors, it is easier to identify the gaps than with value or principle approaches. The gaps may be based on current behaviors that are contrary to what is desired as well as on behaviors that do exist but need to be enhanced or increased. Table 3-4 shows some examples.

Table 3-4 Behavioral Gap Assessment

Future State	Current State	Nature of the Gap
We return phone calls within two business hours.	It currently takes an average of two business hours to return calls, but some take more than 24 hours.	■ Inconsistent call returns. ■ Some employees do not prioritize returning calls.
We ask questions and listen before responding to ensure we understand requests.	Some employees are good at asking questions and listening, whereas others often propose a solution before listening to the customer.	■ Some employees should continue their behaviors. ■ Others need coaching on how to better respond to customers.
We seek feedback and modify our approach if appropriate.	Feedback is collected rarely, and then, only informally.	■ Feedback is not a part of regular procedures. ■ Employees do not recognize its importance.

From this gap assessment, "enablers" may be targeted and actions planned, designed, and implemented. Table 3-5 shows common enablers for culture work.

Table 3-5 Common Culture Enablers

- Organization structure, including department and teaming structures
- Job design
- Leadership style
- Management development
- Education and training
- Performance measures
- Compensation and benefits
- Rewards and recognition
- Communications

From the list in Table 3-5, the company may choose to

- Implement education on how important responsiveness is to customer satisfaction.
- Provide employees with ways to informally monitor their own performance.

Can Two Rights Make a Wrong?
Insights from IBM's Tangible Culture Approach

42

- Prepare a checklist of questions to help prompt effective customer interactions.
- Establish a formal feedback process for following up with customers.
- Establish a recognition system to honor employees who are making a difference with customers, and to acknowledge employees who are improving most rapidly.

The behavior approach has several advantages:

- Behaviors provide a clear way of communicating expectations.
- Behaviors make it easier to identify actionable gaps.
- Behaviors provide an observable way to measure achievement of expectations.

However, it has some disadvantages:

- Behaviors are difficult to craft (they often sound like principles or values).
- Behavior definition takes time, and some business leaders lose patience with the process (or fail to see the business value).
- Behaviors are defined discretely and typically without context, which means that they may be difficult or unclear to apply to specific situations.

This last point is significant. It is plausible to define an expectation that calls be returned within two business hours, but have some transactions that require more research. Following the "rule" may be counterproductive (for example, annoying to customers).

Attributes/Characteristics Approach

A similar approach to behaviors is that of attributes or characteristics. This approach can be a way to quickly diagnose the current state culture.

Attributes or characteristics approaches begin with a cultural diagnostic tool. Some questionnaires are manual, such as the Harrison Culture Assessment (Harrison). Others are automated, such as the

Denison Organizational Culture Survey and Human Synergistic's Organizational Culture Inventory. Many of the automated tools benchmark results against a database. These three are examples, and there are other good ones, too!

> *"Many factors need to align for corporate culture to become a strategic advantage. Our experience (and our research!) shows that focused alignment on business objectives from the top to the bottom of the organization brings the best results. Leading companies clearly position their culture strategy as a part of their business strategy. Those are the ones that get results!"*
>
> **Daniel Denison**
> **Professor of Organization and Management**
> **IMD Business School, Lausanne, Switzerland**
> **and Founding Partner, Denison Consulting, LLC**

These tools seek to describe the culture(s) and target improvement areas. They are used to profile the current state, and sometimes to establish a future state expectation. The gap then becomes the difference between current and future states on specific dimensions.

For example, the tool may indicate relatively low performance in areas such as the following:

- Understanding the vision and goals of the organization
- Customer focus
- Willingness to address issues proactively

Along with target areas, the expected degree of improvement and schedule to measure progress are identified. Actions must then be designed to bridge the gap. For example:

- Develop and deploy communications and training to
  - ◆ Ensure that the organization's vision and goals are well understood.
  - ◆ Emphasize the importance of, and benefits from, focusing on the customer.

Can Two Rights Make a Wrong?
Insights from IBM's Tangible Culture Approach

44

- Implement measure and incentive changes to focus attention on customer satisfaction and achievement of goals.
- Identify and coach the leaders whose styles may be contributing to employee reticence to be proactive (for example, "shoot the messenger").

These tools can also provide a basis for comparing different companies in an M&A or alliance context.

Attribute or characteristic approaches have several advantages:

- They can be administered broadly and thus involve many people.
- They typically come with built-in benchmarks or comparisons, which can help target areas for improvement.
- They provide a baseline for evaluating progress over time.

Unfortunately, this approach is not perfect either:

- Some tools describe the existing culture yet do little to help leaders know what actions to take—and some companies do not take action to "move the needle," failing to realize that the assessment itself provides little (if any) direct benefit.
- Some tools are not tightly linked to business outcomes (that is, "If I improve in the identified areas, how can I be sure my business results will improve?").
- Over time, people can learn the "right" answers for follow-up evaluations.
- It can be difficult to use the information to communicate expectations because the information is general and expressed without reference to "regular" work.

This final point is important, and something inherent to the approach. If a company wants to increase customer focus, it is easy to communicate that point and think it is enough. Employees are even nodding during the presentation! But *how* should they focus on the customer? What is acceptable/unacceptable? How does customer focus compare with other priorities? And more important, *how* should employees handle difficult situations where the customer is impacted yet the best answer is not clear?

Combinations

To gain multiple benefits, some organizations combine approaches. A company may define its values and then the associated behaviors. Another company may begin with an attribute tool, and then use the information to develop principles and/or behaviors.

One reason for combining approaches is to enable a gap assessment, which is difficult with some of the approaches. Another reason is that large efforts may involve multiple leaders, each with a preference. In general, business leaders tend to prefer value and principle approaches, whereas culture experts tend to prefer behaviors and attributes.

Effectiveness of Traditional Approaches

The degree of effectiveness for these approaches is okay. Clearly, all four are logical and have provided benefits over time. However, as indicated in Chapter 1, "Introduction—An Overview of *Tangible Culture*," culture continues to be a problem in many situations, even for companies that have employed one or more of these approaches. This is especially true for multi-enterprise situations, such as mergers, acquisitions, and alliances.

Here's what Larry Bossidy and Ram Charan said about culture change efforts:

> *Most efforts at cultural change fail because they are not linked to improving the business's outcomes. The ideas and tools of cultural change are fuzzy and disconnected from strategic and operational realities. To change a business's culture, you need a set of processes— social operating mechanisms—that will change the beliefs and behaviors of people in ways that are directly linked to bottom-line results.*

We agree. In fact, this chapter lists the issues we sought to overcome. Specifically, we wanted to develop an approach that acknowledged some realities:

- People, individually and collectively, have differing perceptions, experiences, opinions, knowledge, skills, and preferences. When an effort crosses organizational boundaries, these differentials become pronounced.

Can Two Rights Make a Wrong?
Insights from IBM's Tangible Culture Approach

46

- Senior leaders typically clarify their intent at a strategic level and leave operating decisions—where the important *how* question emerges—to middle and lower levels.

- It is easy to assume that agreement on values, principles, and behavior statements means agreement on *how* to execute those expectations. Even if the *how* is discussed, it may remain vague without knowing situational details.

- Most of the time, there are a number of "right" ways to perform work, and unfortunately, these "right" answers often conflict with each other. Reconciling "right" answers can prove difficult, especially in complex, newly formed, and/or evolving circumstances where it is easy for people to see things differently.

- Communicating new expectations so that they are actionable is difficult, especially for large-scale transformations that are often global, multi-enterprise, and complex; however, attempts to clarify the expectations with more detail can be self-defeating (*more* information often means that *less* people will read it).

- Culture is extremely difficult to measure objectively, and it is easy to default to measuring schedule and budget achievement to gauge success.

Shortcomings and all, IBM endorses and uses the four approaches in this chapter. Each has its appropriate application, provides benefits, and addresses certain aspects of culture.

Now that we have *Tangible Culture,* our toolkit has expanded. We have more options, and we can craft more combined approaches, which gives us more flexibility—something extremely valuable in dealing with this difficult topic on complex improvement efforts.

Conclusion

The four traditional approaches to culture change—values, principles, behaviors, and attributes/characteristics—all seek to address the complex topic of culture, yet from different perspectives. Each of these approaches has pros and cons, and even combinations of them do not fully address known issues with culture change.

The next chapter begins to unfold our process for seeking to address these issues, beginning with Outcome Narratives, which help to clarify expectations within the work context and provide a way to objectively measure culture change along the journey.

References

Bossidy, L., and R. Charan. *Execution: The Discipline of Getting Things Done.* New York: Crown Business, 2002, p. 85.

Harrison, R. "Understanding Your Organization's Character." *Harvard Business Review*, May–June 1972.

Palmisano, S. J., P. Hemp, and T. A. Stewart. "Leading Change When Business Is Good." *Harvard Business Review*, December 2004.

4

How to Get to the Right Place the Right Way— Outcome Narratives

By Sara Moulton Reger, Barbarajo Bliss, Jeanette Blomberg, Melissa Cefkin, Eric Lesser, Paul Maglio, and Jim Spohrer

---

Chapter Contents

Can Two Rights Make a Wrong?
Insights from IBM's Tangible Culture Approach

50

Overview

This chapter describes the thought processes and activities that led to the creation of Outcome Narratives, the structured mini-stories used to define expectations. It also compares Outcome Narratives to related thought leadership and techniques. Definitions, examples, and benefits are provided. This is a core chapter, and readers may want to refer back to it when they use Outcome Narratives on their own efforts.

Introduction

Our first development was Outcome Narratives. As we clarified expectations in the complex, global business unit we were creating, we drew on storytelling to make the task easier. We found a way to structure the stories in a particular way that enabled us to see the systemic changes needed for success. Finally, and most important, we found a way to overcome a key problem with culture change: evaluating progress along the journey.

> *"Stories create spheres of influence and fields of engagement. A good story or narrative provides an opportunity to remind us that we are human beings. In highly industrial and post-industrial societies, unfortunately, we need to be reminded about our basic humanity on a regular basis. Stories and narratives are opportunities to find coherence, express our authenticity, and share our humanity."*
>
> **Carolyn Kenny, Ph.D.**
> **Professor of Human Development and Indigenous Studies**
> **Antioch Ph.D. Program in Leadership and Change**

What's the Problem?

Culture change is a notoriously difficult challenge. Imagine this scene and the detailed issues become clear.

A company's top executives are discussing regulatory changes in their industry and how they will respond. The company has been successful to date, but their market has been closed and new regulations will now bring competition.

They have a big concern: They are risk averse. How can everyone at the company learn to take more risks—but not just any risks, mind you, the "right" risks? They hire a culture change consultant to help.

The consultant begins by clarifying expectations. "Do you want to be risk takers?"

"No. We can't be risk takers." All the executives are in agreement.

After lengthy discussions, they have their definition: They want to be "measured risk takers." Sounds clear enough, and to make it even more clear, they identify the behaviors associated with measured risk taking. Each behavior is targeted at overcoming past reasons for failing to accept appropriate risks. For the executive team, this meant the following:

- When consensus is not possible, proposals will be decided on the basis of a simple majority of the executive team.
- The executive team will request additional information from the proposal team no more than twice before making a decision.
- All proposals will be discussed and decided within one month of original submission.

To further clarify the meaning of "measured risk takers"—and to understand the nature of the gap—the consultant looks for a situation where the behaviors were in play. Although not a perfect example, she locates one and presents it, one on one, to the executives.

"That's a great example of measured risk taking," one executive responds.

"That was reckless and irresponsible," another executive exclaims.

Others are in the middle about how well it demonstrates "measured risk taking."

So they go deeper on what they mean by "measured risk taking" before they move forward with their culture change. They work through more definitions of behaviors, and seem to be in agreement. However, something is nagging at them: When applying these definitions and expectations to real life, will they still think it is the right thing to do?

These executives learned something very important early on: They were not in agreement and needed more clarification. In our experience, companies often move forward with assumed agreement while their

Can Two Rights Make a Wrong?
Insights from IBM's Tangible Culture Approach

52

visions are not grounded in the realities of the business context. This is unreliable at best and contrary to what is desired at worst.

It is difficult to ground culture definitions in the business context. There are different "kinds" of culture (for example, mature vs. start-up, bureaucratic vs. informal, risk averse vs. risk seeking), and different types of situations where culture displays itself—often in differing ways (for instance, problems that involve customers, issues across suppliers or partners, personnel conflicts, funding and resource decisions).

We hearken back to Chapter 1, "Introduction—An Overview of *Tangible Culture*," and Harvard Professor John Kotter's second reason why culture is powerful—because it "... exerts itself through the actions of hundreds or thousands of people." This means potential problems on at least two fronts. First, if the culture propels people to act in ways that are contrary to the desired result, the company has a huge barrier to its objectives. Second, if people address the same problem in inconsistent ways—a real likelihood in new, complex and changing situations—the results will be inconsistent, at best.

So how can a company communicate its expectations effectively, especially if there are many, many people involved?

How Were Outcome Narratives Developed?

From the first day of planning for the integration of IBM's BIS business unit with PwCC,[1] members of the Change and Culture team discussed how to clarify expectations. BIS and PwCC had different ways of operating. How could we rationalize this and communicate the new expectations for BCS crisply?

We settled quickly on storytelling. We had used narratives in the past, such as "Day in the Life" descriptions (that is, description of a typical day from one role's perspective), but we needed more. We needed to deal with overlapping responsibilities, which would be the norm, and with situations where reasonable people could disagree on what to do.

---

1. As a refresher: PwCC is the consulting organization IBM purchased. BIS is the consulting business unit that existed within IBM before the PwCC acquisition. BCS—Business Consulting Services—is the current integrated consulting business unit.

> *"I recall in the early 90s when an external executive was hired to initiate IBM consulting. He wore a color shirt with loud stripes to meet IBM's chairman, despite IBM's strict 'blue suit and white shirt' environment. We feared it would spell disaster for consulting, yet his meeting went well—and we went shopping. This story was told and retold—becoming legend and a contributing factor in changing IBM's culture."*
>
> Nirmal Pal
> Former Executive Director, Penn State eBusiness Research Center
> Former Executive, IBM Consulting Group
> Author of *The Agile Enterprise*

Moving forward with the idea of mini-stories, we began to identify likely problems people would face regularly and where BIS and PwCC had handled things differently:

- After approval of proposal terms, the client requests some last-minute changes outside of the partner's level of authority to approve. What should happen?

- Two leaders, a partner from BCS and an executive from another IBM business unit, both hold responsibility at an account. They cannot agree on how to handle a client situation. What should happen?

- A professional hire joins BCS with extensive experience. It is important to train her on the official approach, but there are people with less experience who need the training to be eligible for projects. Who should receive training first?

- Because of some project changes, a consultant's previously requested vacation is coming at a difficult time for the project. The vacation is especially important to him, and he communicated these needs well in advance. What should happen?

Then we began to craft desired outcomes and looked at how BIS and PwCC would have handled the situations to identify gaps and needed actions, as shown in Table 4-1.

Table 4-1 First Iteration

Situation 1	
Situation	After approval of proposal terms, the client requests some last-minute changes outside of the partner's level of authority to approve. What should happen?
Desired outcome	Executives within BCS should have latitude to make these decisions. Their level of authority should be flexible to address timing and broader client impacts. Poor track records for these decisions need to be addressed with consequences.
Current outcome for BIS	Generally, changes outside of the partner's level of authority require additional approvals.
Current outcome for PwCC	Generally, this happens today, within broad limits.
Situation 2	
Situation	Two leaders, a partner from BCS and an executive from another IBM business unit, both hold responsibility at an account. They cannot agree on how to handle a client situation. What should happen?
Desired outcome	The answer could depend on the details, but an escalation mechanism is needed to resolve issues that cannot be resolved quickly across business units.
Current outcome for BIS	Hierarchy resolves these situations. Escalations ultimately lead to the sector decision maker, but issues are often resolved at lower levels.
Current outcome for PwCC	Assigned client ownership makes this situation relatively rare.

Good start, but we knew we needed more to clarify what people should do.

The next generation of mini-stories added roles and behaviors, as shown in Table 4-2.

Table 4-2   Second Iteration

Situation
A disagreement exists between a relationship manager who wants approval for a contract and the finance manager who needs to approve it. The disagreement is about authority levels since the contract value exceeds what the relationship manager can approve.

Desired Outcome
The relationship manager is responsible for the ultimate decision. Exceptions would be for contracts $X or X percent outside the established levels of authority for that position. The escalation process should be used for exceptions and unusual circumstances, with the answer communicated within 48 business hours.

In-Scope Roles	Role Behaviors and Actions
Relationship manager	Needs to work with the intent of true resolution to understand the reasons for objections, and what is best for both the client and company. Needs to help mitigate the risks and impacts by working collaboratively with Finance. Needs to seek others to help mediate the issues before escalation. Should ensure the next higher-level client-facing leader concurs before taking action if mediation has not resolved the issues. As appropriate, needs to support the escalation process and constructively implement the decision from it. Should work to restore any relationships strained during the situation.
Business advisor (for example, Finance)	Needs to be objective and ensure that the risk/issue is serious enough to warrant continued discussion. Needs to work collaboratively to mitigate the risks/issues while meeting the client and company requirements. Should engage in mediation and support the escalation process, as appropriate. Should support and enact the final decision, whether it is made by the relationship manager or the escalation process. Should work to restore any relationships strained during the situation.

Continues

Table 4-2 Second Iteration (Continued)

Categories	Other Considerations
■ Decision making ■ Priorities ■ Client relationships ■ Leadership approach ■ Communications	■ Track record of the relationship manager in making these types of decisions successfully ■ History with the offering, client, and other specifics to help identify the likelihood of success ■ Answers in previous situations with similar details

Now we felt we had what we needed—and we called them Outcome Narratives to emphasize the focus on outcomes. Here are some things we like about them:

■ Outcome Narratives focus attention and action on business outcomes, and help people know what to do within identified boundaries.

■ Outcome Narratives help people get to the right place the right way—especially for sticky issues where multiple people need to make decisions and take action together.

■ Outcome Narratives are flexible for complex requirements, such as justifiable differences across geographies and business units. For instance, for BCS, we defined Outcome Narratives globally, and then let regional teams revise them for local regulations, customs and business priorities.

■ The Outcome Narrative format enables us to integrate important information, such as leadership competencies, operating principles, and value statements, and apply them to daily issues (thus making them more than abstract concepts).

■ Outcome Narratives provide the foundation for systemic gap assessments and an objective evaluation of progress, as you will see in future chapters.

In short, Outcome Narratives make culture definition more than a "soft and squishy, feel good" exercise.

How "New" Are Outcome Narratives?

Standing back, we recognized that Outcome Narratives were related to several important concepts in a business and nonbusiness context. Some were known to us when we were creating them, and some we learned later. For example:

1. Stories are a rich way to convey meaning and help people retain vital information.

   ♦ Religions frequently use stories to communicate important topics. For instance, Jesus told many parables to His followers.

   ♦ As with other cultures, Native Americans used storytelling to communicate history and aspects of their cultures before written language. The importance of storytelling continues today through songs, art and crafts.

   ♦ "Day in the Life" narratives have long been a technique to define future state requirements. These narratives tell a story from one person's perspective in the future performing the new requirements.

   ♦ Rosabeth Moss Kanter of Harvard Business School is a masterful business storyteller. She uses stories to convey business concepts and help companies shape change efforts. Kanter is collaborating with IBM on an effort called Reinventing Education, and has provided vignettes to demonstrate the use and results of certain concepts. The vignettes, which are delivered via automated tool, convey rich meaning and provide examples of her method in action.

   ♦ The Cynefin Framework is a "sense-making device" for unspecified and intractable problems, using new ways of thinking and "group sense-making." The approaches use narrative methods to collect, consider and communicate information. (Kurtz & Snowden)

   ♦ Storytelling is an active part of workplace culture. In *Talking About Machines*, work anthropologist Julian Orr shows how stories (often during supposed "nonwork" times) are the key means for copier repair technicians to demonstrate expertise and experience, and create and share knowledge. Theorists of apprenticeship

Can Two Rights Make a Wrong?
Insights from IBM's Tangible Culture Approach

58

learning (see references in John Seely Brown and others below) often point to storytelling as a key means of learning.

- In addition, here are a few authors and works that emphasize the importance of storytelling for a business context (not an exhaustive list by any means!):

  - Stephen Denning has published a number of works on the importance of storytelling for organizational change and knowledge management, including *The Leader's Guide to Storytelling: Mastering the Art and Discipline of Business Narrative* in 2005.

  - John Seely Brown, Stephen Denning, Katalina Groh, and Larry Prusak published *Storytelling in Organizations: Why Storytelling Is Transforming 21st Century Organizations and Management* in 2004.

  - Peg Neuhauser has published several works on storytelling, including *Tribal Warfare in Organizations*, which applies storytelling to increase the work effectiveness of people from different disciplines and backgrounds. *Corporate Legends and Lore—The Power of StoryTelling as a Management Tool* examines storytelling for strengthening culture and shaping organizational destiny.

2. Beginning with the desired outcome helps to focus efforts and increase understanding of the resolution process.

   - Stephen Covey's seven habits include "Begin with the end in mind." Creating an image of the endpoint helps people to understand what they are seeking to achieve.

   - Rubin, Fry and Plovnick's works on effective team functioning reinforces the importance of clarifying expected outcomes and roles. Their "Goals, Roles, and Process" framework validates the elements of our Outcome Narratives.

3. Modeling how things are supposed to work ahead of time helps to ensure consistent action and success.

   - Use cases, a technique used in systems development, are similar to Outcome Narratives in that they define how things need to work in particular situations. Similar techniques are often called scenarios in a business or process context.

4. Structuring information makes it easier to use for job aids and reference.

 ◆ Organization development disciplines, including our own Organizational Change Strategy and Human Capital Management consulting groups, often develop aids to help people perform their work effectively. Structuring the information makes it easy to quickly identify the needed details.

You may see additional connections, too. So, Outcome Narratives are new in some ways but grounded in thought leadership, which validates them.

Definitions

The elements of Outcome Narratives are as follows:

- **Situation statements**—Descriptions of likely problems
- **Desired outcome**—Problem resolution statements, based on reconciled Right vs. Right (see Chapter 5, "The Good Thing That Can Cause Big Trouble—Right vs. Right") and other input (for example, values, principles, policies)
- **In-scope roles**—Identification of who is needed to achieve the desired outcome (which helps to ensure that the right people get involved at the right time, and avoids the confusion of too many, or the wrong people, getting involved)
- **Role behaviors and actions**—Explanation of how each role should contribute to the desired outcome—which is the key to achieving the outcome the right way
- **Other considerations**—Additional information to help users understand how to handle situations with somewhat different details than those in the Outcome Narrative, which establishes boundaries yet flexibility
- **Reference**—Any information to help explain the content, such as Right vs. Right categories, value statements, competency definitions, guiding principles, and so forth

Can Two Rights Make a Wrong?
Insights from IBM's Tangible Culture Approach

60

Outcome Narratives can be used in a variety of settings and for multiple purposes, such as those described in Table 4-3.

Table 4-3 Example Uses for Outcome Narratives

Use Situation	Purpose for the Outcome Narrative
A company may need to acclimate new employees from an acquisition and help them meet requirements and avoid frustration and rework.	The primary purpose is communication and job support. The Outcome Narratives could be provided in training sessions, procedure manuals and online repositories.
A company may seek to transform its business, and this requires people to handle some situations differently than in the past.	In this case, Outcome Narratives could be used for ■ Communication and job support. ■ Gap assessment. ■ Progress evaluation—an understanding of how close they are to the end state.
Two or more companies may need to integrate their work efforts, either due to a merger or an alliance where the companies need to work together closely.	Outcome Narratives could be used for ■ Communication and job support. ■ Expectation setting (which is extremely important in multi-company situations because previous Business Practices often must be blended for success). ■ Gap assessment and identification of changes needed for any/all companies. ■ Integration effort progress evaluations.

Examples

Defining an Outcome Narrative begins with the situation statement, which represents a likely issue people will face. For communication and job support, the situations need only represent issues that are likely to happen repeatedly across the targeted group. For gap assessments and progress evaluation, they should also represent major ongoing aspects of your change or integration effort and reflect requirements where multiple people need to get involved and where the best answer is unclear.

There is an art to defining a situation for Outcome Narrative purposes. They need to be brief yet actionable, detailed yet broad enough to apply when the circumstances differ somewhat. Table 4-4 shows some examples to help you evaluate yours.

Table 4-4 Example Situation Statements

Adequate Situation Statement	Inadequate Situation Statement
A disagreement exists between a relationship manager who wants approval for a contract and the finance manager who needs to approve it. The disagreement is about authority levels because the contract value exceeds what the relationship manager can approve.	A disagreement exists between a relationship manager and a finance manager about whether to approve a contract.
An employee has escalated an important, time-sensitive project issue to a high level of management without following the prescribed escalation processes.	An employee has failed to follow the escalation processes.
A person assigned to a project previously communicated a scheduled vacation at a time where her presence is now necessary for successful rollout.	A person requests a vacation at a difficult time on a project.

After the situation statements are defined, the rest of the Outcome Narratives can be built. Table 4-5 includes some thoughts for creating definitions for the other elements.

Table 4-5 Guidance for Creating Outcome Narrative Elements

Element	Description
Desired outcome	Approximately two or three sentences that define the end state resolution: who should make the decision and what needs to be considered (not what the decision should be). Exceptions and when they apply are also helpful.
In-scope roles	People who need to help achieve the desired outcome, expressed as categories of roles (for instance, Sales, Finance) or specific job titles (for example, Account Executive, Project Manager).

Can Two Rights Make a Wrong?
Insights from IBM's Tangible Culture Approach

62

Table 4-5 Guidance for Creating Outcome Narrative Elements (Continued)

Element	Description
Role behaviors and actions	Statements mapped to each in-scope role that define how people are expected to contribute to the desired outcome (for example, actions, mindsets, attitudes, intent, and sense of urgency). May include ways to avoid future problems and recurrences.
Other considerations	Information to help people apply the Outcome Narrative, such as things to consider and specific instructions for certain instances.
Reference	Information to "connect the dots" to supporting material, such as reconciled Right vs. Rights, values, principles, and competencies.

Benefits

Outcome Narratives can be likened to using a map when traveling to a place you visit infrequently. You may want to review the map before starting your journey. The map shows you the destination and a suggested route, and it may help you to detour around road construction or take the scenic route.

Outcome Narratives provide a number of benefits, specifically the following:

- They help to reduce delays, inconsistencies, and rework—and employee frustration from being accountable for expectations but not understanding them.
- They provide needed information to systemically identify the gaps and what to do about them—spotlighting both the obvious and the subtle barriers that need to be addressed, and helping to prioritize the actions that will help the most.
- They provide a tangible, objective basis for evaluating progress over time.

Application

Creating Outcome Narratives involves the steps shown in Table 4-6 (visit www.almaden.ibm.com/tangibleculture to download an Outcome Narrative template).

Table 4-6   Work Steps to Create Outcome Narratives

---

1. Identify the purposes and the target audience.

- ◆ Will they be used for communication, job support, gap assessment, and/or progress evaluation?
- ◆ What decisions and actions are needed and by whom?
- ◆ Are there multiple contexts, such as different regions of the world?

---

2. Identify a series of problem situations as candidates for Outcome Narratives.

- ◆ Consider the contexts and expectations you want to clarify.
- ◆ Look for current problems and ones that are likely to arise in the future.

---

3. Select the problem situations.

- ◆ For gap assessments, select a representative, yet manageable number to craft into Outcome Narratives. An appropriate number may be 20 to 40.
- ◆ For communications, select ones that provide broad guidance rather than creating an Outcome Narrative for every possible problem situation.

---

4. Craft answers into the Outcome Narrative template (see Table 4-2 for an example).

- ◆ More detail is okay. For instance, "Should work to restore any relationships strained during the situation, which is usually best done via face-to-face meetings or phone calls. E-mails are rarely a good option."

---

5. Verify the contents of the Outcome Narratives with leaders and other members of the organization(s), and revise as appropriate.

- ◆ Limiting the review to a "friendly" audience can hide problems that will surface later. Include a cross-section of the stakeholders, and begin by explaining the overall effort and decisions that have been made.
- ◆ If you cannot gain agreement for an Outcome Narrative, there may be
  - • Resistance to implications of the stated or implied change.
  - • Valid disagreement or misunderstandings about how reference materials were applied (for example, reconciled Right vs. Right, values, principles, competencies).
  - • Remaining Right vs. Right conflicts that need to be resolved (see Chapter 5).

Continues

64

Can Two Rights Make a Wrong?
Insights from IBM's Tangible Culture Approach

Table 4-6 Work Steps to Create Outcome Narratives (Continued)

6. Communicate the Outcome Narratives as appropriate.

- ◆ Encourage two-way communication (for instance, workshops where people can draft their own answers to—and discuss differences from—the official Outcome Narratives).

- ◆ Use the Outcome Narratives for other purposes identified in Step 1 (see Chapter 7, "Putting It All Together—The Business Practices Alignment Method," and Section II, "The Application," for additional guidance).

- ◆ Revisit and iterate periodically to add more Outcome Narratives, address unforeseen questions and issues, and continue the culture transformation process.

Conclusion

Outcome Narratives are structured mini-stories that define future state expectations. They are powerful for culture transformation or integration because they focus on outcomes and can be used for multiple purposes, such as communications, gap assessment and progress evaluation (more on this in Section II). Outcome Narratives were our first *Tangible Culture* development—and they are greatly enabled by the concept of Right vs. Right, which you will see next.

References

Brown, J. S., S. Denning, K. Groh, and L. Prusak. *Storytelling in Organizations: Why Storytelling is Transforming 21st Century Organizations and Management.* Burlington, MA: Butterworth-Heinemann, 2004.

Covey. S. R. *The Seven Habits of Highly Effective People.* New York: Fireside, 1989, p. 95.

Denning. S. *The Leader's Guide to Storytelling: Mastering the Art and Discipline of Business Narrative.* San Francisco: Jossey-Bass, 2005.

Kanter, R. M. *Evolve! Succeeding in the Digital Culture of Tomorrow.* Boston: Harvard Business School Press, 2001.

Kotter, J. P. *Leading Change.* Boston: Harvard Business School Press, 1996, p. 151.

Kurtz, C. F., and D. J. Snowden. "The new dynamics of strategy: Sense-making in a complex and complicated world." *IBM Systems Journal*, Volume 42, Number 3, 2003, pp. 462–483.

Neuhauser, P. C. *Tribal Warfare in Organizations.* New York: Harper Business of Harper Collins Publishers, 1988.

———. *Corporate Legends and Lore—The Power of StoryTelling as a Management Tool.* Washington: Library of Congress, 1993.

Orr, J. *Talking About Machines: An Ethnography of a Modern Job (Collection on Technology and Work).* Ithaca, NY: Cornell University Press, 1996.

Rubin, I. M., R. E. Fry, and M. N. Plovnick. *Managing Human Resources in Health Care Organizations: An Applied Approach.* Virginia: Reston Publishing Company, 1978.

5

The Good Thing That Can Cause Big Trouble— Right vs. Right

By Sara Moulton Reger, Jeanette Blomberg, Melissa Cefkin, Eric Lesser, Paul Maglio, Jim Spohrer, and Ray Strong

Chapter Contents

Can Two Rights Make a Wrong?
Insights from IBM's Tangible Culture Approach

68

Overview

This chapter describes a key finding during the BIS/PwCC[1] integration effort: There were conflicts left unresolved despite many decisions that were made to guide the new business unit. We describe the events leading up to the creation of the Right vs. Right approach as well as related thought leadership and techniques. Definitions, examples, and benefits are also provided. This is a core chapter, and readers may want to return to it when they use Right vs. Right for their own initiatives.

Introduction

The second, and perhaps most profound, of our developments was that of Right vs. Right. Distinguishing between right and wrong options is easy. But what if two people have reasonable approaches for something, but those approaches conflict? Expand this conflict to many, often thousands, of people involved in business initiatives and there is enormous opportunity for delays, strife, and lost business value.

What's the Problem?

Culture clash is an issue when multiple companies are involved (for example, mergers, acquisitions, alliances). The global move to service-based economies is leading to more culture clash due to co-production between companies and their employees, clients, suppliers, and partners—situations where preferences, methods, and value systems differ (just to name a few).

The studies referenced in Chapter 1, "Introduction—An Overview of *Tangible Culture*," indicate that we are dealing with a universal challenge. However, it has been difficult to pinpoint the reasons, much less define them in an actionable way. Right vs. Right helps us to both understand and act on the issues.

In answer to certain questions, you will hear people describe characteristics of their company's culture. We call them Business Practices,

---

1. As a refresher: PwCC is the consulting organization that IBM purchased. BIS is the consulting business unit that existed within IBM before the PwCC acquisition. BCS—Business Consulting Services—is the current integrated consulting business unit.

and Chapter 6, "The Unseen Hand That Propels Organizational Action—Business Practices," covers them in more detail. For instance, Table 5-1 shows what members of two companies may say.

Table 5-1 Company Traits

Company A	Company B
■ We empower our people and expect them to make decisions and take action.	■ We optimize our processes and use them to guide our work.
■ We focus on keeping our costs low.	■ We focus on the long term and are willing to make difficult short-term tradeoffs.
■ Getting things done quickly is a top priority—we often defer to schedule.	■ We are nice and personable in our communications.
■ We "cut to the chase" in our communications.	■ In new situations, we are cautious and deliberate—this helps us to create an answer that will work in the future.
■ We do whatever it takes to get the job done.	■ We believe that standardization helps us be efficient and effective.

If these two companies merge, their differences would become evident—but not immediately in our experience. At first, the executives craft the merger intent and make strategic decisions about what the new organization will do. They may also define some principles, values, or behaviors to guide action. Table 5-2 shows some examples.

Table 5-2 Merged Company Priorities

Guiding Principles

■ Customers are our top priority.
■ We deliver on our commitments, acting with integrity at all times.
■ We are dedicated to quality and professionalism in everything we do.
■ Speed of execution is a key priority.

These executives are likely to delegate operational decision making to people who are closer to the day-to-day details—and here is where the issues typically begin.

There are numerous ways to achieve the priorities mentioned above and, unfortunately, they often conflict with each other. Let's look at just one of them: Customers are our top priority.

Company A, which encourages employees to do whatever it takes, believes that prioritizing customers means finding a way to do whatever the customer wants, even if it means agreeing to a customized solution. Company B, which focuses on standardization and its efficiencies, believes that it will provide customers with the fastest, lowest-cost solutions by avoiding customization and helping customers select from its menu of options. Both approaches are right, but they conflict.

The problem often manifests when a difficult decision arises—one where reasonable people can disagree about the right thing to do. For instance, a sales leader from Company A has a proposed contract he wants to get approved. The process requires him to get concurrence from a technical leader who came from Company B. The contract is significant—representing 10 percent of targeted revenues for the quarter, but it will require the company to agree to several expensive and technically difficult custom changes.

Both leaders understand and agree with the company priorities mentioned in Table 5-2. And that may be all the guidance available because executives have left the details on *how* to do these things to leaders at this level. Due to habit, and the absence of additional guidance, the sales and technical leaders will refer to their previous ways of doing things—and they are very likely to come up with different answers on what should happen.

Look at the traits in Table 5-1 again, and then see, in Table 5-3, how the leaders are likely to reach different answers based on those traits.

Table 5-3   Likely Responses Based on Company Traits

Sales Leader from Company A	Technical Leader from Company B
Wants a rapid decision since the customer is waiting	Wants to carefully consider the decision because the custom changes have never been tried before
Believes gaining the business is well worth the difficulties, especially because sales are behind quota for the quarter and the order will put them back on track	Believes that the long-term implications are the deciding criteria, especially how the order may impact technical processes and standards
Uses "straight talk" believing that this is not a time for "niceties" but rather one for quick decision and action	Wants to keep communications open and personable, but finds the sales leader's approach brash and offensive

5: The Good Thing That Can Cause Big Trouble
Right vs. Right

71

Sound familiar? These conflicts are almost inevitable where unreconciled Right vs. Right options exist. And do not think you are safe just because you are not merging—Right vs. Right surfaces in various situations (see Section II, "The Application"). The fallout is troubling.

First, there are delays—in both decisions and action. Then, strife creeps in. And it may extend beyond those directly involved due to the rumor mill (which is always active in these types of situations). Then, win/lose patterns emerge. We have seen two different types of win/lose:

- "Winners and losers," which emerges when some group (for example, Company A or a functional area, such as Finance), "wins" on a regular basis and the other "loses." This can negatively impact morale, reduce the ability for certain groups to fulfill their charters, and lead to loss of key personnel.

- "Win/lose, lose/win, win/lose, lose/win," which emerges when the groups take turns winning. It may sound "fair," but it is dangerous. There are inconsistencies that may be obvious to customers and others. Also, employees who do not know who "won" last time are less willing to make decisions, leading to more escalations and disempowerment.

> *"Globally distributed teams are especially fertile ground for subtle differences in assumptions and values about how organizations should operate. If left below the surface, such differences can result in dysfunctional team dynamics that detract from common goals. Using the 'right versus right' approach can surface hidden differences upfront so that they can become sources of creative tension and innovation instead of destruction."*
>
> Marietta L. Baba
> **Dean and Professor of Anthropology**
> **Michigan State University**

What we have here is Right vs. Right—conflicting, yet viable options for achieving the merger intent. Now that we see them that

72

Can Two Rights Make a Wrong?
Insights from IBM's Tangible Culture Approach

way, the options become clearer. Because they are all "right" answers, we could

- Choose one option, and exclude the other.
- Choose one as predominant, and define exceptions where the other is appropriate.
- Choose a combination of both approaches, and carefully define when each applies.

How Was Right vs. Right Discovered?

During the creation of BCS, we looked at continuums of options, each with logical endpoints, and made decisions on a five-point scale. Figure 5-1 shows some examples.

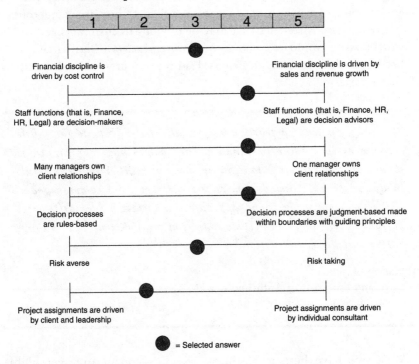

Figure 5-1 Integration continuums.

As we worked with these continuums, a series of interesting observations emerged:

- With the five-point scale, we had to deal with precision that was not needed, or even helpful, for our purposes. For example, some participants would disagree about whether the answer was the left box (1) or the box right next to it (2). When we probed to understand the differences, the participants were clarifying answers that were quite close together—for instance the difference between 16 and 24, which would fall into different boxes but would not be discernibly different.

- Some choices were dilemmas—things we simultaneously needed to do. And with dilemmas, we invariably selected the middle box. For example, to be successful, we would need both cost discipline and a focus on generating revenues. The key was not the choice, but rather to determine how best to do both, yet our continuums did not help with that.

- Other choices represented different ways to perform the work. We found some differences of opinion between BIS and PwCC on some topics. For example, the role of staff functions (for example, Finance, Legal) in decision making was subject to debate because the companies had used different approaches. The ultimate decision meant both companies would need to make changes. Responsibility for client relationships was also debated. IBM did not want standalone consulting; instead, it wanted a business front end for its end-to-end capabilities. This meant multiple managers and some difficulties.

- Others were easy to decide, but meant difficult transition issues. For example, decision processes and whether they should be rules based or judgment based had one appealing (and one not-so-appealing) choice. However, in a large corporate structure, governance is different than in a partnership. Although the preference was for judgment-based decision making, it would not always be under the control of BCS.

- Still others left us with little actionable information because we were dealing with continuums so broad, we invariably selected the middle answer. For example, the continuum that plotted risk averse vs. risk taking was easily plotted smack dab in the middle. But what did it really tell us? In the end, the "answer" was not at all helpful for determining what to do.

- Finally, yet importantly, use of the logical continuum approach required a "right/wrong" combination in several cases. For example, no one believed that individual consultants should make all their own project assignment decisions, so it was not really an option. Using the continuum, however, it became one of the endpoints to acknowledge individual consultants have a role in the process.

What we really needed was a process that would

- Clarify needed information without undue precision.
- Raise realistic options (not just the logical ones) for the needed decisions.
- Surface and help to reconcile differences of opinions that could impede progress.
- Help us to understand and reconcile dilemmas and other trade-offs where different groups had come to contradictory conclusions.
- Clarify and help us to reconcile conflicting operational preferences—different organizational "habits" or norms.

Definitions and Examples

From these observations, Right vs. Right was born. The primary difference between Right vs. Right and the approach we used was a focus on "right" options only—options advocated as feasible for BCS yet in conflict with other advocated, feasible ones.

We also realized that a change to our five-point scale would remove needless precision. Now we would use an uneven scale, as shown in Table 5-4 (be sure to look at the percentage headers).

Table 5-4 Right vs. Right Uneven Scale

1	2	3	4	5
100%	99% to 51%	50% / 50%	51% to 99%	100%
The option to the left is always the answer.	The answer is the left-hand option most of the time.	The answers on the left and right are equally split.	The answer is the right-hand option most of the time.	The option to the right is always the answer.

Table 5-5 shows some examples using the Right vs. Right approach.

Table 5-5 Example Right vs. Rights

	100%	99–51%	50/50	51–99%	100%	
Process adherence and standardization are most important.						Flexibility and speed of execution are most important.
When in conflict, we defer to schedule over cost.						When in conflict, we defer to cost over schedule.
Innovation is equally important to finding cost savings.						Cost savings are more important than innovation.
Leaders make staffing decisions based on customer requirements, company needs, and employee capabilities and preferences.						Staffing decisions are made by leaders, with employees influencing the process by communicating their preferences.
Decisions are to be made via broad-based consensus across all groups impacted.						Decisions are to be made using the advice of the best subject matter experts for the problem.
Decisions, once made, should be considered final.						Previous decisions can be questioned when new information becomes available.

Notice these specifics about the Right vs. Rights in Table 5-5:

■ Some are dilemmas where certain people or groups have identified a decision that conflicts with other decisions, as demonstrated in the first two examples.

- Only viable, advocated options are considered, which means that some endpoints are not opposites or logical endpoints, such as those in the second two examples.
- Some are operational preferences where previous organizational "habits" are different and need to be reconciled, demonstrated in the last two examples.

Right vs. Right also applies to mindsets, priorities, and policies (see Table 5-6).

Table 5-6 Right vs. Right Mindsets, Priorities, and Policies

The right answer is more important than the fast answer.	A fast answer is most important, even if it adds some risk and cost at times.
Standardization and efficiency in our work helps to drive lowest costs, and this is the top priority.	We want low costs, but customer satisfaction is more important, and we are willing to accept some additional expense where customers will notice it.
To avoid even the appearance of compliance questions, there are some procedures we will not adjust.	To meet customer requirements, we will flex almost anything—as long as it is legal and defensible.

To help you see how this works, here is an example from a reconciliation session. Table 5-7 shows the input we collected prior to the session.

Table 5-7 Right vs. Right Data Collected Prior to Reconciliation

	100%	99–51%	50/50	51–99%	100%	
It is best to begin these projects by collecting information from lower levels, and then go to senior leaders for discussion.		RM	TR SM KD	KS LS SP LG WF		For sponsorship and direction, it is best to start with the senior leaders, and then collect relevant information from lower levels.
	Letters above are participant initials.					

The facilitator noticed that the group was split and initiated this discussion:

> Facilitator: "I see you're grouped around the middle, but there are some different opinions about top-down versus bottom-up. Who wants to share their view?"

> Member 1: "Well, I'm the outlier so let me start. I think it's a good idea to better understand the issues. With these projects, I'm concerned that we'll get direction from the senior leaders, and then find things they didn't know and need to amend the project definition. This can waste time and upset expectations."

> Member 2: "Interesting. Historically, we've started from the top, but I see what you are saying about these projects. There may be times when the senior leaders don't know what they're asking us to do and we could waste everyone's time."

> Member 3: "That's true, but how can we even approach the other leaders without the needed sponsor backing? That doesn't make sense to me. We need commitment. We need to direct them on what information we need...."

During the discussion, the facilitator captured key elements of the discussion into a spreadsheet on an LCD projector for the participants to see. Eventually, the facilitator asked whether they were ready to make a decision.

"Remember, our standard is, 'Can I live with this?' not perfection."

An open vote was taken and the group chose the middle answer. The discussion points were documented to demonstrate the thought processes, as shown in Table 5-8.

After the session, the information was refined and documented, and used to create Outcome Narratives.

Table 5-8 Results of Right vs. Right Reconciliation Session

	100%	99–51%	50/50	51–99%	100%	
It is best to begin these projects by collecting information from lower levels, and then go to senior leaders for discussion.			X			For sponsorship and direction, it is best to start with the senior leaders, and then collect relevant information from lower levels.

Historically, we've been top-down, but this project means we'll do more bottom-up. Use bottom-up if senior leaders request more information to understand the issue. Use bottom-up as influence strategy when appropriate—create the business case and sell up based on the nature of the senior leader. It is critical to get senior leader sponsorship, commitment, and follow through—important on the front end.

> *"The business case of BCS-PwCC shows clearly the powers that are unlocked when you are open to the process of enriching each other's [sic] cultures rather than compromising them—capturing the power of 'right versus right' thinking in practice. Linear thought is replaced by cybernetic thought and the results are just amazing."*
>
> **Fons Trompenaars**
> **Founder and Managing Director**
> **Trompenaars Hampden-Turner**

How "New" Is Right vs. Right?

Conflicts where humans are involved are certainly not new, and many ways exist to address them. In reviewing the Right vs. Right approach we had created, we knew we built on some thought leadership, and we uncovered other connections later. For example:

1. There are typically multiple perspectives that need to be considered before a lasting answer can be determined.

- ◆ Stephen Covey's seven habits refer to the importance of win/win and synergy—leveraging differences while finding ways to help everyone feel they can support the decision. Negotiation techniques often emphasize the importance of understanding the other party's perspective so that a "win" can be found for everyone. Right vs. Right looks for differences that lead to conflicts and helps people constructively think through the answers that will work best, often through a combined approach.

- ◆ Game theory, through thought leaders such as Robert Wright and Jorgen Weibull, has an emerging application to designing win/win "games" for all stakeholders in a change situation. Right vs. Right is a way to understand the perspectives needed to design a win/win for all stakeholders.

2. Some choices companies wrestle with are dilemmas—areas without easy answers.

- ◆ When we first used the term *Right vs. Right* in early 2003, we discovered the Institute for Global Ethics, which also refers to Right vs. Right. Their context is ethical dilemmas, and their focus on stories is more akin to Outcome Narratives than how we use the term.

- ◆ While IBM Research was honing these concepts, and unknown to those working on it, IBM engaged Trompenaars Hampden-Turner consulting to help the new BCS leaders with its Dilemma Reconciliation Process (DRP). The method uses the phrases "on the one hand, yet on the other hand" to help leaders work through dilemmas (Hampden-Turner, Trompenaars, and Woolliams). Both Right vs. Right and DRP seek answers for difficult questions, but they use different techniques. Also, Right vs. Right deals mostly with operating preferences. Where dilemmas are included, it is generally where groups have arrived at different answers to those dilemmas.

- ◆ *Polarity Management*, published by Barry Johnson in 1992, is another way to look at organizational problems—specifically ones that need to be managed rather than solved. Although Right vs. Right targets areas where action can be taken, both approaches work on difficult business problems.

3. Many conflicts are based in conflicting values and what is important to people.

   ◆ The Competing Values model was developed through research by John Campbell, Robert Quinn, and John Rohrbaugh, and applied by Kim Cameron and Quinn in *Diagnosing and Changing Organizational Culture*. The model explains different orientations that characterize organizational behavior by looking at competing sets of values and created quadrants of Hierarchy, Clan, Adhocracy, and Market. The concept is similar to Right vs. Right because both are based in what has created effectiveness in the past.

And you may see additional connections not identified above.

So, Right vs. Right is a fresh way for businesses to work through conflicts, and it joins a list of other options for addressing them, too.

Benefits

Right vs. Right establishes boundaries and expectations for people to use in their work. They are similar to lines on a road: They help us to understand where to travel and avoid crashes, but they are flexible and we can drive over them when the conditions warrant it.

We have found a number of benefits from Right vs. Right, specifically the following:

- Simply using the terminology Right vs. Right is constructive, and helps to get the reconciliation effort off to a good start.

- The work is bounded by "right" answers, which helps to narrow the discussion—and ensures success no matter what answer is chosen.

- Focusing on conflict areas concentrates attention where significant benefits can be gained (that is, helping to address productivity drains and increased risks from strife, frustration and dysfunctional norms—such as win/lose).

- It can surface collective mindsets that differ between groups, or that need to be changed within the same organization to achieve new strategies or goals.

There's another benefit to actively managing conflict: creative solutions. In their article "Want Collaboration? Accept—and Actively Manage—Conflict," Weiss and Hughes emphasize that managing conflict effectively can lead to answers that would not have emerged without it. We have seen it happen, so we know they're right!

In fact, we would go further and say that you *must* get to a place of *disagreement* with your vision. At the conceptual level, nearly everything sounds good. If everyone is nodding and there are no conflicts about how to execute your vision, you are likely to have unsurfaced Right vs. Rights. They will rear their ugly heads at some point—and later in the process makes them more difficult and costly to resolve.

Application

Right vs. Right involves the steps shown in Table 5-9 (visit www.almaden.ibm.com/tangibleculture to download a Right vs. Right tool).

Table 5-9 Work Steps for Right vs. Right

---

1. Consider the nature of your effort and the likely Right vs. Rights, for example:

- Do you need to help groups learn to work together, such as in a merger, acquisition, alliance, shared service model, or other restructuring?

- Do you need to surface current Business Practices or mindsets that are no longer effective for your new objectives, strategies, or business model?

---

2. Identify the valid options for achieving the intent, resolving the problems, and so forth.

- Often these options are not readily apparent to those who use them every day—they have become habit. Facilitators can help objectively surface the options. Another approach is ethnography. Derived from the social sciences, particularly anthropology, ethnography provides a means to build a collective, ground-up picture of what actually occurs in the workplace. It is particularly suited to identifying and articulating areas that participants may find hard to see themselves or which may exist at a collective rather than individual level.

---

3. Identify the options that conflict with other options and validate that they are key issues that need to be resolved.

- It is important to cull the list to the key issues that could impede progress and impact many employees. This may be 30 to 50 pairs depending on the scope of your effort. To help prioritize, ask "How difficult is this conflict to resolve when it arises? What is its frequency?"

Continues

Table 5-9 Work Steps for Right vs. Right (Continued)

---

4. Categorize the Right vs. Right pairs by topic, and place them into the Right vs. Right template, as shown in Table 5-5.

---

5. To prepare for reconciliation, ask a selected group of leaders to provide their preferred answers.
   - ◆ Reinforce the uneven scoring described in Table 5-4.

---

6. Convene a small group of decision makers to review the gathered input and decide among the options.
   - ◆ If a combination is chosen, specify when each is appropriate.

---

7. Document the answers on the five-point scale and in key discussion points, and write summary statements about the reconciled answers.

---

8. Validate the decisions with upper level leaders and others, as appropriate.
   - ◆ Limiting the review to a "friendly" audience can hide problems that will surface later. Be sure to include a cross-section of those who will be impacted.

---

9. Communicate the decisions to those impacted, using the format in Table 5-8.

---

10. Use the reconciled answers in other parts of your culture work, and revisit and iterate on the Right vs. Right answers if appropriate.

Conclusion

Right vs. Right is a new way of deciding among available options. It is constructive and focuses attention on ways to avoid delays, strife, frustration, and reduced productivity. It helps to address the culture clash that so often impedes progress and leads to failure on mergers, acquisitions, alliances, and restructuring.

Right vs. Right can be applied to dilemmas, tradeoffs such as cost-quality-schedule, operating preferences, and mindsets. And as you will see in the next chapter, it is especially applicable to Business Practices.

References

Cameron, K. S., and R. E. Quinn. *Diagnosing and Changing Organizational Culture.* Reading, MA: Addison-Wesley Series on Organization Development, 1999.

Covey, S. R. *The Seven Habits of Highly Effective People.* New York: Fireside, 1989.

Hampden-Turner, C., and F. Trompenaars. *Building Cross-Cultural Competence: How to Create Wealth from Conflicting Values.* New Haven: Yale University Press, 2000.

Institute for Global Ethics. www.globalethics.org.

Johnson, B. *Polarity Management: Identifying and Managing Unsolvable Problems.* Amherst: HRD Press, 1996.

Trompenaars, F., and P. Woolliams. *Business Across Cultures.* West Sussex, UK: Capstone Publishing, 2003.

Weibull, J. W. *Evolutionary Game Theory.* Cambridge: MIT Press, 1997.

Weiss, J., and J. Hughes. "Want Collaboration? Accept—and Actively Manage—Conflict." *Harvard Business Review*, March 2005.

Wright, R. *Non-Zero: The Logic of Human Destiny.* New York: Vintage Publishing, 2001.

6

The Unseen Hand That Propels Organizational Action— Business Practices

By Sara Moulton Reger, Barbarajo Bliss, Jeanette Blomberg, Melissa Cefkin, Ron Frank, Eric Lesser, Paul Maglio, and Jim Spohrer

---

Chapter Contents

Can Two Rights Make a Wrong?
Insights from IBM's Tangible Culture Approach

86

Overview

This chapter describes the overarching concept of Business Practices and how we came to recognize it as a surrogate for culture. It provides a definition of Business Practices and how they apply in various settings, along with examples and a discussion about related thought leadership. This is a core chapter and may be valuable for future reference.

Introduction

In applying Outcome Narratives and Right vs. Right, we realized we were overlooking a concept—the one that made culture tangible and actionable. Business Practices are not anything new *per se*; they have been lurking around the edges of culture transformation all along, and enable us to describe the unseen hand[1] (that is, organizational expectations and habits—the autopilot) that propels people to act in certain ways. They also make culture accessible and relevant to business people and give us a new lens for peering at it.

What's the Problem?

One of the biggest issues with culture is definition. A group of 10 people may give 12 different definitions! In fact, as early as 1952, two anthropologists from Berkeley, Alfred Kroeber and Clyde Kluckhorn, identified nearly 200 different culture definitions.

Organizational culture is a complex subject. In Chapter 1, "Introduction—An Overview of *Tangible Culture*," we included a list of 11 culture categories from Schein's book *Organizational Culture and Leadership*. The topics again are as follows:

- Observed behavioral regularities when people interact
- Group norms
- Espoused values

---

1. Our meaning of the unseen hand is simpler than Adam Smith's concept of the invisible hand. We are referring to the undocumented guidance and rules that compel people to act in particular ways.

- Formal philosophy
- Rules of the game
- Climate
- Embedded skills
- Habits of thinking, mental models, and linguistic paradigms
- Shared meanings
- "Root metaphors" or integrating symbols
- Formal rituals and celebrations

> *"Corporate culture plays a huge role in a company's success or failure. But as a practical matter, you cannot run a business by examining culture every day. That's where business practices come in. Business practices are the fundamentals of how work gets done. Focusing on them provides a level of clarity that drives results—and at the same time strengthens the culture."*
>
> **Bob Moffat**
> **Senior Vice President, Integrated Operations**
> **IBM Corporation**

The culture definition we most often hear in business is "the way we do things around here" (according to Deal and Kennedy, this is attributable to Marvin Bower—the man referred to as the "father" of modern management consulting). Interestingly, in Schein's list, this definition is associated only with rules of the game. Also interesting is that many culture transformation efforts concentrate on *what* (that is, priorities through values and principles) and not *how* (specific actions people are to take)—despite the focus on *how* in their definition.

Schein provides an elegant definition of culture:

> *... a pattern of shared basic assumptions that was learned by a group as it solved its problems of external adaptation and internal integration, that has worked well enough to be considered valid and, therefore, to be taught to new members as the correct way to perceive, think, and feel in relation to those problems.*

Can Two Rights Make a Wrong?
Insights from IBM's Tangible Culture Approach

88

That's a mouthful, but elegant because it brings the relevant dimensions, and indicates how culture develops and is sustained over time. We might humbly suggest expanding the definition a bit into notions such as tacit culture development, creativity and innovation (rather than just problem solving), and "catching" the culture (because it is often learned from participating rather than through explicit teaching activities). However, these additions would make the definition more complex and harder to apply.

In simplifying these complexities for business, the iceberg analogy is often used. As with the iceberg, only small parts of culture are visible, such as behaviors, norms, and cultural artifacts (for example, dress, office structures, and artwork). The majority—such as beliefs, assumptions, shared values (as opposed to stated values), and expectations—are important but harder to see and more difficult to act on directly.

For business people, this is often confusing and even frustrating. They know culture is important. They may have joined, or left, a company based on "cultural fit." They may remember a project failure where culture was a villain. They may think that culture is a current barrier to business performance.

How We "Discovered" Business Practices

We uncovered the power of Business Practices as a surrogate for culture as we wrestled with our integration challenge. In Chapter 2, "We Can't Do This the Traditional Way—IBM's Acquisition of PricewaterhouseCoopers Consulting," we mentioned a debate about the cultural alignment between BIS and PwCC.[2] The assessment data told us that we had work to do, but common elements indicated to some that we had the same cultures.

One exchange was fateful. It went something like this:

"The Operating Committee has asked for some culture information. I think we should remind them of the operating principles they have developed. Agree?"

---

2. As a refresher: PwCC is the consulting organization IBM purchased. BIS is the consulting business unit that existed within IBM before the PwCC acquisition. BCS—Business Consulting Services—is the current integrated consulting business unit.

"Well, we really want to tell them about our culture assessment and make sure that they understand we have some work to do."

"We don't all agree with those assessment results. Don't forget—we had the same value statements. Our organization structures were almost identical, and the Operating Committee quickly agreed to the operating principles—all strong indications we have the same cultures. No need to concern them unnecessarily."

"Could we set aside the C word for a minute? I am beginning to think that calling it culture is part of the problem. Let's take a look at one operating principle. How about, 'We execute with speed.' They're agreed on it, right?"

"Yes."

"Here's our concern: BIS has historically executed via process. They have a process for everything and make sure everyone knows his or her role—then they do-it-as-fast-as-they-can. Here's PwCC's approach: They may or may not have a process, and if they have one, partners can go around it if they need to."

"You mean we have to fix that?"

"Well, I don't know how to honor process and go around it at the same time—at least not unless we clarify when each applies. And we need the top leaders to make this kind of decision."

"Well, I agree we need to work on that. But I wouldn't call it culture."

"What would you call it?"

"Business Practices."

Eureka! We found terminology we could agree on—and simply using *Business Practices* rather than *culture* changed our interactions. The Culture team saw Business Practices as a good representation of what needed to be addressed (even though a subset of the overall topic of culture). Others on the Integration team thought we were *finally* getting to some real business issues, not soft, squishy, feel-good stuff.

This was a pivotal moment—one that addressed an important and frustrating issue.

90

Can Two Rights Make a Wrong?
Insights from IBM's Tangible Culture Approach

> *"The culture you have results from what you do. Therefore, what you do—Business Practices—determines your culture (and your culture determines your Business Practices). Not to knock books, articles, training on culture—they are of some value. But everything I've learned really worthwhile about anything—including culture—was learned by doing. No different: It is culture by doing."*

Jack Grayson
Chairman, APQC
Co-author of *If Only We Knew What We Know*

Definitions

Business Practices are the rarely documented *how* that propels *what* people do. They are patterns of behavior and action—an inertial guidance system, so to speak—shared across the organization. They are often communicated to new people by someone "showing them the ropes." They are truly what make organizations unique. This is what Lou Gerstner referred to in Chapter 1. Even though companies may describe themselves in similar ways to other companies, what they actually do will differ because the people are responding to distinct sets of unwritten rules.

Business Practices exist everywhere—for every type of work the company does, from establishing strategy, to executing processes, to using technology, to applying policies, to leading people, to identifying what achievements will result in what rewards, and on and on. They represent expected actions in certain situations, although not necessarily because they are the best or "official" answer (in fact, some are practiced despite the fact they cause problems). For example:

- The Business Practices for processes often tell people

  - Who should get involved in what specific work steps and in what ways.

  - How certain decisions are made.

  - When escalations should occur and why, and how they are to be handled.

- ◆ What mindsets people are to hold when making key decisions.
- ◆ How mistakes and problems are to be handled.
- ■ The Business Practices for policies often include
  - ◆ Expected degree of adherence.
  - ◆ When and how policy exceptions will be entertained.
  - ◆ Who decides what to do for exceptions.

When we ask people how their company handles certain things, they readily highlight the Business Practices through statements such as

- ■ "Our senior leaders often get involved in operating-level decisions— it's the quickest way to get the help we need as we grow rapidly."
- ■ "We're expected to resolve things at this level and ask for senior leader help only if we can't decide what to do."
- ■ "We work to cultivate relationships with our customers, so we assign people to an account and leave them there for years."
- ■ "We concentrate our attention on the biggest deals, which means we'll change sales assignments fairly frequently."
- ■ "Leaders at all levels need to focus first on making sure we meet our business commitments."
- ■ "Leaders need to balance their attention on achieving business results and making sure people feel they are adequately supported and morale is strong."

You probably recognized some Right vs. Rights—and they often are. And you may have found yourself asking a few questions—which is part of understanding Business Practices.

Business people easily tell you these things about their businesses, although they probably do not call them Business Practices. What the definition of Business Practices does is simply put a label on business dialogue and knowledge that already exists.

Here are some questions that will solicit the Business Practices statements previously mentioned:

- ■ How do you prefer to make decisions within your organization?
- ■ How do you handle problems and disagreements?
- ■ How do you prioritize competing requirements?

Now compare those questions to these:

- What are the values around here? And I don't mean the ones on that poster over there—rather, what are your *real* values?
- What are your company's norms?
- Are there any important assumptions and beliefs we need to consider?
- What are your mental models?

You get the picture.

> *"It is very difficult to 'show' the tangible culture levers that drive companies' transformation. The concept of 'Business Practices' comes as a lifesaver to demonstrate how important is this force that, rightly applied, propels business ideas and projects into success."*
>
> **J. Randall MacDonald**
> **Senior Vice President, Human Resources**
> **IBM Corporation**

The primary benefit we get from Business Practices is tangibility to business people. And they are flexible enough to incorporate other important considerations such as mindsets and different expectations for certain circumstances. For example:

- "We believe the best way to motivate our workforce is through work-life balance."
- "The contract is for five years, but we think about it as a permanent partnership between our companies."
- "Generally, we expect Finance and Legal to advise on decisions, but when compliance or significant business risks are involved, they are decision makers."

Business Practices are a new lens to use for identifying areas to improve and for ensuring that planned changes will work well. They shine a spotlight on important drivers of action. Like flying over a city, you can see the smog that you could not see while you were on the ground—perspective allows you to see it clearly. The definition of Business Practices helps people to see and discuss things that have been around them all the time.

Business Practices are also complementary to other techniques, such as values, principles, or behavior statements. In fact, we would say these other techniques provide direction, and Business Practices help people apply them to daily action.

Without considering the Business Practices, it is too easy to assume agreement when it does not actually exist. Remember our integration effort? Agreement on key priorities led to the assumption there was agreement on *how* to fulfill those priorities. With Business Practices, it is easy to probe deeper.

Here's one discussion we facilitated that proves the point:

> "So, we've agreed to create and sustain trust through keeping our commitments, valuing our differences, admitting mistakes, and apologizing and accepting responsibility while avoiding blame. Great decisions so far. Let's take it to the next level and consider the Business Practices we expect to see."

> "Well, this is great for me because now I can quit giving everybody status on everything. I waste a lot of time keeping people informed, especially when I'm on track with everything. I'm glad we've finally agreed to trust each other."

> "Now wait a minute. Status is still important. Remember that I get questions from my leadership team. And if I'm not close to the details and can't tell them the latest—well, you know what happens...."

Without a discussion of Business Practices, these assumptions would not have surfaced—at least not until they had caused problems. And that would have been a double whammy—remember these people were working on trust! Discussing *how* people should fulfill these agreements helped to surface disconnects before they caused trouble.

94

Can Two Rights Make a Wrong?
Insights from IBM's Tangible Culture Approach

Examples

Business Practices are both common across an organization and somewhat different among the organization's business units, often based on charters. For instance, Business Practices for decision making may differ significantly between Finance and Marketing. Creative decisions are often expected in Marketing, but because of compliance requirements they cause much trouble in Finance and Accounting.

Table 6-1 shows some example Business Practices. To demonstrate variance between organizations, we show some contrasting examples on the same subjects (which could become Right vs. Rights if these organizations needed to work together).

Table 6-1 Example Business Practices

We believe in commitment and are willing to take longer to make some decisions to get everyone on board.	Speed is critical so we expect leaders to make fast decisions, and consider employee input if it will improve the decision.
Customer requirements always come first, even if internal requirements slip.	When we receive a directive from headquarters, the deadlines are firm.
We expect people to closely follow our policies.	Some of our policies are strict, but many are guidelines and we expect employees to exercise their best judgment.
Relationships are important, and we work hard to ensure that everyone feels included and comfortable during discussions.	We believe in "straight talk"—which means that we tell it like it is and do not politicize or sugarcoat the information.
When a priority becomes a metric, leaders are expected to "sell" its importance to employees through communications, discussion, work priorities, and so forth.	We allow our leaders to decide how they are going to handle metrics within their own departments as long as they meet our business requirements

Another way to surface Business Practices is to consider how stated expectations are to be acted out within the organization. In this way, Business Practices can support principles, values, and behavior statements. Table 6-2 shows some examples.

Table 6-2 Questions to Surface Business Practices

Principle, Value, or Behavior Statement	Does This Mean...
We will discuss issues openly, honestly, and professionally	■ Employees should prioritize outcomes over relationships, or should "niceties" be honored? ■ Tough issues can be discussed in a group setting, or should people meet privately to air differences? ■ Employees should be dispassionate to be professional, or can emotions be shown at times?
We seek better ways of doing things.	■ Employees are expected to try out new ideas on their own, or do they need approval before making changes? ■ Processes do not always have to be followed, or do process changes or workarounds require special approvals?
We take appropriate risks.	■ All employees are expected to take some risks, or are "appropriate risks" expected to be decided by leaders? ■ Risks are evaluated carefully and planned thoroughly, or can action be taken on the basis of informed intuition?

How "New" Are Business Practices?

Well, a strong case could be made that Business Practices are not new at all. In fact, we recognize that the term does come up periodically, although without consistent meaning. Our confidence that Business Practices are a helpful proxy for culture has grown since we first began to use the term in 2002.

As with Outcome Narratives and Right vs. Right, there are connections to thought leadership. For example:

1. Business Practices are a reflection of what actually occurs within organizations.

   ◆ A study area in business ethnography is work practices—what people actually do. Work practices consider influences on how work gets done and what happens while work is being done— beyond what people say about it. Several thought leaders are important here, including Julian Orr, Harold Garfinkel, and Harvey Sacks, as well as IBM Researchers Jeanette Blomberg, a founding member of the Work Practice and Technology Area at the Xerox Palo Alto Research Center, and Melissa Cefkin, formerly of the Institute for Research on Learning. We consider Business Practices to be collective work practices that have bubbled up to a level of conscious awareness (if the right question is asked).

- Communities of practice also reflect the significant role of practice for businesses. Communities of practice were first identified by Jean Lave and Etienne Wenger in *Situated Learning*, and have been encouraged through the Institute for Research on Learning and by John Seely Brown and others. Although often implicit, an important aspect is how practices become shared among people, which connects with our notion of Business Practices.

- Carleton and Lineberry mention types of practices: organizational practices, leadership/management practices, supervisory practices, and work practices. In their examples, the relevant questions frequently begin with "how." All of these practices are covered within our definition of Business Practices.

2. Business Practices are a manifestation of what people believe will work best given a context and set of circumstances.

- Chris Argyris and Donald Schön developed an approach called Theory in Action, which "is founded upon the importance of programs stored in our heads that are activated by human beings as they are needed." (Argyris) The associated concept of theory-in-use is a set of governing variables or values. Clearly Business Practices represent these kinds of "programs" and are learned over time on the basis of what has been successful.

- In their book *The Shape of Actions*, Harry Collins and Martin Kusch look at variations that do and do not matter in different contexts. They have developed a framework for determining whether variations matter, and if so, to whom and in what context. Business Practices are adapted to contexts over time, which helps to explain differences across the same company.

3. Business Practices are a norm—a mode of action shared by many people.

- Internally, IBM uses a framework called the Business Leadership Model, which focuses attention on strategic and execution elements to address performance and opportunity gaps. The execution element is adapted from the work of Michael Tushman and Charles A. O'Reilly III in *Winning Through Innovation*. Within execution exists a component called Climate and Culture where the primary focus is on norms. Business Practices are a type of norms, and we believe, a more tangible business expression of the idea.

♦ Terrence Deal and Allan Kennedy, in *Corporate Cultures*, validate the importance of Business Practices by describing the manner in which strong culture companies communicate how they expect people to behave, handle procedures, and even have fun. They call these rites and rituals of behavior.

You may see additional connections not identified here.

We hope Business Practices will soon be discussed as frequently and as knowledgeably as business processes are today, and that business leaders will better recognize what actions to take because of this more tangible definition of business culture.

Benefits

A number of the benefits derive from surfacing and considering Business Practices.

■ Business Practices raise the collective awareness of how people actually do their work. Often, the things that are assumed and not discussed cause the problems (Rubin, Fry, and Plovnick). Talking about Business Practices can identify risks early and enable constructive discussions.

■ Business Practices provide a common, relevant definition of culture. Certainly culture is much bigger and broader than our definition of Business Practices, but it is a nice surrogate because it reflects what business leaders typically care about when they talk of culture. And they can be phrased to include some of the "below-the-water" culture elements such as mindsets.

- Business Practices help people to recognize whether planned changes will work within the culture. Specifically considering the existing Business Practices can uncover important risks early—when they can be most easily addressed and/or the decision reconsidered.

- Business Practices, when communicated, can help new members become self-sufficient more rapidly. Without this, they learn the organization's expectations by trial, error, and observation, which takes longer and is more frustrating.

- Business Practices can help you collaborate more effectively across organizations. Business Practices are automatic and can be the source of conflict. By knowing their Business Practices, organizations can highlight expectations and begin to address differences.

Application

The concept of Business Practices is foundational, so there are many ways to apply it, each depending on the ultimate use of the information.

If you ask the right questions, it is relatively easy to surface Business Practices. People may even tell you the difference between what *should* happen in certain instances and what actually *does* happen.

Table 6-3 documents some business topics and questions to uncover the associated Business Practices.

Table 6-3 Questions to Identify Business Practices

Decision processes / governance	■ Who are the decision makers and for what specific types of decisions? What is the role of staff functions in decision making?
	■ Is consensus preferred, and if so, among whom? Do people expect to "vote" on certain decisions?
	■ What decisions are made centrally? Locally?
	■ Once made, who ensures the decisions are fulfilled?
	■ What drives governance (for example, regulations, organization's history)? Are some topics more sensitive; if so, which ones and why?

Financial / investments	■ How are funding decisions made?
	■ Is information shared openly, or held closely among a few leaders?
	■ Who is involved in budgeting and other financial plans?
	■ What happens when results exceed, or fall short, of expectations?
	■ What is the relative importance of financial results to other areas such as customer satisfaction, brand image, and employee satisfaction?
Problem solving	■ How are exceptions handled? How are they perceived?
	■ When determining solution alternatives, is it better to identify and discuss all options, or only the best ones?
	■ Who needs to be involved in what types of problems?
	■ How much planning is needed before action should be taken?
	■ How are people expected to handle conflicts?
Processes	■ To what degree are employees expected to follow processes versus exercise their own judgment? Are some roles allowed more latitude, and if so, under what circumstances?
	■ Are some processes and circumstances handled differently, and if so, who decides?
	■ Who needs to get involved with what aspects of processes as they are being executed?
Accountability, monitoring	■ How are measures used throughout the organization?
	■ How should people respond to measures?
	■ What rewards and recognition are given to people who meet or exceed specific objectives? Which objectives?
	■ What happens when people fail to meet objectives?
Priorities	■ How are employees expected to view customers? The market? The organization's mission?
	■ When handling global issues, do local or global answers rule?
	■ How are priorities identified and reinforced?
	■ Is it best to focus on the long term or short term?

Continues

Can Two Rights Make a Wrong?
Insights from IBM's Tangible Culture Approach

100

Table 6-3 Questions to Identify Business Practices (Continued)

Nature of relationship	■ How important are interpersonal relationships, and how should they be nurtured? ■ How important are titles, and how should people interact across different organizational levels? ■ How should teamwork and individual work be applied? ■ When working outside the company—such as with customers, vendors, alliance partners, and so on—what is the orientation and expected relationship?
People decisions	■ How is work assigned? Who makes the decisions? ■ What is the hiring strategy (for example, promote from within, "best and brightest," diversity)? ■ What is the preference for tenure vs. "new eyes?" ■ How are employees developed (for example, training, mentoring, apprenticeship)?
Policies	■ To what degree are employees expected to follow policies versus exercise their judgment? ■ Who can exercise judgment and when? ■ Do the policies apply differently in various circumstances, and if so, who decides?
Leadership process, approach and style	■ Are leaders primarily people managers, or are they also involved in the hands-on work of their groups? ■ How should they interact with subordinates, peers, and superiors? ■ How are leaders expected to communicate? How often and through what processes and communication media? ■ How much openness is expected, and on what topics? ■ What power is invested, and in what leadership positions?

Finally, recognize there may be "blind spots"—areas where people will tell you things happen one way, but they don't. There are a number of reasons, including workarounds and inconsistencies between stated expectations and what the organization rewards. For example, the values may say one thing, but recognition says something else, as it did in one company with a stated value of operational excellence yet with frequent recognition and rewards to "heroes"—those who went around the processes and standards. In other cases, "it depends" may muddy the picture. Two techniques to help: direct observation and outside, objective project resources.

Conclusion

Business Practices are a tangible representation of culture. They tell members *how* work should be carried out. However, because they are rarely documented, people must learn them on the job. Making Business Practices more visible can help explain what makes a company unique and effective, and even identify what gets in the way. Business Practices have a variety of uses, such as clarifying the meaning of principles, values, and behavior statements, and helping to surface conflicting expectations before they become problems.

Now we have all the elements: Business Practices, Right vs. Right, and Outcome Narratives. Let's bring them together and show how they can be applied.

References

Argyris, C. *Reasons and Rationalizations: The Limits to Organizational Knowledge.* Oxford: Oxford University Press, 2004, p. 8.

Carlton, J. R., and C. S. Lineberry. *Achieving Post-Merger Success: A Stakeholder's Guide to Cultural Due Diligence, Assessment, and Integration.* San Francisco: John Wiley & Sons, Inc., 2004, pp. 72–73.

Collins, H., and M. Kusch. *The Shape of Actions: What Humans and Machines Can Do.* Cambridge, Massachusetts: MIT Press, 1999.

Deal, T. E., and A. A. Kennedy. *Corporate Cultures: The Rites and Rituals of Corporate Life.* New York: Basic Books, 2000, pp. 4, 59–60.

Kroeber, A. L., and C. Kluckhohn. "Culture; a critical review of concepts and definitions." Papers of the Peabody Museum of Archaeology and Ethnology, Harvard University, 1952, 47(1):1–123.

Lave, J., and E. Wenger. *Situated Learning: Legitimate Peripheral Participation (Learning in Doing: Social, Cognitive & Computational Perspectives).* Cambridge, New York: Cambridge University Press, 1991.

O'Reilly, C. A., and M. L. Tushman. *Winning Through Innovation: A Practical Guide to Leading Organizational Change and Renewal*. Boston: Harvard Business School Press, 2002.

Rubin, I. M., R. E. Fry, and M. N. Plovnick. *Managing Human Resources in Health Care Organizations: An Applied Approach*. Virginia: Reston Publishing Company, 1978.

Schein, E. H. *Organizational Culture and Leadership*. San Francisco: Jossey-Bass, 2004, p. 17.

7

Putting It All Together— The Business Practices Alignment Method

By Sara Moulton Reger and Michael Armano

Chapter Contents

104

Can Two Rights Make a Wrong?
Insights from IBM's Tangible Culture Approach

Overview

This chapter shows how the concepts of Business Practices, Right vs. Right, and Outcome Narratives come together. You will be taken on a hypothetical journey back through the BCS integration effort as if we had applied the method in its current form—after the development described in Chapters 4 through 6 ("How to Get to the Right Place the Right Way—Outcome Narratives," "The Good Thing That Can Cause Big Trouble—Right vs. Right," and "The Unseen Hand That Propels Organizational Action—Business Practices," respectively). The benefits, including those gained during the journey, are described. This chapter will help readers understand and distinguish between *Tangible Culture* and other culture approaches.

Introduction

The three concepts—Business Practices, Right vs. Right, and Outcome Narratives—are valuable by themselves. And they can provide an end-to-end approach through the Business Practices Alignment method—a way to overcome the culture issues that wreck business case assumptions and put initiatives at risk.

Business Practices Alignment Method

The Business Practices Alignment method (BPA) is a logical, progressive approach to culture integration or transformation. It is an end-to-end method that facilitates the entire effort—even if it will require several years.

Figure 7-1 shows the high-level steps for BPA:

1. Identify conflicting alternatives.
2. Craft and reconcile the Right vs. Right alternatives.
3. Consolidate the decisions into a practices charter, and communicate it.
4. Prepare Outcome Narratives, and communicate them.
5. Identify the gaps between current handling and the Outcome Narratives.

6. Identify and prioritize an action plan to address the gaps.
7. Evaluate progress and identify additional actions.

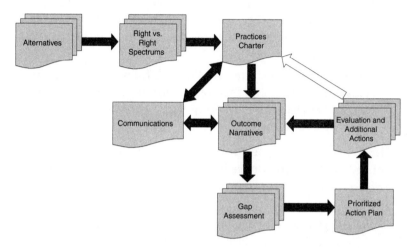

Figure 7-1   Business Practices Alignment method.

Looks robust, you say? Well, it is, and we do not apologize for that. When it comes to culture, quick-fix methods are plentiful, and some one-off solutions may help, but they are far from a total solution. BPA includes sequential steps, yet provides for—and encourages—iteration because significant culture work cannot be completed in one pass.

The process can be likened to a house remodeling project. For example:

1. First, some key decisions are needed about the project, which are similar to identifying conflicting alternatives, reconciling the Right vs. Rights and consolidating those decisions into the practices charter.

   ◆ Some new rooms may be planned and room functions changed (for example, from bedroom to office), which are similar to executive-level Right vs. Rights.

   ◆ Detailed decisions, such as flooring and counter materials, cabinet and window styles, light fixtures, and paint colors, are similar to the Right vs. Rights often delegated to middle and lower levels.

Can Two Rights Make a Wrong?
Insights from IBM's Tangible Culture Approach

106

2. Next come detailed blueprints. These are similar to the Outcome Narratives.

   ♦ It is important to indicate how the decisions should be carried out. For instance, when some tiles arrive, the workers can look at the plans and determine where to install them rather than ask the supervisor.

   ♦ These blueprints help to avoid rework from incorrect assumptions and information. Incorrectly installing the tiles on the floor rather than the countertop will cause both frustration and extra expense to correct.

3. Next, the existing building needs to be evaluated, materials ordered, and resources identified, similar to the gap assessment and prioritized action plan steps.

   ♦ The building may require changes or repairs. For instance, the electricity may not pass current code or the owner may want to build an observation deck that requires roof reinforcement. It is important to understand the gaps that need to be addressed for the project's success.

   ♦ A plan is needed to detail what activities, materials, and craftspeople are needed at what time. Interdependencies need to be identified and everything sequenced to ensure things are ready when needed—not too soon and not late. This is a representation of the prioritized action plan.

4. Progress must be evaluated and, because things will not go as planned, adjustments will be needed. This is a representation of evaluation and the method's iterative nature.

   ♦ Water damage may be discovered while removing shower tiles. It must be fixed before the new tiles can be installed. This is like an Outcome Narrative not working as intended and additional work that needs to be done.

   ♦ While painting the kitchen walls, the owner may notice that the paint is not what she expected, even though everything looked okay in the design center. She likes the general color but wants it to be brightened up a little. This is analogous to a slight adjustment needed in the practices charter.

◆ When ordering the cabinets, some sizes are not available. It is possible to get the right sizes, but only with an expensive custom order. Another option is to reface the existing cabinets instead of replace them. This is similar to a new Right vs. Right that needs to be reconciled.

If assessed, planned, executed, and monitored well, this house remodeling project will achieve its desired effect. However, it will not be a "smooth" process—there will be unexpected issues that require attention (ask anyone who has done it). This is similar to a culture transformation process, and the Business Practices Alignment method provides a practical framework for defining and integrating the work needed for success.

If We Could Do It Over Again

Hindsight is valuable, especially when it becomes learning for the future. IBM is continually acquiring companies, although a purchase like PwCC[1] may not happen anytime soon. However, this learning is applicable to smaller acquisitions, and can help our clients, too. So, let's journey back and consider how we might have handled the BCS culture integration if BPA had been available to us in its current form. (Remember, we used the approach to help create BCS, and then honed it in IBM Research.)

Remember from Chapter 2, "We Can't Do This the Traditional Way—IBM's Acquisition of PricewaterhouseCoopers Consulting," that IBM acquired PwCC to bolster its business consulting capabilities, brand image, and client relationships. IBM wanted to leverage the best that both companies could bring, and do it globally with 60,000 people in 160 countries. This meant that the effort looked like a merger from the vantage point of those in BCS.

The culture work was performed in a workstream that addressed both Change and Culture, tethered closely to the Communications and other integration workstreams. To be concise, we will narrow our discussion to

---

[1]. As a refresher: PwCC is the management consulting organization IBM purchased. BIS is the management consulting business unit that existed within IBM before the PwCC acquisition. BCS—Business Consulting Services—is the current integrated consulting business unit.

Can Two Rights Make a Wrong?
Insights from IBM's Tangible Culture Approach

108

the culture work and provide some key connection points with other integration components.

> *"The partnership between Business Consulting Services, IBM Research and all the rich technical heritage of IBM is driving innovation at the intersection of business and technology—innovation we apply to our own challenges, leverage to help clients solve their hardest problems, and in the process, open up entirely new ways of working and a new services culture."*
>
> **Ginni Rometty**
> **Senior Vice President, Enterprise Business**
> **IBM Corporation**

Step 1: As we made the high-level decisions about whose way to adopt

- **Without Business Practices Alignment**

  An assessment was performed to determine which way was best— how IBM's BIS had performed each function historically, or how PwCC had performed it. The method—"adopt and go"—meant that each organization's approach was reviewed and one chosen for BCS.

- **With Business Practices Alignment**

  After we knew the "adopt and go" decisions, we would have delved deeper, acknowledging that we needed to know the implicit Business Practices and likely Right vs. Right conflicts embedded in the operating preferences chosen. And we would have acknowledged that compromise was not likely to be a sustainable solution because it would not provide an adequate answer to anyone's needs.

  We would have begun the dialogue about Business Practices early, and we would have begun to communicate some known Business Practices for the "adopt and go" decisions to help people understand the new expectations.

Step 2: As we worked to understand what the high-level decisions would entail

■ **Without Business Practices Alignment**

We performed an as-is culture assessment to document elements of both cultures as well as surface and assess the key "people" risks we needed to address. We assessed the implications of the culture differences and used the as-is data and the team's collective intuition to identify the likely gaps and their magnitude.

■ **With Business Practices Alignment**

We would have pushed further into the to-be culture using "adopt and go" decisions and Business Practices, knowing we would get back to the as-is culture later.

We would have spoken with leaders, both those helping with integration and others familiar with each company's Business Practices, to surface and understand the differences and likely conflicts. We would have looked at the Business Practices topics identified in Chapter 6's Table 6-3 and asked questions such as these:

♦ How are employees expected to perform this work today?

♦ Which current Business Practices will be especially important to BCS success?

♦ What are some difficult problem situations you have seen so far, or believe are likely to happen, within BCS?

From this information, we would have created the following outputs, and communicated them to other members of the integration effort:

♦ Right vs. Right Business Practices that needed to be reconciled

♦ Conflicting Business Practices for which an explicit or implicit answer had been chosen via "adopt and go" and needed to be communicated

♦ Likely problem situations that could be used for Outcome Narratives

Focusing on Business Practices would have helped us express the culture challenge to the executives and members of the integration team through business language and in the context of business transactions. And it would have helped us communicate important decisions more effectively to the employees.

Can Two Rights Make a Wrong?
Insights from IBM's Tangible Culture Approach

110

Step 3: As we incorporated the high-level decisions into the to-be culture

- **Without Business Practices Alignment**

  A list of to-be cultural dimensions was developed and clarified through a series of decision continuums. The dimensions included client relationships, decision processes, leadership approach, people and development, communications, and financial discipline. The continuum answers were drafted by the Change and Culture team based on the "adopt and go" decisions and the operating principles.

  Once drafted, the dimensions and continuums were validated and refined with other integration team members. Although this process enabled others to get involved, most of the information was still at a very high level, so agreement was easy despite the differences surfacing simultaneously in the as-is culture assessments.

- **With Business Practices Alignment**

  After clarifying and prioritizing the Right vs. Rights, we would have decided how to reconcile them and who should participate. Because of size, geography, and leadership dynamics (specifically that many BCS leaders were partners/owners in PwCC), it would have been important to collect input from a broad range of leaders. This input would have been used to guide decision makers, and would have helped the Change and Culture team know where significant change issues would exist. Members of the other integration workstreams would have been included due to their in-depth knowledge of the new BCS design.

  The selected reconciliation leaders would have been brought together to discuss perhaps 30 Right vs. Right options—ones where the "adopt and go" decisions were not fully adequate to answer *how* things needed to be done. The decisions would have been identified, and key discussion points documented. This information would have been communicated to the integration team to incorporate into their designs.

Step 4: As we documented the to-be culture and its attributes

- **Without Business Practices Alignment**

  We documented the high-level to-be culture and its attributes based on the decision continuum answers, and assessed the magnitude of change. This was helpful, but not "rich" enough for broad communications so it was used by the Culture team, other integration workstreams, and was disseminated to the geography and change leaders only.

- **With Business Practices Alignment**

  After Right vs. Right reconciliation, we would have created a practices charter that included outputs from the reconciliation, Business Practices where one company's approach was selected, and information on what these key decisions meant.

  Then the practices charter would have been given to members of BCS through their leaders, and to the integration team (to augment earlier information). We would have ensured the information was communicated broadly throughout BCS because it would have helped everyone to better understand the expectations.

  We would have also analyzed the leader input collected before the reconciliation process and used it to help geography leaders and change teams understand their challenges. We would have provided recommendations on how they could best communicate and reinforce the decisions documented in the practices charter.

Step 5: As we clarified what the to-be culture would mean on a daily basis

- **Without Business Practices Alignment**

  We created a set of about 80 Outcome Narratives to address problems the Culture team believed were likely to arise. The Outcome Narratives included transition issues (that is, ones applicable for six months or so) and ongoing issues.

- **With Business Practices Alignment**

  The Culture team would have drafted the Outcome Narratives, using the list of problem situations collected from leaders earlier and input from other integration members. Two sets of Outcome Narratives would have been created and validated:

+ *For the gap assessment*—Outcome Narratives (perhaps 30) that represented key aspects of BCS, selected to include a broad range of working areas.

+ *For communication purposes (a lower priority)*—Outcome Narratives about transition requirements and/or responses to feedback and questions received.

The Outcome Narratives would have been drafted at the global level and given to the geographies for refinements. The Outcome Narratives would also have been communicated to the integration team, and to members of BCS through their leaders.

Step 6: As we compared the as-is and to-be

■ **Without Business Practices Alignment**

Because we had launched an as-is culture assessment effort right away, we were "stuck" with the information collected. It was helpful, but we then knew many more questions we would have liked to ask but would not get the chance.

■ **With Business Practices Alignment**

At this point, we would have compared the Outcome Narratives to corresponding as-is answers. Because two companies were involved, we would have identified two sets of answers: how BIS would have done it, and how PwCC would have done it.

Step 7: As we identified the gaps and decided the path forward

■ **Without Business Practices Alignment**

The Culture team prepared a gap assessment using information from the as-is culture assessment and other integration teams. A plan with specific actions was created and status milestones with leaders were scheduled. Outcome Narratives were used as a discussion point in these check-ups, but they were not primary for evaluating progress and identifying mid-course corrections.

- **With Business Practices Alignment**

  The earlier comparison of Outcome Narratives to current handling
  would have formed the basis for the gap assessment. It would have
  been important to understand the types of gaps for prioritization and
  planning purposes. For instance:

  ◆ Does this gap exist for both companies or for one company only?

  ◆ What is the degree of gap between the two companies in this area?

  ◆ How big is the gap between what is desired and what is happen-
    ing today?

  We would have prioritized the gaps into a manageable list, with
  input from various sources such as other integration members, and
  identified actions to address them. Finally, a project plan would have
  been created and the actions launched. At the same time, milestones
  for evaluating progress would have been established.

---

*"The integration of PwCC was a watershed opportunity for IBM
Research. Not only did it help enhance our partnership with IBM's
services unit, but it also proved a real catalyst for our efforts to
develop a 'science of services' in concert with leading universities.
Applying the rigor of scientific and engineering approaches to services, we hope to create new technologies, tools and skill sets to help
our consultants and clients—we even hope to create the services practices of tomorrow."*

Paul Horn
Senior Vice President, Research
IBM Corporation

At the milestones, an evaluation would have been completed and discussed with geography leaders. The evaluation would have been
based on how members of BCS were handling the situations and how
this compared to the official answers in the Outcome Narratives.
Progress would have been identified, additional actions prioritized,
and areas that had earlier been put on hold would have been reconsidered. Each of these evaluation milestones (covering at least two

114

Can Two Rights Make a Wrong?
Insights from IBM's Tangible Culture Approach

years or so) could have launched the development of new Outcome Narratives, clarifications to the practices charter and/or additional Right vs. Right reconciliation.

Because Hindsight Is 20/20

So, the process we developed for the integration effort was okay, but we now know several improvements that could have helped us. Business Practices Alignment could have

- Given us common terminology.
- Helped our information collection to be more targeted and better timed.
- Given us more "meaty" issues to discuss and decide.
- Better clarified our to-be culture and the challenges we would face achieving it.
- Provided more useful information to communicate—to leaders, to the integration team, and to members of BCS.
- Provided a more objective basis for evaluating progress and determining additional actions.

Benefits

To complex efforts, Business Practices Alignment brings a number of benefits:

- It addresses strife, frustration, resistance, confusion, and "change fatigue"—all barriers to productivity.
- It helps leaders focus on important business issues, such as addressing customer concerns and leading employees, rather than handling escalations and repeated decisions on the same topics.
- It decreases the risk of failure by removing culture barriers and reasons for culture clash, and helps the organization achieve "full functioning" as quickly as possible.

In addition, perhaps Business Practices Alignment's finest feature is the value generated along the way (which helps justify its robust nature!):

1. Crafting and reconciling the Right vs. Right alternatives

   - Helps people recognize the sources for issues. As one leader mentioned, "No wonder we've got problems—look at the issues on these pages! Seeing them laid out like this is helpful."

   - Solicits a constructive mindset, which helps with reconciliation, because all the options are "right" answers.

   - Builds commitment and helps leaders understand the challenges and their needed role through participation in the Right vs. Right decisions.

2. Consolidating the decisions into a practices charter

   - Gives everyone the chance to clarify and ensure agreement before the information is communicated. Organizations that fail to perform this step may later find disconnects that cause confusion and require rework.

   - Provides a helpful reference for employees to use in their daily work. Also, new employees, whether from the outside or other internal positions, need to understand expectations and this information can increase their confidence and ability to perform.

3. Preparing Outcome Narratives

   - Builds awareness of current issues as well as those likely to crop up, which is the first step in taking actions needed for success.

   - May uncover additional disagreements early when they are most easily addressed. These disagreements may be because additional Right vs. Right decisions are needed, a misunderstanding exists about the meaning of previous Right vs. Right decisions, and/or there is resistance to the implications.

4. Performing a gap assessment based on Outcome Narratives

   - Ensures that subtle and systemic gaps are recognized. Often organizations jump quickly into identifying gaps and actions. This may seem proactive and results-driven, but it often leaves fundamental gaps unrecognized and unaddressed. A leader on one such initiative complained, "We've changed the process,

Can Two Rights Make a Wrong?
Insights from IBM's Tangible Culture Approach

116

procedures, measures and incentives. We've changed the way we manage this work—I could go on and on. But the performance hasn't changed. It's really frustrating." This indicates unaddressed gaps—probably the subtle ones that can be readily discovered through Outcome Narratives.

5. Developing and prioritizing the action plan based on Outcome Narratives

   ◆ Makes prioritizing the actions easier. Without Outcome Narratives, decisions may be based on debating capability or organizational clout. Choosing actions based on the frequency and severity of the gaps identified through Outcome Narratives helps to ensure that the most valuable actions will be chosen.

6. Evaluating progress and taking additional action based on Outcome Narratives

   ◆ Provides a tangible basis for handling the eventual "are we done yet?" question. Historically, this has been a thumb-in-the-air exercise based on high-level definitions, so disagreements are common—as are delays in taking needed action. Using Outcome Narratives as the basis for evaluating progress makes it clear what results have been achieved and where additional work is needed.

   ◆ Helps to pinpoint specific issues that need additional work through the elements of the Outcome Narratives, specifically the following:

     • Are we getting to the right outcome? If not, when, where and why are disconnects happening?

     • Are the right people getting involved at the right time?

     • Are the people taking action in expected ways, and properly enacting our principles, values, competencies, and so forth?

Conclusion

The Business Practices Alignment method—an integrated approach using Business Practices, Right vs. Right, and Outcome Narratives together—builds on IBM's lessons learned in integrating a huge and complex acquisition. It is an end-to-end method that can bring tremendous value to companies needing to integrate diverse cultures.

You have seen how we would have tailored Business Practices Alignment for our integration needs. Now let's move on to how this basic approach can be modified to address a variety of initiatives where culture is important, starting with mergers and acquisitions.

II

The Application

W e recognize it is unlikely you will need to handle the cultural integration of 30,000 people into a global organization of more than 300,000—our primary focus in Section I. Section II should be right up your alley—it is a "show and tell" for how *Tangible Culture* can be applied to a variety of efforts where culture is important. Each of these topics could fill volumes, so we briefly explain the business and culture challenges, and then demonstrate how *Tangible Culture* can help, using examples compiled from our experiences. You may want to select chapters most applicable to your current needs and return to other chapters as future needs arise. At the sake of some repetition, Chapters 8 through 11 are designed to be complete coverage of what you need to apply *Tangible Culture* to that chapter's topic—from a discussion of the issues through an example and specific actions to take.

8

Mergers and Acquisitions— Managing the Common Sources of Culture Clash

By Sara Moulton Reger, Barbarajo Bliss, Sue Blum, Andrew Duncan, and Pat McDonnell

Chapter Contents

Can Two Rights Make a Wrong?
Insights from IBM's Tangible Culture Approach

122

Overview

This chapter applies *Tangible Culture* to mergers and acquisitions. The business and culture challenges are discussed, along with steps and examples of applying Business Practices, Right vs. Right, and Outcome Narratives, using our composite experiences to create sample outputs. This chapter will help people who are strategizing about future mergers and acquisitions (M&As), contemplating a pending merger or acquisition (for example, due diligence), or dealing with an integration underway.

Introduction

M&As are a permanent fixture—at least in today's environment. In fact, many companies, including IBM, use acquisitions to propel growth and innovation strategies, and sell off older capabilities to open funding and attention for new areas.

However, M&As are challenging—always. Chapter 1, "Introduction—An Overview of *Tangible Culture*," mentioned culture clash as a top reason for M&A failure. New approaches are needed—and this chapter provides one.

Business Challenges

Mergers and acquisitions promise many benefits: economies of scale, removal of entry barriers, easier market penetration, and access to new knowledge and resources. They may help prevent or resolve organizational rigidity, which could hamper future success.

However, M&As bring additional costs from integration activities and takeover premiums of 20 to 40 percent. In addition, they divert top management attention away from other activities, and may be undertaken for questionable reasons without adequate consideration of what is necessary to manage them (Vermeulen and Barkema).

Hmm. Sounds like a mixed blessing.

Then there are the financial results, which are more of a curse for many. Taking into account the estimates we have seen, it appears that mergers and acquisitions have—at best—a 50/50 chance of achieving their objectives. A 2004 KPMG report indicates that 34 percent of major deals completed in 2000 and 2001 enhanced value for shareholders, and this number is up from previous studies. Improvement is good, but these numbers mean many companies are better off before all that tough integration work—double whammy!

Joseph Bower of Harvard identifies five reasons for acquisitions:

- To deal with overcapacity through consolidation in mature industries
- To roll up competitors in geographically fragmented industries
- To extend into new products or markets
- As a substitute for R&D
- To exploit eroding industry boundaries by inventing an industry

The business cases and integration strategies differ depending on the reasons for the deal. For instance, overcapacity typically means layoffs, and extending into new products or markets typically requires aggressive strategies to retain employees with vital knowledge.

Each merger or acquisition is unique, but there are some common business challenges:

- Determining the best operating model and organizational structure to support it
- Selecting the right leaders (and with each appointment, there is likely disappointment for those who weren't selected)
- Deciding how the organization should be governed and run
- Determining the best human resources strategies and execution, which often require retaining key talent and motivating employees while effectively exiting others from the business
- Ensuring everyone understands the new environment and responsibilities, which often means global training and even communicating with customers
- Ensuring customer and market focus to retain the customer base and market share
- Maintaining focus on the rest of the business to ensure that momentum is not lost

In many mergers, nearly everything changes—new strategies, products, processes, customers, management, systems, and locations.

Although frequently less pervasive, acquisitions often bring broad-based changes, too. In other words, many things need to be reconsidered and changed, while juggling all the balls currently in the air.

Philippe Haspeslagh, Professor of Corporate Strategy at INSEAD and expert in M&A, raises some interesting points in "Maintaining Momentum in Mergers." Frequently, members of each side, as well as members of each organization, perceive the deal differently, and this can be troublesome later. Also, value is not created by the dealmakers, but rather by those who operationalize it; however, there are different cultures, terminology, ways of doing things (which can block collaboration), and a sense of loss (which can reduce motivation to collaborate).

These are great points to segue into our next discussion.

Culture Challenges

On top of the business challenges is the strong potential for culture clash. No two organizational cultures are alike. Even if they are similar in many ways, there will be important and potentially contentious differences.

When culture has surfaced during preliminary discussions, some executives have been unable to describe their cultures (Grossman, Haines). Haines cites one example in which a lean, decentralized, field-based company merged with a centralized, well-controlled, office-based one. Despite these seemingly obvious distinctions, no one prepared the people for the differences—or for the mistrust and strife that followed.

GE, well known for acquisition success, provides an important lesson. During the final stages of due diligence, senior executives from GE Capital and a British company met to discuss GE's expectations for the merged company. The discussion surfaced some key differences, which prompted GE to look more closely at the target's culture. Its conclusion: The integration was likely to be difficult and contentious. Its decision: Walk away despite the favorable financials (Ashkenas, DeMonaco, and Francis).

This story reinforces the importance of choosing M&As wisely. The GE executives understood culture challenges and used that knowledge in their decision. Perhaps some of the questions in Table 6-3 in Chapter 6, "The Unseen Hand That Propels Organizational Action—Business Practices," came to mind—the ones that identified the target's Business Practices.

> *"As IBM exploits new growth opportunities, we'll become a more aggressive acquirer. Several factors will enable our success. First, we need a clear strategic plan. Second, the targets need to share our vision. Finally, and perhaps most important, IBM and the target need a common approach to executing the strategy—which is where focusing on business practices becomes beneficial."*
>
> Jim Liang
> **Vice President, Strategy and Business Development**
> **IBM Global Services**

Three additional questions are also important:

- How do these answers align with the strategy for this merger or acquisition?
- How do these answers compare to our company's answers?
- Are any national/regional cultural norms important to consider?

These questions are important because they impact what is appropriate. For instance:

- The nature and intent of the deal drive the alignment needed. M&As are often one step in a transformation journey. When this happens, as it did for creating BCS,[1] it means that both companies need to change, just in different areas.
- Different answers between the companies and across national boundaries are always relevant because they drive expectations and chances for culture clash. In many cases, the acquired company is expected to adopt the acquirer's answers. In other situations, opportunities exist to leverage what both can bring. In either case, recognizing and understanding the differences is an important first step.

If you are not careful, one culture may quash elements of the other, even though (and perhaps because) some of those elements were

---

1. BCS—Business Consulting Services—IBM's current integrated consulting business unit.

126

Can Two Rights Make a Wrong?
Insights from IBM's Tangible Culture Approach

intended as part of the future state. In one financial services acquisition, the acquirer sought to overcome its rigid decision making through adopting the acquisition's streamlined process. Instead, the acquirer's go-slow processes were eventually adopted by the acquisition despite the original intent. Also, some acquirers' managers default to "our way or the highway." We believe they do it because they do not know any other way to deal with the differences and want to move on quickly, even though they typically create plenty of problems with that approach.

So, what can be done?

> *"Mergers and acquisitions of services businesses (where ultimately people are the product) are extremely difficult. Unaddressed differences in culture can lead to missed expectations and value erosion. Making the intangible tangible—by identifying and addressing the specific differences in norms, behaviors, and operational and management methods early—can be the difference between winning and losing in M&A."*
>
> Eric Pelander
> Partner
> Waterstone Management Group LLC

Handling Related "People" Risks

Let's start with some brief advice about important "people" areas in an M&A:

- No matter how much communication you do, we can safely say it is not enough. To address employee needs for information (from strategic to tactical messages), you will need different communication strategies for the initial stages (that is, post-announcement through due diligence), the early stages of integration (that is, the first 100 days), and for later stages of integration. Dedicating an ongoing team with communications expertise is vital, as is ensuring two-way communications and thoughtful, quick responses to questions and feedback received.

- Human Resource plans need to help align and enact the intent and objectives. With M&As, some staff reductions may be required at the same time retention of key personnel is a primary concern. Plans are needed to assign employees to job classifications, determine compensation and benefits, and decide career progression schemes—just to name a few. Some of these details are top of mind for employees, yet they take time to decide, so communicating the decision timetable can be just as important as communicating the decisions.

- You will want a strong focus on organizational change management to help reduce your risk. M&As are disruptive, which means you will experience resistance—even from those who think it is the right thing to do. Be sure to think broadly when you consider the stakeholders who are impacted (for example, you will likely need to include your customers in your plans). Also, recognize the importance of defining the new organization structure and roles/responsibilities quickly. People want to know where they fit in—and are likely to be very distracted until they know.

In addition, the organization may want to develop some new operating or guiding principles, values and/or behavior expectations. Several studies have found that during early stages of M&A transitions, management fails to communicate ground rules that create a context for learning (Gibson and Love; Haines). Operating principles can also communicate the intent and begin the important process of setting expectations.

Finally, remember that the benefits are not secured by signing the deal—they are created in the following months and years. You will need active leadership from both organizations to create a powerful company.

Let's get down to how Business Practices, Right vs. Right, and Outcome Narratives can help address culture clash in two key phases for M&A: due diligence and integration.

Applying *Tangible Culture* to Due Diligence

In due diligence, companies evaluate success potential from a number of important perspectives—culture fit being one. However, human due diligence is often short-changed.

A Hewitt Associates study among European multinationals indicated less than 10 percent of management time was devoted to the human side during due diligence—this despite respondents acknowledging that human issues, including cultural fit, are the most critical and difficult to resolve during integration. This study also indicated that companies tended to focus on what could be easily measured within the first six months. Certainly, a full cultural integration of two companies is not achieved during that timeframe.

Carleton and Lineberry also mention the pattern that cultural factors are least likely to be included in due diligence even though a great barrier to success. They identify two potential causes: assuming cultural compatibility rather than testing for it, or believing that nothing can be done about it. Neither sound like good excuses, do they?

To address the risk, it is vital that due diligence includes a culture assessment and that actions be planned for integration. Business Practices and Right vs. Right can enhance understanding of cultural fit. Table 8-1 shows some key steps for both companies to perform during due diligence.

Table 8-1 Work Steps to Assess Culture During Due Diligence

---

1. Consider the deal intent and the nature of the integration that will be needed.

- If an acquisition, to what extent will the acquired company need to adopt the Business Practices of the acquirer, and in what areas?
- If a merger, will the Business Practices of both be leveraged? If so, in what areas? Has a strategy been prepared for leveraging both companies' capabilities?

---

2. Prioritize areas for assessing cultural fit through the Business Practices lens:

- Decision-making processes and authorities
- Financial practices: funding, investments, budgeting and reporting
- Management style and practices
- Performance monitoring and management
- Problem solving and conflict resolution
- Process and policy expectations and practices
- Technology expectations and practices
- Formal communications, style and processes
- Interpersonal relationships and communications
- Operating preferences, including the degree of openness and candor, needed planning before taking action, and expected management and employee latitudes

---

3. Discuss the priority areas and how each company currently performs the work.
   - How important is this area to you? In comparison to other areas?
   - What actions are people expected to take and why?
   - Are there differences based on organizational level, functional area, urgency, and so forth?
   - What would be considered to be a problem in this area? How have these problems been handled in the past?

4. Identify Business Practices that will require change for one of the companies.
   - Be specific. Saying "Company B will need to change its decision-making approach" is less actionable than "Company B uses consensus for many decisions we won't delegate in the future. We need to communicate the change and indicate how employees will participate in decision making."

5. Identify the Right vs. Rights to be reconciled. For example:
   - "Both have good funding and investment approaches, but they conflict and need to be reconciled, particularly on how priorities are established, funding is secured, and who resolves disagreements."

6. Assess overall cultural fit and provide appropriate recommendations:
   - Rank each priority area on importance (high, medium, or low).
   - Rate each priority area on cultural fit (high, medium, or low).
   - Use the assessment to provide a go/no-go recommendation, as appropriate.
   - Identify actions to address the culture risks if the deal proceeds.
   - Ensure the business case takes these findings into account.

Applying *Tangible Culture* to Integration

The 2004 KPMG report says that prioritizing synergies and integration planning favorably impact M&A outcomes. Good due diligence can jump-start the integration process. In general, two types of culture gaps must be addressed:

1. A gap where one side needs to change, meaning the other company's Business Practices will be fully adopted, as identified in Table 8-1 Step 4
2. A gap where both companies have viable options and where Right vs. Rights need to be reconciled, as identified in Table 8-1 Step 5

Due diligence cannot tell you everything, so these are starting places. Figures 8-1 and 8-2 show the workflows. Figure 8-1 works with the first bullet above (Table 8-1 Step 4) and Figure 8-2 with the second bullet (Table 8-1 Step 5).

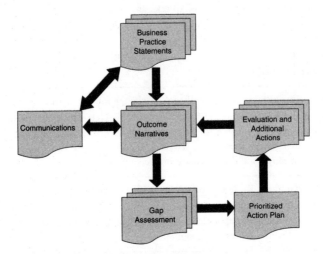

Figure 8-1 Method where one side needs to change.

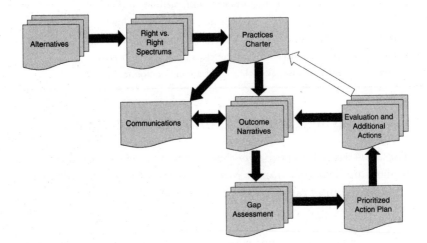

Figure 8-2 Method where Right vs. Rights need to be reconciled.

Example

Let's look at some output examples, then the steps to get you there. The following example shows *Tangible Culture* applied to a small acquisition. (Remember that there are additional M&A experiences in Chapters 4 through 7, "How to Get to the Right Place the Right Way— Outcome Narratives," "The Good Thing That Can Cause Big Trouble— Right vs. Right," "The Unseen Hand That Propels Organizational Action—Business Practices," and "Putting It All Together—The Business Practices Alignment Method," respectively.) Because mergers and acquisitions come in various types, we begin with an explanation of the context and overall intent.

Note that the following details are a compilation from a number of relevant situations.

Context: The deal is an acquisition of a European company (Company B) with similar products and services to the acquirer (Company A). Company A operates mainly in the United States, with limited operations in Europe and Asia. Its growth strategy includes global expansion through targeted acquisitions. Company A is very interested in Company B's European customer base and its sales/marketing organization. Because many of Company B's products and services are similar, an evaluation will be done to determine which should be retained or eliminated because Company A does not want a complex portfolio.

Excerpts from Due Diligence

Business Practices that need to change for the acquired company:

- Company B will need to adopt the more rigorous approach to sales opportunity management. This will require updating the sales-tracking tool weekly, attending bi-weekly sales review calls, and participating in detailed territory reviews quarterly. Today, Company B's approach is ad hoc and locally managed.

Business Practices that will require reconciliation of Right vs. Rights:

- Both companies have excellent approaches to sales compensation and incentives. Although switching to the U.S. approach might seem efficient, we risk losing the motivation of the European sales force if we make changes in this sensitive area.

Table 8-2 shows an example Outcome Narrative where Company B needs to change.

Table 8-2 Example Outcome Narrative Where One Company Needs to Change

Situation

Territory sales have slipped from targets and previous results. The territory executive has scheduled an off-cycle opportunity review to understand the problem and identify actions. The representatives believe the issue is simply one of customer face time and do not want to take the time away from the field, especially during prime customer hours.

Desired Outcome

Customer face time is vital and should be prioritized. The bi-weekly and quarterly reviews are scheduled during noncustomer hours to capitalize on this. However, when warranted, the territory executive may call special reviews, and representatives are expected to attend. To meet both goals, the representatives are encouraged to suggest times to avoid customer conflicts and to identify specific areas in which the territory executive and others can assist in improving results.

In-Scope Roles	Role Behaviors and Actions
Territory executive	Needs to be judicious in calling special reviews. Needs to seek input from the representatives to identify best times before scheduling them. Needs to adopt a problem-solving and supportive style, asking what actions he/she can take to help. Needs to be open to requests for schedule changes and other adjustments based on what best serves the customers.
Sales representative	Needs to be constructive when additional reviews are called. Needs to proactively suggest times that will work best. Needs to come to the review prepared to explain the facts, issues, actions taken, and what could help get results back on track. Needs to be candid and not tell the territory executive what he/she wants to hear. Needs to help revise the forecast and reporting as requested by the territory executive.

Business Practices	Other Considerations
■ Decision making ■ Customer relationships ■ Priorities ■ Leadership ■ Financials	■ Degree of slippage against targets and other territories' results (indicators of severity) ■ Length of time the slippage has been seen ■ Experience levels of the sales representatives ■ Customer base for that territory ■ Economic and other relevant external conditions

Table 8-3 shows excerpts from the practices charter and the Right vs. Right decisions.

Table 8-3 Practices Charter Excerpts

	100%	99–51%	50/50	51–99%	100%	
Decision Making						
Territory executives should make key decisions for the territories, after gathering representative input.			X			Collaborative decision making is best, with territory executives and sales representatives driving to consensus in most cases.

Territory executives are responsible for strategic and financial decisions. Sales representatives should be actively involved in operational and execution decisions. We will frequently seek consensus for operational and execution decisions. If consensus is not possible, the territory executive will use input received to make the decision.

Customer Relationships						
Sales representatives will maintain primary customer relationships.				X		All employees with customer access should build customer relationships.

The customer relationships, and who can best nurture them, need to be decided with specific customers in mind. In general, the sales representative role continues to include primary customer contact. However, depending on the roles of sales engineers and delivery professionals for a particular customer, general roles may be expanded. It is vital to avoid customer confusion, and sales representatives will coordinate efforts.

Priorities						
Achieving near-term results is most important.					X	A balance between near-term and long-term results is best.

Our move into non-U.S. geographies is a long-term investment. We cannot risk prioritizing short-term results at the expense of making this successful. Some quarterly results may be impacted, so we will communicate our strategy externally to support the stock price.

Can Two Rights Make a Wrong?
Insights from IBM's Tangible Culture Approach

134

Table 8-4 shows an example Outcome Narrative to describe the future state.

Table 8-4   Example: Outcome Narrative 1

Situation

The sales representative and sales engineer on an account disagree on how best to approach a customer with a potentially significant issue. The sales engineer believes it is best to raise it early. The sales rep wants to wait until it is clear that the problem exists.

Desired Outcome

In general, on implementation decisions, the sales engineer is responsible. When customer relationships may be impacted, the sales representative's views should be considered. The decision needs to be in line with the sales engineer's "trusted advisor" role. Either the rep or engineer can request the territory executive be consulted before proceeding. All three are expected to participate constructively, focusing on what is best for the customer.

In-Scope Roles	Role Behaviors and Actions
Sales engineer	Needs to put the customer first, while considering the potential impact on sales opportunities. Needs to objectively consider the sales rep's views. Needs to participate actively and constructively in consulting with the territory executive, if appropriate. Should evaluate the best timing and method for the customer communication. Needs to actively reconcile any relationships, internal or with the customer, which may have been negatively impacted by the situation.
Sales representative	Needs to recognize the sales engineer's "trusted advisor" role and how easily this relationship can be damaged. Needs to carefully consider the sales engineer's concerns and prioritize sold work over pending sales if the engineer's concerns are valid and the customer is best served by early notice. Needs to be judicious in asking the territory executive to participate. Needs to constructively support the final decision, and take needed action to help resolve the potential or impending issue. Needs to work actively to reconcile any relationships, internal or with the customer, which may have been impacted.

In-Scope Roles	Role Behaviors and Actions
Territory executive	Needs to be judicious about engaging in the situation, and then participate as a neutral party, seeking the best overall answer for the customer first and company second. Should not make the decision (except in extreme cases), but can give recommendations to the sales engineer. Should promote customer focus and effective relationships between the sales engineer and sales rep. Needs to offer personal assistance to communicate to the customer, if appropriate. Needs to encourage the resolution of any lingering relationship issues.

Right vs. Right Categories Referenced	Other Considerations
■ Decision making ■ Customer relationships ■ Priorities ■ Leadership ■ Communications ■ Financials	■ Length of time each person has served that customer ■ History of other implementations with the customer and its responses to similar issues in the past ■ Number of other situations at this customer that have also been escalated to the territory executive ■ The sales engineer's tenure, history and experience with similar situations

Table 8-5 shows excerpts from the gap assessment and the areas that need change.

Table 8-5   Gap Assessment Excerpts

Gap Assessment for Outcome Narrative 1

■ Sales representatives and territory executives tend to push for answers that benefit sales opportunities only, neglecting the potential impacts of delivery and implementation issues on customer relationships.

■ Most of the time, disagreements are quickly escalated, and often decided in favor of the sales rep by the territory executive.

■ Many past situations have overturned sales engineer decisions, so many "give in" immediately and some have lost "trusted advisor" status with their customers.

■ Territory executives are acting as decision makers and not decision advisors.

Continues

Table 8-5 Gap Assessment Excerpts (Continued)

Gap Assessment for Outcome Narrative 2

■ The answer deemed best for the current quarter is nearly always selected...

Table 8-6 shows excerpts from the prioritized action plan.

Table 8-6 Prioritized Action Plan Excerpts

Prioritized Enablers and Actions

Outcome Narrative 1	Priority
1. Broadly communicate the sales engineer's responsibility for implementation decisions, and how the sales representatives and territory executives are to support and interface with this role.	High
2. Review the sales and territory commission programs and add elements to balance sales and delivery success.	High
3. Communicate that territory executives need to engage these situations as decision advisors and not decision makers.	High
4. Hold a joint workshop on conflict management techniques with sales engineers and sales reps, including a module on "trusted advisor."	Medium

Outcome Narrative 2	
1. Communicate the long-term priorities...	Medium

Table 8-7 shows excerpts from the progress evaluation and additional actions needed.

Table 8-7 Progress Evaluation Excerpts

Progress Evaluation: Outcome Narrative 1

Situation statement: The sales representative and sales engineer on an account disagree on how best to approach a customer with a potentially significant issue. The sales engineer believes it is best to raise it early. The sales rep wants to wait...

Outcome Narrative Expectations	Actual Results and Practices
Desired outcome: In general, on implementation decisions, the sales engineer is responsible. When customer relationships may be impacted, the sales representative's views should be considered. The decision needs to be...	In general, the desired outcome is happening. However, some sales engineers quickly override their best judgment if the territory executive may get involved. Situations where large deals were pending were particularly contentious.
In-scope roles: Sales engineer, sales representative, territory executive.	The right people were involved in the actual situations reviewed.

Role Behaviors and Actions	
Sales engineer: Needs to put the customer first, yet consider the potential impact on sales opportunities. Needs to...	■ In a few situations, needed customer notice was delayed to avoid difficult internal discussions. Each resulted in unwelcome, last-minute surprises for customers.
Sales representative: Needs to recognize the sales engineer's "trusted advisor" role and how easily this relationship can be...	■ Some territory executives continue to make decisions, and in all cases reviewed, they sided with the sales rep.
Territory executive: Needs to be judicious about engaging in the situation, and then participate as a neutral...	■ In most situations in which relationships were strained, those problems continued because no effort was put into resolving the issues.

Additional Actions Needed

■ Coach the territory executives still making decisions on their expected role.

■ Probe each situation that resulted in customer issues to document lessons learned for sales engineers, sales representatives and territory executives.

■ Contact those with ongoing relationship issues to identify what support could help.

Work Steps

To create the outputs for gaps involving one company (Figure 8-1), follow the steps in Table 8-8. To leverage both companies' answers (Figure 8-2), use Table 8-9. Visit www.almaden.ibm.com/tangibleculture to download applicable tools and templates.

Table 8-8   Work Steps Where One Side Needs to Change

Develop Business Practices Statements

---

1. Review the due diligence results.
2. Identify Business Practices from one company to be adopted by the other.
3. Prioritize the Business Practices, as appropriate, and craft into statements. Include detail so that employees will understand what is expected and why.
   - For example: "In general, 'straight talk' is the best way to communicate, even if it is uncomfortable. We encourage employees at all levels to state their views openly and constructively, and we expect others to constructively consider those views. 'Straight talk' improves decisions and encourages employee commitment. Although 'straight talk' can't ensure everyone will agree, we'll be more likely to understand the considerations."

Develop Outcome Narratives

---

4. Identify problem situations that convey the new expectations.
   - Seek to convey multiple Business Practices whenever possible. For example, a Business Practice about "straight talk" may be easily combined with ones on decision-making and management style.
5. Develop Outcome Narratives for these new expectations (see Table 8-2).

Develop and Deploy Communications

---

6. Develop a communications plan for this stage and other stages of the effort.
   - Incorporate a feedback loop for formal and informal input. It will increase commitment and identify areas that need additional clarification.
7. Communicate the Business Practices statements and Outcome Narratives.
8. Consider whether the communications will be enough or if barriers may inhibit the change. A gap assessment is needed if there are barriers.
   - For example, if management style expectations are different, but many of the same managers will fill positions, it may be advisable to look at the gaps.

Perform the Gap Assessment and develop the Prioritized Action Plan

---

9. Perform the gap assessment, as appropriate.
10. Identify and prioritize the actions needed to bridge the gaps.
    - For example, for a management style change, education, coaching and mentoring may be appropriate, along with a self-assessment job aid.
11. Establish the appropriate timeframe for evaluating progress.

Evaluate Progress and Identify Additional Actions

12. At the identified milestones, gather information about actual situations and compare them to the Outcome Narratives.

13. Identify any continuing gaps, and determine if additional actions are needed.

Table 8-9   Work Steps Where Right vs. Rights Need to Be Reconciled

Identify and Reconcile the Right vs. Rights

1. Review the due diligence results.

2. Identify the areas that surfaced Right vs. Right options to be reconciled.

3. Meet with key members of both organizations and probe into existing Business Practices in these areas, as well as related areas not covered during due diligence.

4. Gather example problem situations and how each company handles them.

5. Identify Business Practices that are advocated yet conflict with other advocated Business Practices, and validate their importance.

6. Craft the Right vs. Right pairs into the Right vs. Right template (see the first three rows of Table 8-3).

7. Gather inputs from selected people on the answers they believe are most appropriate.

  ◆ It is important to reinforce the uneven scaling in the template. See Table 5-4 in Chapter 5 for additional explanation.

8. Convene the decision makers to select the Right vs. Right answers. Collect the final decisions and discussion details to clarify the decisions.

9. Validate the decisions, as appropriate.

Clarify and Communicate the Practices Charter

10. Craft summary statements to communicate the Right vs. Right decisions.

11. Combine the Right vs. Right decisions, discussions, and summary statements into a practices charter.

12. Communicate the practices charter.

Develop, Validate, and Communicate the Outcome Narratives

13. Identify problem situations (approximately 20 to 30) that represent the reconciled Right vs. Rights.

  ◆ Focus on situations where people must collaborate on decisions and action, and where answers are unclear or reasonable people can disagree.

  ◆ Select problem situations that demonstrate multiple elements of the practices charter.

Continues

Table 8-9   Work Steps Where Right vs. Rights Need to Be Reconciled (Continued)

Develop, Validate, and Communicate the Outcome Narratives

14. Use the practices charter to create Outcome Narratives, clarifying

- Desired outcome
- In-scope roles
- Desired behaviors and actions for each role
- Additional considerations that could impact the desired outcome
- References, including Right vs. Rights, values, and principles

15. Validate the Outcome Narratives, as appropriate.

16. Communicate the Outcome Narratives.

- Cascade them through managers to reinforce the new leadership positions.
- Consider a workshop format to enable people to develop, compare and discuss their answers to the official Outcome Narratives.

Identify and Prioritize the Gaps

17. Identify differences between current handling and the Outcome Narratives.

18. Clarify the gaps, looking for both obvious and subtle aspects, and recognizing there will be multiple gaps as each company starts from a different place.

19. Summarize and prioritize the gaps, looking for areas applicable to multiple Outcome Narratives.

Build and Launch the Prioritized Action Plan

20. Identify and design actions for the prioritized gaps.

21. Build an action plan, along with an appropriate timetable for evaluating progress.

22. Implement the actions in the prioritized action plan.

Evaluate Progress and Identify Additional Actions

23. At the identified milestones, gather information on how situations were handled.

24. Compare handling of actual situations to the Outcome Narratives.

- Was the desired outcome achieved in the desired timeframe?
- Did the right people get involved at the right time?
- Did the people perform the identified actions in the described way?
- Are there indications of additional Right vs. Right conflicts?
- Are clarifications needed for some Outcome Narratives?
- Do Outcome Narratives need to be written for new problem situations?

Evaluate Progress and Identify Additional Actions

---

25. Identify additional actions needed to address ongoing gaps.
26. Identify any new or ongoing Right vs. Right issues that need reconciliation and initiate the process.
27. Launch definition of additional Outcome Narratives to address new issues and/or issues that were tabled earlier.

Benefits

In general, *Tangible Culture* can help to mitigate the culture clash inherent when bringing multiple companies together. The activities are a proactive approach and, in addition to the benefits listed in Chapters 4 through 7, help to

- Broaden the options for dealing with the culture challenges.
- Enable the companies to consider multiple views, which helps to avoid mandated decisions—often the default when issues linger on.
- Better leverage what both companies can bring to the combined organization.
- Reduce the chances of alienating and losing key personnel.

Conclusion

Many organizations will experience a merger or acquisition, and for some, it is a way of life. Bringing multiple organizations together always risks culture clash, so a proactive approach is needed. *Tangible Culture* can be used to improve both due diligence and integration. In particular, it can facilitate decisions to leverage both companies' capabilities and communicate new expectations. Now, let's move on to another situation where companies join forces: alliances.

Can Two Rights Make a Wrong?
Insights from IBM's Tangible Culture Approach

142

References

Ashkenas, R. N., L. J. DeMonaco, and S. C. Francis. "Making the Deal Real: How GE Capital Integrates Acquisitions," *Harvard Business Review*, January–February 1998, pp. 169.

Bower, J. L. "Not all M & As are Alike—and That Matters," *Harvard Business Review*, March 2001.

Carleton, J. R., and C. S. Lineberry. *Achieving Post-Merger Success: A Stakeholder's Guide to Cultural Due Diligence, Assessment, and Integration*. San Francisco: John Wiley & Sons, Inc., 2004, pp. 14–15.

Davenport, T. O. "The Integration Challenge." *American Management Association International*, January 1998.

Gibson, S., and P. Love. "Hidden sore points that can thwart a culture match," *Mergers and Acquisitions*, May–June 1999.

Grossman, R. L. "Irreconcilable Differences," *HR Magazine*, April 1999.

Haines, L. "After the honeymoon." *Oil & Gas Investor, (Suppl. Performance powered: The new value drivers for the energy industry)*, Second Quarter 1997.

Haspeslagh, P. "Maintaining Momentum in Mergers," European Business Forum. www.europeanbusinessforum.com, pp. 2–3.

Hewitt Associates, "Is HR a Mergers & Acquisitions Deal Maker or Breaker?" November 2003, http://was4.hewitt.com/hewitt/worldwide/europe/uk/.

KPMG International, "Beating the Bears: Making global deals enhance value in the new millennium." 2004.

Lublin, J. S., and B. O'Brian. "Merged firms often face culture clash—Businesses offer advice on ways to avoid minefields." *Wall Street Journal*, February 14, 1997, p. A9A.

Panko, R. "After the Ink is Dry," *Best's Review*, June 1999.

Vermeulen, F., and H. Barkema. "Learning through acquisitions," *Academy of Management Journal*, June 2001.

9

Alliances—Finding Ways to Leverage Your Collective Capabilities

By Sara Moulton Reger, Cheryl Grise, and Lisa Kreeger

Chapter Contents

Can Two Rights Make a Wrong?
Insights from IBM's Tangible Culture Approach

144

Overview

This chapter applies *Tangible Culture* to business alliances. The business and culture challenges for alliances are discussed, then Business Practices, Right vs. Right and Outcome Narratives are applied to them, using composite examples from our experiences. We will also provide a list of benefits. Those planning or implementing a multi-enterprise venture will find value in this chapter.

Introduction

Alliances are essential in today's business environment. Few, if any, companies can perform all capabilities needed to compete globally. Unfortunately, alliances often suffer from culture clash (see Chapter 1, "Introduction—An Overview of *Tangible Culture*"). Choosing to "go it alone" is not an effective option for most companies, so business leaders need ways to address the inherent culture risks.

Business Challenges

Partnerships and alliances' come in many different flavors, from joint ventures to strategic alliances to outsourcing to joint teaming. Some alliances are strategic, whereas others are primarily transactional; some involve multifaceted multi-organizational linkages, whereas others are relatively simple with straightforward connections.

In the 1990s, many alliances were formed to outsource noncore activities to providers offering lower cost. Today, for several reasons, business leaders are rethinking notions of core and noncore, and driving instead to achieve world-class capabilities in every area:

- Economic and competitive pressures are escalating and compelling companies to seek new sources of productivity and growth.
- Open standards are more widely adopted, which enables interconnectivity within and among companies.

---

1. Some experts use *interorganizational relationships* to overcome terminology overlaps. For simplicity, we use *alliance* for any type of interorganizational relationship and *partner* for the parties.

- Free trade agreements, and explosive skills growth in emerging nations, are opening new opportunities.

These factors point toward even broader interorganizational relationships, and to new relationship models, in the hunt for productivity and effectiveness gains.

In addition, alliance structures are becoming more complex. Many companies partner and compete with the same companies in different markets and for different products. And there are multi-partner alliances. Think about the cross-organizational requirements for Homeland Security and current military efforts, which cross military branches and governmental agencies—and, increasingly, allies. Although many business alliances tend to be one on one, indications are for more multi-organizational alliances in the future.

Alliances are important, with a typical corporation relying on them for 15 to 20 percent of revenues, assets, or income. Although many alliances are successful, others are not, and the overall success rate is about 50 percent over an average life of five to seven years. (Ernst and Bamford) "To add to CEOs' woes, research suggests that 40 to 55 percent of alliances break down prematurely and inflict financial damage on both partners." (Dyer, Kale, and Singh)

An early business challenge is ensuring all partners understand and agree to the nature of the relationship. Every alliance should be unique because the objectives and parties are specific to that relationship. Even new alliances among existing partners should differ because of new objectives.

After agreeing to the objectives and relationship, the partners may face other challenges:

- Priorities that shift over time
- Lack of skill in dealing with alliance complexities
- Lack of technology to manage the communications and content of the relationship (for example, portals, repositories, collaborative software)
- Difficulty in establishing planning protocols (for example, perform the work separately and later combine, or perform jointly; one approach or varied situational approaches)

- Differences in organizational ability to adapt to the changes
- Loss of key experts
- Unforeseen problems with the viability of the project
- Ineffective relationships

Arguably, this last challenge is a culture challenge—so we cover that topic next.

Culture Challenges

Let's go deeper on relationships. After negotiation, the alliance deal teams are disbanded and an execution team is assembled, sometimes with little overlap. The execution team may know little about the detailed discussions that led to the words in the agreement and how performance and success are to be measured—this is where many relationship issues begin. We strongly believe that real relationships are built on more than service level agreements—and that relationships are needed at many levels, not just among executives.

> *"Right vs. Right business practices sound so basic, but I can say from experience that it's hard to determine what's happening when cross-organizational teams clash or are at a stand still. Business leaders often don't think about culture, and they often lack the background and tools to address the culture challenges that lead to issues and risks."*
>
> **Cindy Berger**
> **Vice President**
> **American Express**

To better explain what goes into an effective relationship and further describe the culture challenge, Table 9-1 mentions some important, and difficult, alliance elements.

Table 9-1 Alliance Elements

Decision Making

- Translate the central intent of the relationship into goals and effective decisions.
- Agree on decision-making protocols and who has power for what decisions.
- Jointly set mutually appropriate priorities and timetables.
- Agree on competitive positioning for new offerings.

Knowledge Sharing and Communication

- Define the level and nature of information exchange.
- Decide the best way to communicate decisions to impacted personnel.
- Decide handling of intellectual capital, especially what is created together.
- Agree on the appropriate level and type of documentation for created knowledge.

Governance and Relationships

- Define how joint roles and responsibilities will be navigated.
- Define how conflict will be resolved.
- Agree on appropriate types of interpersonal interaction.
- Agree on how the relationship will evolve over time and as situations change.

Given the types of alliances and their potential complexities, Table 9-1 lists just a sample. However, this list hints at some reasons for culture risk: Intertwined with each element is a series of Business Practices that define how best to decide, communicate, enact, resolve, and manage them. Each company brings its own answers—and they need to decide some together, which may give the partners their first taste of culture clash.

When deciding what to do together, each is likely to expect its own preferences will be adopted—because, indeed, they are right answers. Unfortunately, these often-assumed expectations promote direct conflict between the partners. No matter how well the agreement is written and what has been clarified through principles, values, and behavior statements, unreconciled Right vs. Right Business Practices can lead to failure, even dissolution and major losses.

If you think companies walk away from deals that indicate poor cultural fit, you may be surprised. The Corporate Strategy Board indicates that cultural differences rarely stop alliances from going forward. Their recommendations: Assess cultural fit, and then plan and deal with the

148

Can Two Rights Make a Wrong?
Insights from IBM's Tangible Culture Approach

issues through effective governance, accountability, and performance management. We agree and believe even more can be done.

> *"Alliances mean no longer owning the work—and often changing preferred ways of working. Assuming you know how your partner operates—and that it is just like you do—destines your partnership to failure. It is essential for both partners to understand each other's practices, and the change impacts. Right vs. Right enables a neutral discussion to resolve the predictable tension."*
>
> **Janet Young**
> **President**
> **Change Edge Consulting, LLC**

In some ways, alliances share M&A culture risks. However, there is one key difference: The partners often carry responsibilities that interlock only in specific areas, whereas in M&As, groups often blend by functional area. Although some alliances do that (see Chapter 8, "Mergers and Acquisitions—Managing the Common Sources of Culture Clash," where that is the case), many are crafted to leverage diverse capabilities. This means, for culture purposes, a combination strategy is needed: reconciling Right vs. Right for interdependent areas, and acknowledging and managing expectations in areas where each company will retain its own Business Practices.

Handling Related "People" Risks

A number of actions are needed to address inherent alliance challenges. The rest of the chapter focuses on culture, so here we offer some brief advice on related topics:

- Governance is vital, and how it is initially established sets the tone for the relationship between the companies and people involved. Structures, decision making, roles and responsibilities, and performance measurement are just a few of the elements that need to be covered. Facilitators can help the partners know what is needed and can help set an environment where trust can be built.

- Communications are tricky because they cross organizational boundaries and are often extra sensitive. Each partner needs its own communication team, and these teams need to coordinate. During the initial stages, be sure to answer: "Who are the key players on the other side? What are the objectives? Who does what?"

- Organizational change management helps employees achieve full functioning as quickly as possible. Remember that you are enabling a transition that is new for many people—participating in a cross-organizational team. Selecting leaders with strong influence skills and compatible working styles is critical. Also, do not assume that little needs to be done if people will perform the same work they have done in the past (for example, in outsourcing). Alliances bring interaction complexities, which often require additional knowledge and skills.

Alliances that skimp on these vital steps increase their risk of failure. Even if one partner does extremely well at addressing the risks, the alliance may fail if the other partner does not. Holding each other accountable is an important risk mitigation strategy.

In addition to these vital steps, companies are encouraged to jointly develop principles, values, and behavior expectations. It is good to compare and discuss existing values and other stated expectations to understand how they are the same or different. These discussions promote effective relationships and cross-organizational transparency.

When these efforts are launched, it is appropriate to turn to the sources of culture clash and proactively address them before ineffective norms become entrenched. *Tangible Culture* applies to two alliance phases: research/negotiation and leverage. Research/negotiation starts when the alliance is explored and continues until an agreement is signed. Leverage picks up when the partners begin working together.

Applying *Tangible Culture* to Research/ Negotiation Phase

Effective alliances begin with careful partner selection. It is like premarital discussions: Ask the right questions before the big day, and hope to experience fewer surprises later.

During research, the partners evaluate each other's ability to perform. This often involves a series of discussions about capabilities on topics that could include markets, products and services, processes, technology, and human resources—just to name a few. Cultural fit is relevant but tends to be under-represented in the discussions.

> *"After interviewing dozens of CIOs about outsourcing, AMR Research recognizes that most companies lack a structured evaluation process, and therefore they don't adequately evaluate cultural fit when selecting a partner. Offshore outsourcing exacerbates the problem—not only must you must consider work-related alliance elements (decision making, knowledge sharing, and governance), but also the broader geography and historical cultural issues."*
>
> Lance Travis
> Vice President, Research
> AMR Research

A Vantage Partners study of 130 cross-industry companies involved in alliances showed that only 9 percent have an institutionalized capability to evaluate relationship fit, corporate culture, and operating style. Instead, many rely on the intuition or "gut senses" of those involved with the deal. (Ertel, Weiss, and Visioni) This seems hard to believe given the acknowledged failure rates for alliances. Perhaps people do not know what to ask.

We advocate that each party assess cultural fit during research/negotiation using the lens of Business Practices and Right vs. Right. These concepts provide specific questions to ask and can identify areas where action will be needed if the alliance goes forward. See Table 9-2 for ideas on how to assess cultural fit.

Table 9-2 Work Steps to Assess Cultural Fit

---

1. Consider the intent of the alliance, and what areas need to be leveraged.

- ♦ How closely do the partners need to work together and in what areas?
- ♦ Will the partners bring what they currently do into the alliance, or will new capabilities, processes, and so on be created for the alliance?

---

2. Identify priority areas for assessing cultural fit and Business Practices alignment:
   ◆ Decision-making processes and authorities
   ◆ Financial practices (for example, funding, investments, and reporting)
   ◆ Management style and practices
   ◆ Governance structures, processes, and mechanisms
   ◆ Performance monitoring and management
   ◆ Problem solving and conflict resolution
   ◆ Process and technology expectations and practices
   ◆ Communication mechanisms and processes
   ◆ Operating preferences, including degree of openness and candor, required planning before taking action, and expected management and employee latitudes

3. Discuss the priority areas, with emphasis on how the work is currently performed and what will be best for the alliance. Some good questions to ask:
   ◆ Generally, how does this topic work within your organization today?
   ◆ Do you believe that this is a viable approach for the alliance? If not, what adjustments do you think are warranted?
   ◆ What actions are people expected to take on this topic?
   ◆ What priority does this topic have for you?
   ◆ What constitutes problems in this area? How do you handle them?

4. As possible, identify Business Practices that need to change for each partner.
   ◆ Be specific. Saying "Company A will need to change its approach to problem solving" is less actionable than "Company A prefers subject matter experts to resolve problems. The alliance will need collaborative problem solving for people to understand the problem and avoid repeats."

5. Identify and evaluate the types of Right vs. Rights to be reconciled—for areas where the partners need to work interdependently yet their approaches differ. For example:
   ◆ "Expectations about process adherence need clarification. Company A expects close adherence for consistency and risk mitigation. Company B expects employees to use the process, but apply judgment as they deem appropriate. We need the benefits of both to achieve our objectives."

6. Assess overall cultural fit, and provide appropriate recommendations:
   ◆ Weigh each priority area as high, medium, or low importance.
   ◆ Assess each priority area as high, medium, or low cultural fit.
   ◆ Contribute to the overall recommendation of go/no go, as appropriate.
   ◆ Identify actions to address the culture risks if the alliance proceeds.
   ◆ Provide input to hone the business case objectives and schedules.

A Vantage Partners study of negotiation best practices reinforces that research and selection should be done by both sides. Also, frequently done in parallel with research, negotiation needs to be collaborative and undertaken as a foundation for building good working relationships rather than as an opportunity for each company to push for its own very best deal. (Hughes and Gordon) We agree.

Applying *Tangible Culture* to Leverage Phase

The leverage phase incorporates three stages: transition, manage/measure, and advance/grow. We focus on transition and into the manage/measure stages, but many of the same steps can help the partners advance and grow their relationship, too.

Figure 9-1 shows the overall process for leverage, expressed in key outputs.

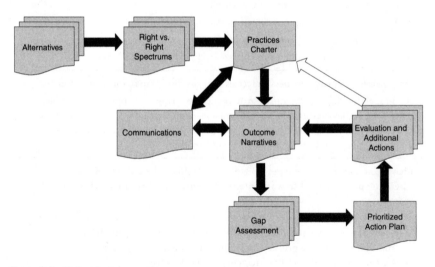

Figure 9-1   Method for leverage phase.

Let's start with an example of how the outputs would look, and then identify the steps in getting there. We use an outsourcing context for this example. The story line is not taken from any one situation; instead, it represents a composite of relevant experiences.

Example

Context: The agreement is for outsourcing a company's technology operations. The primary goal is immediate cost reduction. The company is growing and also wants to ensure that operations are a progressively smaller percentage of total costs. The company is also expanding into new markets and product areas and wants the outsourcer to help them in areas that may be innovative for both companies. Finally, the CIO wants the outsourcer to help instill a greater degree of standardization and process adherence.

Table 9-3 shows excerpts from the practices charter and the Right vs. Right decisions.

Table 9-3 Practices Charter Excerpts

	100%	99–51%	50/50	51–99%	100%	
Decision Making						
Employees should make decisions and take action with the idea that this is a permanent alliance.		X				Employees should consider the five-year term of this contract in making decisions and taking actions.
Employees at all levels are expected to think of this as a "blended family." The term of the contract is not relevant to most employees' daily decision making. Employees are expected to trust senior leaders for handling the contract, and consider the contract only when they are brought into specific discussions where it is identified as relevant.						
Priorities						
Achieving fast results is more important than following consistent procedures.				X		Adherence to processes/procedures is vital to mitigate risk and decrease costs.
Within Operations, employees need to adhere to processes and procedures. This will mitigate risk, contain costs, and enable consistency, all of which are vital for problem detection, resource back fills, and transfers. On occasion, there will be reasons to deviate from stated processes and procedures, and approval from a director or above will be required.						

Continues

Table 9-3 Practices Charter Excerpts (Continued)

	100%	99–51%	50/50	51–99%	100%	
Governance						
When deciding what to do in difficult situations, the company has more clout than the outsourcer.			X			When deciding what to do in difficult situations, the companies drive to consensus and escalate only when contractual issues are in play.

The intent is a strategic alliance, and will be managed that way. However, Operations are not the purpose of this company, rather an enabler to it. We expect employees of both companies to care deeply about our customers. The company is in a better position to make some decisions, particularly when lines of business impacts are in play. We will seek consensus, but the company will decide when consensus cannot be achieved.

Table 9-4 shows an example Outcome Narrative to clarify future-state expectations.

Table 9-4 Example: Outcome Narrative 1

Situation

A line-of-business leader has requested a project due date that an outsourcing leader believes is aggressive and is likely to be missed. The due date is important for a new customer program. The outsourcer is concerned about following the procedures necessary to ensure against negative impacts on availability and current capabilities.

Desired Outcome

In general, availability and current capabilities are top priority, and the outsourcer is responsible for them. However, for significant market responses, the governance leader may agree to accept some risks as long as there are mitigation plans and the risks can be isolated to that line of business. The companies are expected to agree on the earliest date that appropriately mitigates the risks.

In-Scope Roles	Role Behaviors and Actions
Company governance leader	Needs to help the line of business and outsourcing leaders assess the situation, functioning as an independent mediator to find the best overall answer. Helps to assess the market requirements versus the potential for negative impacts. Makes the decision where the line of business and outsourcing leaders cannot agree. Needs to ensure that documentation and plans are completed to handle the risks and any potential exposures accepted by both companies.
Line-of-business leader	Needs to objectively assess the market requirement and compare it to the availability and current capability risks. Needs to be open to negotiating a date that meets all needs. Needs to help mitigate risks whether or not the dates are revised. If the risks cross lines of business or are too significant, needs to defer to the governance leader's decision on a revised date and avoid the temptation to escalate the decision except under extreme situations.
Outsourcing leader	Needs to be flexible, within reasonable limits, to process and procedure changes to help the line of business meet its requirements. Needs to be willing to modify priorities, with the concurrence of the governance leader, to put resources on the project if deemed appropriate. Needs to remain responsible for the availability and current capabilities, but defer to the decisions made by the governance leader in accepting some risks. Needs to help the governance leader gather and complete the risk plans and documentation.

Right vs. Right Categories Referenced	Other Considerations
■ Decision making ■ Priorities ■ Governance ■ Leadership approach ■ Communications ■ Measures	■ Nature and degree of availability and capability risks ■ Stage of life cycle for the line of business ■ Other exceptions underway and their potential impact on availability and current capability ■ History of line of business in declaring market necessities and the justification for those declarations ■ Recent history with availability and capabilities: Are things stable at the time of this request?

Table 9-5 shows excerpts from the gap assessment.

Table 9-5 Gap Assessment Excerpts

Gap Assessment for Outcome Narrative 1

- The decision that availability and current capabilities are top priorities is not widely known, and where known in the lines of business, is not always accepted.
- Few outsourcing leaders have authority to make process and procedure changes. Sometimes they do not "feel" they have authority even when they do (or are concerned about personal risk), so decisions are typically escalated and slow.
- Lines of business deem most projects to be "significant market responses."
- Governance leaders typically defer to the lines of business to avoid being escalated and incurring internal political risks.
- It is not clear how to adjust the service level agreements (SLAs) for risks and exposures accepted by the company.
- Priorities cut across lines of business, and changing priorities to address one line of business may cause resource exposures in another.

Gap Assessment for Outcome Narrative 2

- Executives have not provided guidance about the cost implications...

Table 9-6 shows excerpts from the prioritized action plan to align the environment with the future state expectations.

Table 9-6 Prioritized Action Plan Excerpts

Prioritized Enablers and Actions

Outcome Narrative 1	Priority
1. Revise the levels of authority for outsourcing leaders to make appropriate process and procedure changes in identified situations.	High
2. Ask the CIO to communicate to senior line of business executives that availability and current capabilities are top priorities and why.	High
3. Develop criteria for projects to be "significant market responses."	High
4. Communicate with senior executives that we want to avoid these escalations and ask them to delegate back rather than get involved.	Medium

Prioritized Enablers and Actions	
Outcome Narrative 1	**Priority**
5. Establish guidelines for when and how SLAs should be adjusted.	Medium
Outcome Narrative 2	
1. Ask the CIO to provide priorities in handling cost implications for ...	High

Table 9-7 shows excerpts from the progress evaluation and additional actions needed.

Table 9-7 Progress Evaluation Excerpts

Progress Evaluation: Outcome Narrative 1	
Situation statement: A line of business leader has requested a project due date that an outsourcing leader believes is aggressive and is likely to be missed. The due date is ...	
Outcome Narrative Expectations	**Actual Results and Practices**
Desired outcome: In general, availability and current capabilities are top priority, and the outsourcer is responsible for them. However, for significant market ...	Generally, the desired outcome happens. In a few situations, the line of business leader did not accept the governance leader's decision for later dates.
In-scope roles: Governance leader, line of business leader, outsourcing leader	The right people were involved in the actual situations reviewed.
Role Actions and Behaviors **Company governance leader:** Needs to help the line of business and outsourcing leaders assess the situation ... **Line of business leader:** Needs to objectively assess the market requirement and compare it to the availability and ... **Outsourcing leader:** Needs to be flexible, within reasonable limits, to process and procedure changes to help ...	■ When dates were pushed out, one line of business escalated to senior executives, who sometimes made decisions without exploring both sides. ■ Significant time was spent determining what to do with SLAs when the company chose to accept risks. ■ Some outsourcing leaders did not quickly make the needed adjustments, and expressed discomfort that these changes could "set precedence" and result in future risks.

Continues

Table 9-7 Progress Evaluation Excerpts (Continued)

Additional Actions Needed

- Monitor the line of business where escalations occur frequently to determine the source and whether it will continue over time. Consider a meeting to understand why the escalations are happening so frequently and seek a resolution.

- Develop a reference repository of SLA changes from various situations, along with an assessment of their effectiveness after implementation.

- Meet with the outsourcing leaders who were reticent to make adjustments to understand their concerns and address them.

Work Steps

To create the outputs above (for Figure 9-1), follow the steps in Table 9-8. And, visit www.almaden.ibm.com/tangibleculture to download applicable tools and templates.

Table 9-8 Work Steps for Leverage Phase

Identify and Reconcile the Right vs. Rights

1. Meet with key partner leaders and ask questions that probe into Business Practices in areas important for alliance success. The list may include
   - Decision-making.
   - Funding and investments.
   - Measures and accountability.
   - Problem solving.
   - Priorities.
   - Processes, procedures and policies.
   - Escalation.
   - Resourcing and assignments.
   - Leadership and communication styles.
2. Gather examples of problem situations and preferred partner handling.
3. Compare the partner's Business Practices to your own company's Business Practices to identify Right vs. Rights that need to be clarified and resolved.
4. Craft the Right vs. Right pairs into the Right vs. Right template. (See the first three rows of Table 9-3.)
5. Gather input from selected people on the answers they believe are most appropriate.
   - It is important to reinforce the uneven scaling in the template. See Table 5-4 in Chapter 5, "The Good Thing That Can Cause Big Trouble—Right vs. Right," for additional explanation.

Identify and Reconcile the Right vs. Rights

6. Convene decision makers to select the most appropriate answer for the alliance. Collect final answers and discussion details to clarify the decisions.

7. Distinguish between Business Practices that require change for one or more partners and other Business Practices that are different but will continue and need to be acknowledged and accepted by the other party.

8. Validate the decisions with appropriate leaders.

Clarify and Communicate the Practices Charter

9. Document the decisions and craft summaries to communicate the decisions into a practices charter.

10. Develop a communications plan to be used at this stage as well as later.

   ♦ Incorporate a feedback loop for formal and informal input. It will increase commitment and identify areas that need additional clarification.

11. Communicate the decisions documented in the practices charter.

Develop, Validate, and Communicate the Outcome Narratives

12. Identify problem situations (approximately 20 to 30) that represent the reconciled Right vs. Rights.

   ♦ Focus on situations where people must collaborate on decisions and action, and where answers are unclear or reasonable people can disagree.

   ♦ Select problem situations that demonstrate multiple elements of the practices charter.

13. Use the practices charter to create Outcome Narratives, clarifying

   ♦ Desired outcome

   ♦ In-scope roles

   ♦ Desired behaviors and actions for each role

   ♦ Additional considerations that could impact the desired outcome

   ♦ References, including Right vs. Rights, values, and principles

14. Validate the Outcome Narratives, as appropriate.

15. Communicate the Outcome Narratives.

   ♦ Cascade them through managers to reinforce their leadership positions.

   ♦ Consider a workshop format to enable people to develop, compare and discuss their answers to the official Outcome Narratives.

Identify and Prioritize the Gaps

16. Identify differences between current handling and the Outcome Narratives.

17. Clarify the gaps, looking for both obvious and subtle aspects.

18. Summarize and prioritize the gaps, being careful to prioritize those applicable to multiple Outcome Narratives.

Continues

160

Can Two Rights Make a Wrong?
Insights from IBM's Tangible Culture Approach

Table 9-8 Work Steps for Leverage Phase (Continued)

Build and Launch the Prioritized Action Plan

19. Identify and design actions to address the prioritized gaps.

20. Build an action plan, along with an appropriate time table for evaluating progress.

21. Implement the actions in the prioritized action plan.

Evaluate Progress and Identify Additional Actions

22. At the identified milestones, gather information on how situations were handled.

23. Compare handling of actual situations to the Outcome Narratives.

- ◆ Was the desired outcome achieved in the desired timeframe?
- ◆ Did the right people get involved at the right time?
- ◆ Did the people perform the identified actions in the described way?
- ◆ Are there indications of additional Right vs. Right conflicts?
- ◆ Are clarifications needed for some Outcome Narratives?
- ◆ Do Outcome Narratives need to be written for new problem situations?

24. Identify additional actions needed to address ongoing gaps.

25. Identify any new or ongoing Right vs. Rights that need reconciliation and initiate the process.

26. Launch definition of additional Outcome Narratives to address new issues and/or issues that were tabled earlier.

Benefits

The overall benefit of applying *Tangible Culture* to alliances is risk mitigation. In addition to the benefits we have mentioned in earlier chapters, you will find

- ■ The health of the alliance is less vulnerable to leadership changes and the personal relationships between key individuals.
- ■ Consistency is enhanced, which establishes and manages expectations (especially important for large alliances and ones that function in multiple geographies).
- ■ Confusion is reduced, particularly role confusion about who needs to do what.

Conclusion

At some point, most organizations will engage in the risky business of alliances—and many rely on them extensively. Although they take many different forms, all alliances must acknowledge and address culture risks to be successful. Using *Tangible Culture* starting with the research/negotiation phase, and continuing into the operations of the alliance, the partners can enhance their chances of achieving their original expectations and fully capitalizing on the alliance's potential.

Now that we have discussed two types of multi-enterprise situations, let's look at culture within a single enterprise, starting with restructuring efforts.

References

Corporate Executive Board. "Joint Venture Toolkit," Corporate Strategy Board, November 2002, p. 3.

Dyer, J. H., P. Kale, and H. Singh. "When to Ally & When to Acquire," *Harvard Business Review*, July–August 2004, p. 109.

Ernst, D., and J. Bamford. "Your Alliances Are Too Stable," *Harvard Business Review*, June 2005, p. 133.

Ertel, D., J. Weiss, and L. J. Visioni. *Managing Alliance Relationships: Ten Key Corporate Capabilities*. Boston: Vantage Partners, 2001, pp. 12, 34.

Hughes, J., and M. Gordon. *Negotiating and Managing Key Supplier Relationships: A Cross-Industry Study of 20 Best Practices*. Boston: Vantage Partners, 2003, p. 11.

Hughes, J., and J. Weiss. *Making Partnerships Work: A Relationship Management Handbook*. Boston: Vantage Partners, 2001.

Kosits, M., D. Hawk, and D. Ing. *Relationship Alignment: Reducing Friction, Realizing Value*. IBM Corporation, 2004.

Kreeger, L. D. "Alliance Leadership: Intersecting Two Indistinct Borderlands," 2004.

Lajara, B. M., F. G. Lillo, and V. S. Sempere. "Human resources management in the formulation and implementation of strategic alliances," *Human Systems Management 21*, IOS Press, 2002, pp. 205–215.

Parkhe, A. "Interfirm diversity, organizational learning, and longevity in global strategic alliances," *Journal of International Business Studies*, 1991, pp. 579–601.

10

Major Restructuring— Gaining Sustained Value from Your Reorganization

By Sara Moulton Reger, Cheryl Grise and
Dave Lubowe

Chapter Contents

164

Can Two Rights Make a Wrong?
Insights from IBM's Tangible Culture Approach

Overview

This chapter applies *Tangible Culture* to major restructuring efforts, using shared services as an example. The business and culture challenges are discussed, along with steps and examples of applying Business Practices, Right vs. Right, and Outcome Narratives using our composite experiences. This chapter will help people who are planning and executing major restructuring efforts. Also, depending on the nature of their restructuring, readers may also benefit from insights in Chapters 8, 9, and 11 ("Mergers and Acquisitions—Managing the Common Sources of Culture Clash," "Alliances—Finding Ways to Leverage Your Collective Capabilities," and "Major Transformation—Addressing Your Plan's Hidden Barrier," respectively).

Introduction

Often triggered by a specific event, companies restructure their operations in a fairly significant way. The triggering event could be

- Change in the market (either threat or opportunity).
- Indication that costs need to be significantly reduced (for example, drop in stock price).
- Regulatory change.
- Change in leadership.

This list represents only a fraction of the possible triggers.

By definition, restructuring takes what currently exists and rearranges it into a new, and often a smaller, form. Restructuring can be unsettling and is often much like internal mergers and alliances. Companies that want good success with their restructuring efforts are wise to consider culture as a risk that needs to be proactively evaluated and addressed.

Business Challenges

The business challenge for restructuring depends greatly on the intent. For example, there may be the need to

- Create collaboration and reduce silos by combining previously separate groups.
- Integrate earlier acquisitions that are operating autonomously for consistency and efficiencies.
- Consolidate fragmented capabilities to manage business risks or respond effectively to regulatory requirements.

Also, the centralization/decentralization pendulum swings back and forth. Sometimes it is driven by a specific event, but often it is simply an acknowledgement that the current choice is not perfect. However, the alternative is not perfect either—hence the swing.

Because restructuring is so vast, we use shared services throughout this chapter because it is a good example of the benefits companies seek by restructuring.

Shared services combine functional groups into one or more centralized units, and often target reduced costs and improved delivery through standardization, control, and integration—which enable process rigor over time. When regulations change (for example, Sarbanes-Oxley), this rigor helps companies to quickly and effectively implement the requirements.

Shared services are a way for companies to consolidate capabilities and knowledge, which can improve insights and decision making, and provide better career paths for professionals. They can also be a route to outsourcing and additional benefits.

By adopting shared services, companies have produced savings of 25 to 50 percent and an average ROI of 27 percent. These benefits are impressive alone, and even more impressive because they often come with improved service and increased customer satisfaction. (Fahy)

Shared services can help companies rapidly implement technology. Because changes are made in fewer locations, less time and coordination are needed. Also, companies growing through acquisition may find that simply having the shared services center can reduce the number of integration decisions—all applicable functions go directly to the shared services center. For many reasons, shared services are growing both in

Can Two Rights Make a Wrong?
Insights from IBM's Tangible Culture Approach

166

the number of companies using them and in the size and breadth of the functions covered.

Most often, companies implement shared services for their support functions, although some companies have expanded into other cross-organizational areas. Table 10-1 shows some examples.

> *"Cost savings can't be the sole objective for shared services—quality of service from the internal customer's perspective is equally, or sometimes more, critical. Why? Because the quality of service provided internally can have a ripple effect that influences productivity, employee morale, and satisfaction, and ultimately the satisfaction of end customers. A shared services strategy initiated without a customer focus may actually cost more than it saves."*
>
> **Mary Jo Bitner, Ph.D.**
> **Petsmart Chair in Services Leadership**
> **Academic Director, Center for Services Leadership**
> **W. P. Carey School of Business, Arizona State University**

Table 10-1 Common Shared Services Functions

■ Finance	■ Learning Services
■ Accounting	■ Information and Technology Services
■ Accounts Payable	■ Project Management
■ Accounts Receivable and Collections	■ Process Reengineering
■ Travel Management and Expense Services	■ Order Fulfillment
■ Procurement	■ Real Estate and Facilities Management
■ Human Resources and Employee Services	■ Document Imaging

Shared services can take on many forms, such as consolidating Finance and Accounting functions for the entire enterprise, or providing all of the back-office functions for a particular business unit. Another shared service model creates a separate business to provide the services to the company and external customers.

It is easy to see that the effort depends greatly on the shared services details and intent. However, no matter the type, several business challenges need to be addressed:

- Leaders need to be selected.

- An overall strategy needs to be created that includes the approach to shared services and targets for standardization vs. tailoring to business unit requests.

- Locations need to be selected, built out as "greenfields" and/or shut down.

- Funding, budgeting, and transfer prices need to be designed and implemented.

- Organizational structures and roles/responsibilities need to be designed.

- Governance mechanisms need to be created, including service level agreements.

- Processes need to be selected, combined, redesigned, and rolled out.

- Technologies need to be selected, and migrations and shutdowns handled.

- Employees need to be selected for positions, and layoff plans may be required.

- Relocation packages may be needed and/or new employees may need to be hired and trained (typically within very compressed timeframes).

And there are other challenges. Companies implementing shared services for the first time should consider getting support from those who have experienced the challenges.

Culture Challenges

Despite its benefits, restructuring is disruptive to all involved. It often requires new relationships, processes, technologies, and roles and responsibilities. It may require a physical relocation, which may change commutes or uproot families. And, it typically requires new expectations and ways of working, which is where culture gets into the act.

Not every restructuring effort has culture risk, but many do. Anytime there is a change to how people need to perform their work, team with others, or respond to new expectations, Business Practices are in play and culture may be a barrier to success.

168

Can Two Rights Make a Wrong?
Insights from IBM's Tangible Culture Approach

Within organizations, subcultures typically exist and need to be considered. These subcultures may be based on leaders' styles, history (for example, a previous acquisition where the prior culture is still prevalent), occupational practices, and the tenures, nationalities, genders, and ages of employees, just to name a few.

Shared services run the risk of two types of culture clash. First, shared service centers are often created by merging two or more internal groups. Each group will have its own subculture, and often will have some differing Business Practices. And, if that is not enough, there is the chance for an alliance culture clash between the shared service organization and its internal "customers." Culture clash inside an organization can be just as damaging as between organizations—and two types simultaneously is double trouble.

Compounding the culture clash risk, shared services often seek to change some parts of the existing culture. For instance, there may be lack of customer focus, an unbalanced view of the importance of administration, or near oblivion to the market and important external events. Implementing shared services centers may be an opportunity to help change these culture issues by infusing a customer mindset, clarifying organizational priorities, and motivating external interest through benchmarking.

Finally, part of the culture challenge may be to infuse motivation for continuous improvement. Status quo is comfortable, and just changing this expectation may be one of the greatest challenges to be faced.

Handling Related "People" Risks

As with other efforts, there are important "people" aspects to address. We spend time on culture in the rest of this chapter, so here we offer these other pieces of brief advice:

- Organization design is vital to create a shared services structure that will stand the test of time yet be flexible to changing requirements. Departments and groups need to be identified, reporting relationships need to be clarified, linkages need to be devised, and role and responsibility definitions need to be developed. Then, all of it needs to be communicated thoroughly because these changes tend to be very important to employees at all levels. Often, the organizational infrastructure needs to be tailored to the requirements of specific countries or regions, and many human resource issues need to be navigated (for example, employee selection, processes for layoffs). The organizational infrastructure also needs to support key decisions such as the chosen overall strategy and location.

- Governance both inside the shared service organization, and between the organization and its internal customers, is a key to success. As with alliances, service level agreements are needed, as well as ways to coordinate and communicate across the impacted parts of the enterprise. Governance structures, roles and responsibilities, processes, measures, and policies are all part of a well-designed governance function for shared services.

- Organizational change management can really help address peoples' hearts and minds during restructuring, which can be a key driver of a successful transition. Recognize that former colleagues and peers will now have a "customer/service provider" relationship and this shift needs to be nurtured, perhaps through new knowledge and skills.

In addition, it may prove helpful to develop some principles, values, or behavioral statements to convey the new expectations. Finally, remember that it is important to reduce the sense of loss that people may feel (especially because it helps reduce the potential for exaggerating how good things were before).

"We outsourced most 'noncore' functions to deal with semiconductor economic cycles. We recognized we'd need new competencies to manage a 'variable virtual company,' new approaches to dealing with long-term business partners, and new ways to manage 'core' functions. Results have been excellent—along with some unexpected benefits: 'Core' employees' morale and retention have improved; management focuses more time on customer requirements; [sic] and, as a result, market share has significantly improved."

Steve Newberry
President and CEO
Lam Research Corporation

Applying *Tangible Culture* to Shared Services

Tangible Culture is applicable to two stages of shared services: (1) creating and transitioning to an effective shared services organization, and (2) establishing a workable partnership with internal customers. Let's start with the transition to shared services.

Creating a shared services organization is much like an internal merger, so the steps from Chapter 8 are generally applicable. Figure 10-1 shows the overall process.

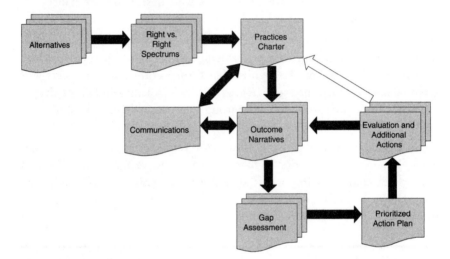

Figure 10-1   Method for shared services.

Example

Let's start with some sample outputs, and then move on to the steps to get there. We will use the following story line, which is a composite example from our experiences.

Context: The effort is to initiate an enterprise shared services center for Finance, Accounting, and associated reporting functions. The company wants to reduce costs and enhance information provided to managers about financial results. The company is publicly traded and based out of Chicago, and has decided to consolidate the functions into one shared services center in Chicago. The center will support all three of the company's business units, two of which were the result of earlier acquisitions. Currently, each business unit has its own Finance and Accounting functions, which have operated relatively autonomously reporting into the business unit and dotted line to the CFO.

Table 10-2 shows excerpts from the practices charter and the Right vs. Right decisions.

Table 10-2   Practices Charter Excerpts

	100%	99–51%	50/50	51–99%	100%	
Problem Solving						
Business unit and shared services leaders need to collaboratively decide the best way to handle situations.			X			The shared services center will make all final decisions on how situations should be handled.

Whenever possible, the business unit preferences will be honored. This is possible more frequently with internal financial reporting and less frequently when external accounting rules are in play. The shared services leaders will explain the constraints if it is not possible to honor requests. And when it is feasible to consider the business unit preferences, the response needs to be, "Let's look into it and find out what we can do."

Management Style						
Managers should be involved in situations where A- through C-level leaders are involved.	X					Managers should only be involved in situations where someone asks for help.

Anytime an A-, B-, or C-level leader is involved, the managers need to be aware. Not only are these delicate service situations, they are opportunities to build relationships. Finance and accounting professionals need to immediately notify their manager when an A- through C-level leader becomes involved. The manager is encouraged to keep the professional involved as much as possible for continuity, relationships, and understanding of the actions needed.

Continues

Table 10-2 Practices Charter Excerpts (Continued)

	100%	99–51%	50/50	51–99%	100%	
Execution						
It is most important to follow the specified process.				X		Quality outputs are most important, even if some steps need to be modified.

We drive for quality most of all. Our outputs need to conform to the highest standards of our professions and to the expectations for accuracy, timeliness, and relevance that our business demands. At times, we will modify process steps to achieve the quality, and managers need to be actively involved in all situations where this is required.

Table 10-3 shows an example Outcome Narrative to define the future state.

Table 10-3 Example: Outcome Narrative 1

Situation

A level-B business unit leader has called to ask an amount be transferred to another business unit for an internal agreement. He has documentation about the agreement for the charges, but cannot provide details, which are needed to assign costs to proper accounts. The leader insists that the amount is small and should simply be booked to a particular account, yet the accountant is concerned due to lack of detail provided.

Desired Outcome

Because a level-B leader is involved, the accountant's manager needs to be notified. Proper documentation is vital because accounting rules are involved, and the definition of "proper" is a decision for the shared services manager to make. The shared services manager needs to help with the needed documentation, or decide whether the transaction can be booked. If necessary, the external auditor may be consulted.

In-Scope Roles	**Role Behaviors and Actions**
Accountant	Needs to immediately notify his/her manager when the level-B leader becomes involved. Needs to constructively provide the history (just the facts) and viable options. Needs to participate in additional conversations and rapidly implement the chosen decision. Should seek feedback on ways to better approach similar situations in the future, if applicable.

In-Scope Roles Role	Behaviors and Actions
Business unit leader	Needs to recognize that even small transactions are covered by rules that need to be followed. Needs to fully explain the situation and constructively engage with the shared services manager and accountant on the options for dealing with it. Needs to accept and support the final decision made by the shared services manager. Should ask for ways to avoid the situation in the future, if appropriate.
Shared services leader	Needs to prioritize the situation, and thoroughly research it. Needs to keep the accountant involved going forward as much as possible. Needs to seek out the implications and ensure an understanding of available options, even if difficult to implement. Needs to explain the implications and options to the business unit leader, and seek his/her ideas, too. Needs to reach consensus if possible yet be firm in making the best decision, even if difficult.

Right vs. Right Categories Referenced	Other Considerations
■ Problem solving	■ Nature of the transaction itself
■ Management style	■ Previous handling of similar situations
■ Execution	■ Accountant's tenure and experience
■ Relationships	
■ Communications	

Table 10-4 shows gap assessment excerpts and areas to address.

Table 10-4   Gap Assessment Excerpts

Gap Assessment for Outcome Narrative 1

■ Managers tend to take over and leave the accountant out of problem solving.

■ Accountants tend to work problem situations too long, some believing that it reflects poorly on them that they cannot resolve the issue themselves.

■ Business units often express a belief that internal transactions do not need much documentation, so they frequently neglect the details.

■ Some managers opt for the most stringent answer and expect the business units to meet that standard, even when it is unnecessary.

Gap Assessment for Outcome Narrative 2

■ During the monthly close process, responses may take up to 48 hours ...

Table 10-5 shows excerpts from the prioritized action plan.

Table 10-5 Prioritized Action Plan Excerpts

Prioritized Enablers and Actions	
Outcome Narrative 1	**Priority**
1. Communicate that managers should engage when A-through C-level leaders are involved. Explain the benefits of this approach and how it will not be viewed as a failure on the part of the accountant.	High
2. Communicate to managers the importance of keeping the accountant involved throughout.	High
3. Prepare a checklist of transactions and decision latitude for reference, and provide it to business unit leaders as appropriate.	High
4. Coach the shared services leaders who tend to opt for stringent answers about balancing financial and business requirements.	Medium
5. Identify some resolved situations as learning opportunities and use them during the "lunch and learn" sessions.	Medium
Outcome Narrative 2	
1. Review how responses are prioritized and routed ...	Medium

Table 10-6 shows excerpts from the progress evaluation and additional actions needed.

Table 10-6 Progress Evaluation Excerpts

Progress Evaluation: Outcome Narrative 1
Situation statement: A level-B business unit leader has called to ask an amount be transferred to another business unit for an internal agreement. He has documentation ...

Outcome Narrative Expectations	Actual Results and Practices
Desired outcome: Because a level-B leader is involved, the accountant's manager needs to be notified. Proper documentation is vital because accounting rules are involved, and the definition of "proper" is a decision for the shared services manager to make. The shared services manager ...	In most situations, the desired outcome happens. However, a pattern is emerging where proper documentation is frequently lacking for one business unit, and the situations are escalated rapidly. Also, some shared services managers do not keep the accountants involved in the process.
In-scope roles: Accountant, business unit leader, shared services leader.	The right people were involved in the actual situations that were reviewed.
Role Actions and Behaviors **Accountant**: Needs to immediately notify his/her manager when the level-B leader becomes involved. Needs to ... **Business unit leader**: Needs to recognize that even small transactions are covered by rules that need to be followed. Needs ... **Shared services leader**: Needs to prioritize the situation, and thoroughly research it. Needs to keep the ...	■ Some accountants start with a stringent answer rather than problem solving, which often causes quick escalation within the business unit. ■ Some shared services managers used e-mails to communicate with A- through C-level leaders, which has led to delays and misunderstandings. ■ A few isolated situations became contentious because the business unit leader did not accept the shared services manager's decision.

Additional Actions Needed

■ Coach the accountants whose actions have led to immediate escalations on the importance of resolving issues at lower levels and on approaches to use.

■ Convene a discussion among the shared services managers on how best to approach A- through C-level leaders.

■ Set up an appeals process for reviewing disputed decisions.

Work Steps

To create the outputs above (for Figure 10-1), follow the steps in Table 10-7. And, visit www.almaden.ibm.com/tangibleculture to download applicable tools and templates.

Table 10-7 Work Steps for Shared Services

Identify and Reconcile the Right vs. Rights

---

1. Meet with key members of the in-bound groups and ask questions about existing Business Practices. Some areas to include are
   - Decision-making processes and authorities
   - Management style and practices
   - Performance monitoring and management
   - Problem solving and conflict resolution
   - Process expectations and practices
   - Communications, style and processes
   - Interpersonal relationships
   - Operating preferences, including degree of openness and candor, required planning before taking action, and expected management and employee latitudes
2. Gather examples of problem situations and how each group handles them.
3. Based on the strategy and intent, determine
   - Business Practices that are "best" and should be adopted.
   - Areas where Right vs. Right Business Practices exist.
4. Launch efforts to implement the "best" Business Practices.
5. Identify the contexts for which the Right vs. Rights need to be reconciled.
   - Note that multiple shared service centers may require that some of the following steps be performed for each of the centers.
6. Craft the Right vs. Right pairs into the template (see the first three rows of Table 10-2).
7. Gather input from selected people on the answers they believe are most appropriate.
   - It is important to reinforce the uneven scaling in the template. See Table 5-4 in Chapter 5 "The Good Thing That Can Cause Big Trouble—Right vs. Right," for additional explanation.
8. Convene the decision makers to select the Right vs. Right answers. Collect the final decisions and discussion details to clarify the decisions.
   - If each shared service center is making its own decisions, coordinate the answers to bring consistency across the service centers.
9. Validate the decisions, as appropriate.

Clarify and Communicate the Practices Charter

---

10. Craft summary statements to communicate the Right vs. Right decisions.
11. Combine the Right vs. Right decisions, discussions, and summary statements into a practices charter.
12. Communicate the practices charter.
    - Incorporate a feedback loop for formal and informal input. It will increase commitment and identify areas that need additional clarification.

Develop, Validate, and Communicate the Outcome Narratives

13. Identify likely problem situations that represent the reconciled Right vs. Rights.

- Focus on situations where people must collaborate on decisions and action, and where answers are unclear or reasonable people can disagree.
- Select problem situations that demonstrate multiple elements of the practices charter.

Develop, Validate, and Communicate the Outcome Narratives

14. Use the practices charter as input to create Outcome Narratives, clarifying

- Desired outcome
- In-scope roles
- Desired behaviors and actions for each role
- Additional considerations that could impact the desired outcome
- References, including Right vs. Rights, values, and principles

15. Validate the Outcome Narratives, as appropriate.

16. Communicate the Outcome Narratives.

- Cascade them through managers to reinforce their leadership positions.
- Consider a workshop format to enable people to develop, compare and discuss their answers to the official Outcome Narratives.

Identify and Prioritize the Gaps

17. Identify differences between current handling and the Outcome Narratives.

18. Clarify the gaps, looking for both obvious and subtle aspects.

19. Summarize and prioritize the gaps, looking for areas applicable across multiple Outcome Narratives.

Build and Launch the Prioritized Action Plan

20. Identify and design actions for the prioritized gaps.

21. Build an action plan, along with an appropriate timetable for evaluating progress.

22. Implement the actions in the prioritized action plan.

Evaluate Progress and Identify Additional Actions

23. At the identified milestones, gather information on how situations were handled.

24. Compare handling of actual situations to the Outcome Narratives.

- Was the desired outcome achieved in the desired timeframe?
- Did the right people get involved at the right time?
- Did the people perform the identified actions in the described way?

Continues

Table 10-7 Work Steps for Shared Services (Continued)

Evaluate Progress and Identify Additional Actions

- ◆ Are there indications of additional Right vs. Right conflicts?
- ◆ Are clarifications needed to some Outcome Narratives?
- ◆ Do Outcome Narratives need to be written for new problem situations?

25. Identify additional actions needed to address ongoing gaps.
26. Identify any new or ongoing Right vs. Right issues that need reconciliation and initiate the process.
27. Launch definition of additional Outcome Narratives to address new issues and/or issues that were tabled earlier.

Partnering with Internal Customers

In parallel with creating the shared services organization, it is appropriate to launch an effort to build effective relationships with internal customers. If neglected, this area can quickly lead to dissatisfaction. When business units do not receive the support they expect, or they do not like the approach taken, they often "complain high," which can negatively impact the effort. Instead, we suggest that companies proactively surface the conflicts, using approaches identified in Chapter 9.

When initiating this process, it is important that the strategy and intent of shared services are clear so that topics and boundaries may be established. In some cases, a customer-vendor relationship is appropriate. Accounting is a good example where this arrangement may work well and where governance, service level agreements, and problem solving will be important. However, if a collaborative relationship is needed, such as with Application Development or Learning Services, an open discussion is necessary to determine the type of internal partnership to be created.

The best timing to initiate this work is a key decision itself. In general, it is good to move forward quickly, but there may be more important considerations in the near term. However, do not neglect this work, because waiting may cause lingering negative impacts. Also, use the opportunity to identify baselines to gauge progress on the metrics and influence the designs underway in the early stages of the shared services implementation.

Benefits

In general, applying *Tangible Culture* to shared services and other major restructuring is a way to proactively address culture clash. In addition to the benefits you have read about in earlier chapters, *Tangible Culture* helps to

- Support interpersonal relationship both inside the shared services center and between the center and the internal customers it serves.
- Prepare employees for taking action, knowing what is expected of them.
- Achieve consistency, even across multiple centers and geographies, which is often a key requirement to achieve the shared services objectives.

Conclusion

Major restructuring often is a path to improvements, and shared services are an example of how companies achieve cost savings while enhancing performance. Despite their benefits, shared services are challenging to implement and run from a cultural perspective. *Tangible Culture* can help a company merge internal groups into the shared services center(s) as well as crafting effective partnering relationships with internal customers. Organizations that proactively approach the culture challenge will speed their time to benefits and avoid many issues that cause internal customer disappointment.

Now let's turn our attention to transformation efforts.

Reference

Fahy, M. "Getting shared services right," The Shared Services and Business Process Outsourcing Association, www.sharedxpertise.org/, September 2, 2003.

II

Major Transformation— Addressing Your Plan's Hidden Barrier

By Sara Moulton Reger, Sue Blum, Ron Frank,
Kris Pederson, and George Pohle

Chapter Contents

Can Two Rights Make a Wrong?
Insights from IBM's Tangible Culture Approach

182

Overview

This chapter applies *Tangible Culture* to major transformations. We cover the business and culture challenges for transformation along with examples of how Business Practices, Right vs. Right, and Outcome Narratives may be applied. IBM's recent transformation history will be an example, as will composites from our other experiences. This chapter is helpful for those planning or implementing transformation or other changes that require new employee mindsets and actions. Readers may also want to reference Chapters 8, 9, and 10 ("Mergers and Acquisitions—Managing the Common Sources of Culture Clash," "Alliances—Finding Ways to Leverage Your Collective Capabilities," and "Major Restructuring—Gaining Sustained Value From Your Reorganization,") if their transformation incorporates external organizations and/or restructuring.

Introduction

Companies transform for a variety of reasons—some voluntary and others foisted by circumstances beyond the company's control and preference. One company may be facing current problems, such as bankruptcy or a stock-price drop. Another may anticipate future problems, such as increased competition and commoditization. Still others may see current or anticipated opportunities, such as the ability to move into a market-dominating position or create entirely new markets.

Whatever the trigger, transformation is difficult, and culture is relevant. In some cases, a company's culture may prove helpful in achieving the transformation. However, culture is frequently perceived as a barrier to objectives—and much of the time, it is.

Business Challenges

Transformation takes a number of forms. To make the point, let's look at IBM history.

IBM experienced near death in the early 1990s. The company contained loosely connected, independent business units with an unwieldy management system, redundancies, and disconnected technology. Driven by drastic cost-reduction needs, the company undertook an ambitious reengineering effort—and further reintegrated IBM, redesigned core processes, and refocused the company on customers and the market.

In the mid-1990s, the Internet led to new uses for information technology. Being the world's largest information technology company, IBM needed to establish a leadership position, and point of view, on the Internet. Was it only for browsing and online shopping, or was it something more important and enduring? IBM's view: The Internet would transform the fundamental nature of transactions—in commerce, education, health care, and government—under the umbrella term *e-business*. And this meant IBM needed to transform its own strategy, operations, and investment priorities—touching every aspect of the company from research to product development, services, workforce enablement, and talent development. All this would be necessary to make e-business a unifying strategy, and not simply good marketing. This second transformation came on top of the earlier company-wide reengineering and transformation still underway.

Early in the new century, IBM's third transformation began—one based not on disruptive technology but on broad-based marketplace requirements. Clients wanted increased flexibility and a variable cost profile for technology and other support functions. They spoke of a competitive and market environment more volatile than anything they had experienced, and how systems and modes of operation needed to be far more responsive and resilient. These client requirements led IBM to On Demand Business—a view of the future for both business and computing infrastructure. As just one example, in a discussion between IBM's CEO, Sam Palmisano, and Procter & Gamble's CEO, A. G. Lafley, Lafley said that P&G might be able to function with only 25 percent of its current workforce—yet transform into a much more competitive enterprise—by relying on a network of sophisticated partnerships with third-party providers. (Hamm and Ante)

At this writing, IBM is three years into a journey to becoming an On Demand company—a journey that may take 15 years. So what is IBM's vision for On Demand Business?

> An On Demand Business is an enterprise whose business processes—integrated end to end across the company and with key partners, suppliers, and customers—can respond flexibly and with speed to any customer demand, market opportunity, or external threat.

For IBM, this means changes in inter- and intra-company interactions, working styles, and organizational infrastructure—just to name a few. And IBM is not alone—most companies face these same challenges.

- **Extended enterprise networks**

  Companies are using multiple sourcing arrangements to rapidly gain new capabilities, flexibly respond to growth and fluctuations, and achieve a variable cost structure. This multi-sourced environment means alliances—both internally and externally—with all the challenges mentioned in Chapter 9.

  Integration is difficult even within one company (especially large global ones). "If each entity in the network works only within the context of its own mission, strategies and management processes, conflict will be a constant and cooperation an accident" (Street et al). For IBM, this means relationships with 35,000 suppliers and 45,000 business partners in a multitude of different types of business arrangements.

- **Variable, virtual work**

  Increasingly, employees are mobile and work on teams that come together for specific projects, and then disband. Often the people come from different geographies and companies. Use of contractors is growing as a way to supplement the workforce with specific skills while avoiding fixed costs.

  Also, jobs are not what they used to be. Now they are frequently a compilation of roles, often tailored to capabilities of the individuals, making it more challenging to manage, deploy, hire, and replace employees. The best leadership for this environment is hands-on, entrepreneurial, customer centric, and focused on coaching and enabling others virtually, no matter who the employees work for. For IBM, this means a workforce where 40 percent do not go into an IBM office regularly, and where most people take direction from multiple leaders.

- **Flexible, distributed organizational infrastructures**

  To enable the variable, virtual workforce, many capabilities are needed. These include modular and voluntary organizations (for example, business "components," communities of interest), distributed authorities, flexible measures and incentives, and mechanisms to locate expertise and assign staff. Restructuring is often needed, bringing the issues cited in Chapter 10.

One IBM example involves business solution professionals chartered with developing industry solutions for the long term. They report into one group, are funded by another, and have distinct measures, compensation mechanisms, and organizational arrangements to enable their work.

These core challenges place stresses on governance, communications, and relationships—at all levels. And they set up the potential for brand misalignment and inconsistencies in customer experience, especially where value chains of organizations are in play.

IBM faces a series of implementation challenges in achieving On Demand:

- **Funding and roadmap**—IBM does not have a pot of money tagged for transformation. (If you have one, we envy you!) In lengthy, large-scale, complex global transformations, deciding where to begin is tough. Certainly payback for reinvestment is important, and so is weaving in foundational capabilities where return may be difficult to calculate. Agreeing to these priorities is "fun."

- **True integration**—For IBM's On Demand Business vision, it is necessary to go beyond running parallel workstreams on structures, processes, technologies, and so on. The workstreams must be woven together into an integrated, seamless capability so that nothing blocks rapid response to customer demands and changing market conditions.

- **Governance**—Making key decisions, guiding the process, and tracking performance are necessary for success. Although tempting (because they're easy to measure), implementation dates and budgets are certainly not enough to measure true success. It is necessary to track real business results and not just the steps toward them.

But it's worth it. One example: IBM's supply-chain results to date include savings of nearly $20M over three years through integration of 30 supply chains into one. This generated $500M in cash over two years through reduced inventories while simultaneously achieving IBM's lowest unfilled order level.

186

Can Two Rights Make a Wrong?
Insights from IBM's Tangible Culture Approach

However, we are still working on a few things, such as fostering a collaborative culture; breaking down the business and cultural barriers in our global, multi-sourced environment; reaching out seamlessly to customers, suppliers, and business partners; and differentiating business value.

> *"To address our biggest challenge—collaboration—we're pulling the levers that influence people and enable teamwork—new tools, processes, education, compensation, and rewards. But they're only effective if people collaborate naturally—as we must in our networked world. Employees need to think, 'Who else can benefit from what we're doing? Who should I contact to gain new perspectives for this project?' Once collaboration moves from ad hoc to ingrained behavior, culture change makes a step-function improvement across the organization."*
>
> **Linda Sanford**
> **Senior Vice President, Enterprise On Demand Transformation**
> **IBM Corporation**

At the core of these challenges, a "people" element emerges. And for IBM, and any company engaged in transformation, this means that people need to change how they think about the business.

Culture Challenges

Major transformation, no matter the trigger or type, faces some culture challenge. By its very definition, transformation implies changes in many directions, from what to do, how to do it, who does it, and so forth. When we think about the basic business building blocks—people and organization, processes, and technology—it seems logical that real transformation in one will drive transformation in at least one of the other two.

In recent IBM market research, companies told us that a mindset shift was critical to achieve the On Demand Business characteristics of resilience, flexibility, responsiveness, and horizontal integration. What mindset shifts in particular? Well, one was a move away from the reliance on hierarchy and control mechanisms, and another was focus on sensing the market and not simply responding.

This meets our own experience: It is mindsets that drive the Business Practices deemed appropriate for a given situation. For this reason, for transformation, Right vs. Right *mindsets* are the starting place. This differs from every other type of effort we have described so far, where the starting place has been Right vs. Right *Business Practices*.

To trace IBM's three transformations is to uncover a series of progressive mindset shifts:

- In the early 1990s, IBMers needed to

  - Shift their focus to customers and the external market.
  - Prioritize "one IBM" and not individual business units or regions.
  - Motivate and reward results, not simply efforts.

- To become leaders in the e-business era, IBM needed to

  - Steer attention toward products and services that enabled an Internet-based business environment.
  - Shift to a blended focus on technology and business.
  - Regain confidence in its ability to lead (remember that this transformation started while IBM was still recovering from near death).

- For On Demand Business, IBM is working on additional changes that also require mindset shifts:

  - Focus on industries and integrated solutions (and shifting away from brand focus).
  - Business-led sales and delivery (augmenting technology-led sales and delivery).
  - Shift from a full portfolio of products and services to one focused on innovation and value (which means regular pruning and divestitures).
  - "Seamless" delivery, no matter the brands, geographies, and delivery entities involved (including external partners).

> *"IBM's experience with continuous reinvention is unparalleled—and its culture, especially the mindset of its people, is a critical factor. My research indicates other inhibiting factors that may be just as important as mindset, including flexibility and variety of resources, skills, alternative uses for technologies, ability to redeploy physical assets, and the firm's financial ability to weather the storm.*
>
> Richard D'Aveni
> Professor of Strategic Management
> Chairman of the Strategy and Technology Group
> Tuck School of Business at Dartmouth College
> Author of *Hypercompetition*

We are navigating these changes with a global workforce of more than 300,000 where 50 percent have joined in the past 5 years—many due to acquisitions and outsourcing arrangements. (And remember, 40 percent do not go into IBM facilities on a regular basis.) Driving consistent mindsets in this type of environment is especially challenging.

To align the business environment with these mindset shifts, changes in Business Practices are needed. Here are a few relevant questions IBM is answering:

- Who should be the primary client contacts when multiple brands, lines of business, and/or geographies are involved?
- Who should lead cross-organizational sales opportunities and project deliveries?
- How should brands, business units, and geographies be structured and measured?
- How should experts be identified and engaged (including those outside IBM)?
- Where should standardization be required, and where can judgment be applied?

We hope this brief discussion explains how transformation often starts with mindset shifts, which then lead to the appropriate Business

Practices. Then—and we would assert, only then—is it possible to effectively identify the changes needed to make it all work.

> *"It can be very difficult to assess the existing organizational mindset by solely relying on internal perspectives. Enterprises often delude themselves regarding their relationships with customers, employees, and other key stakeholders, as well as the strength of their value propositions with these stakeholders. A structured, visible methodology, augmented with external perspectives, can help to identify and mitigate such delusions."*
>
> **William B. Rouse, Executive Director and Professor**
> **Tennenbaum Institute, Georgia Institute of Technology**
> **Author of** *Don't Jump to Solutions: Thirteen Delusions*
> *That Undermine Strategic Thinking*

Handling Key "People" Risks

During transformation, "people" aspects must be addressed. Before we focus our attention on culture, we want to offer some brief related advice.

- Stakeholder strategies are increasingly important in an extended enterprise network because many more people are likely to be impacted (directly and indirectly), and the needed sponsor network is complex. If those who need to change are beyond the company's direct control, it is risky to assume the partner will take needed actions (or that you can address your partner's shortcomings with negative consequences). We suggest it is better to consider all impacted people as under one organizational change umbrella (no matter who they work for), and start with well-conceived stakeholder strategies as the first step.

- Future-state visioning is vital to successful transformation because the journey is often long. Let's demonstrate this simply: Suppose you want to move. If you are not sure where you want to go, your effort will be more difficult. Do you want to stay in the same city or move across the country? Do you want to keep your lifestyle, or change it—and if so, how? Without these answers, you will not know where to begin or how to set a reasonable timeframe. Simple example, but many companies embark on major transformation efforts and either fail to make the end-state clear or make it clear for only a small group of people.

■ Transition strategies are needed to sustain the changes over time. Although compliance is sometimes appropriate (that is, "We'll tell you what to do, monitor your compliance, and dole out appropriate positive and negative consequences"), leaders often use this approach when it will not work well. How can you tell? Ask the following:

+ How well can we really monitor compliance with the new requirements?

+ Are we able and willing to monitor them, and apply appropriate positive and negative consequences, over the long term?

If monitoring will be difficult or expensive over the life of the requirements, you need commitment (that is, workers taking action because they believe it is right, not because someone is watching them). If you are working to achieve an On Demand Business, for instance, you need to build commitment to that vision.

Consider the value of principles, values, and behavioral statements for conveying the new expectations and communicating your intent. And remember that you need active support from formal and informal leaders for credibility and motivation for change.

Let's now look at how *Tangible Culture* concepts can be applied to transformation.

Applying *Tangible Culture* to Transformation

Figure 11-1 shows the general workflow. It is similar to what we have covered in other chapters, but with one very important difference: beginning with mindsets.

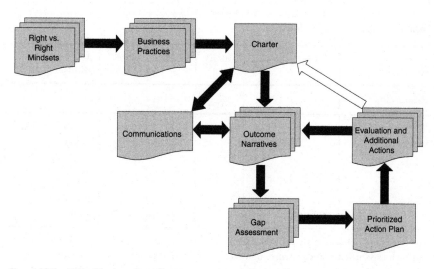

Figure 11-1   Method for transformation.

Let's start with an example of how some of the outputs would look, and then give you the steps to get there, using the following story line.

Example

Senior executives have identified changes they want to pursue. They are concerned that the company is bogged down in old approaches to the market, and they want to radically transform—from the company's structure to how people interact with one another to capability sourcing. Today, they are fully in-sourced with only customer-supplier relationships with other companies. They want to outsource parts of the Technology group and other administrative functions to reduce costs and allow the company to grow without delays. Their biggest concern: the ability to collaborate. Even internal cross-organizational efforts are slow and difficult, and they have few external experiences. They plan to simultaneously build collaboration capabilities and pursue outsourcing.

Table 11-1 shows excerpts from end-state mindsets in the charter.

Table 11-1   Charter Excerpts: Mindsets

Current Mindset	100%	99–51%	50/50	51–99%	100%	Alternative Mindset
Resourcing						
We need to be self-sufficient.				X		We need to fully leverage internal capabilities, and build selected external relation-ships for some requirements.

For our core—what is truly differentiating—we will predominantly develop and use our own capabilities. For noncore, however, we will look to new options—many of which will be external—to help us grow faster and move toward a variable cost profile.

Markets						
We have done well in this mar-ket, and we need to keep doing what's worked for us in the past.			X			We need a fresh approach to this market—and will even change some things that have worked in the past.

Our customers expect excellence and consistency from us—and we are dedicated to delivering them. We also recognize that this market is changing, as are our customer needs, and we cannot just rely on what has worked in the past. So we are willing to consider any change deemed beneficial for our customers and the company.

Priorities						
Internal competi-tion drives us to be better.					X	Internal competi-tion causes redun-dancy and harms collaboration.

In the past, internal competition brought benefits, but often at the expense of relation-ships and collaboration—both of which we need today. Everyone needs to collaborate on similar needs and find common ground rather than drive toward their own unique solutions. Our new governance process will help identify overlapping projects early and bring the groups together.

Current Mindset	100%	99–51%	50/50	51–99%	100%	Alternative Mindset
Leadership						
I am responsible to my direct manager and his/her management chain.				X		I am responsible to my management chain and to leaders for other efforts I work on.

Most people have regular and project responsibilities. This requires reporting into both managers and project leaders. Employees should seek help from both sets of leaders to overcome conflicts that may arise. If necessary, the manager's decision will prevail.

Table 11-2 shows excerpts from the Business Practices decisions in the charter.

Table 11-2 Charter Excerpts: Business Practices

Current Business Practices	Transition Business Practices	End-State Business Practices
The first response to new requirements is to begin developing the capabilities.	For identified functions, the first response will be to identify internal and external alternatives.	For all new requirements, the first response will be to consider the internal and external alternatives.
Departments tailor systems and processes to ensure their needs are fully met.	Everyone recognizes the importance of standardization and carefully considers the cost-benefit value before proposing customization. (Note: End-state Business Practices apply to the transition.)	
For new requirements, department experts are consulted.	For new requirements, company subject matter experts are consulted.	In addition to internal subject matter experts, external expertise is considered and consulted.
Projects outside of "regular work" and run by other leaders have lower priority.	Department managers help to prioritize workload and ensure that all projects get coverage.	Department managers and project leaders collaborate, along with external alliance partners, to determine appropriate priorities.

194

Can Two Rights Make a Wrong?
Insights from IBM's Tangible Culture Approach

Table 11-3 shows an example Outcome Narrative to describe the future state.

Table 11-3 Example: Outcome Narrative 1

Situation

Two groups independently identified a technology requirement and selected software. They selected different packages—ones that were best suited to their own group's needs. The packages cover redundant functionality, but do so in different ways. The groups are ready to purchase and have applied to the Project Funding Board for approval and funding. The Board is concerned about the redundancy and wants to purchase only one package; however, both groups strongly believe they need the package they selected.

Desired Outcome

The top priority is to select one package to avoid duplicate costs—and to find the one that best meets the needs of both groups, as well as other groups who may later need that functionality. An independent team, selected by the Project Funding Board, will be chartered with researching the situation and making a recommendation. The team's recommendation will be final unless the Board overrides it, which should be rare.

In-Scope Roles	Role Behaviors and Actions
Group leaders	Need to remain open to what is best for the company's current and future needs. Need to put forward concerns and requirements in a balanced light, and be constructive in working with other group leaders, the independent team and the Board in identifying and assessing the requirements. Need to openly support and enact the final decision.
Project Funding Board members	Need to assign members to the independent team who are perceived as objective by the group leaders. Need to stay involved closely enough to understand and guide the work as necessary. Need to accept the team's recommendation unless there are very important reasons to do something else.
Independent team members	Need to be objective—in appearance and substance. Need to analyze the situation broadly, including needs of other groups and future requirements. Need to include recommendations on how to help both groups to implement the decision most effectively.

Referenced Right vs. Right Categories	Other Considerations
■ Leadership ■ Priorities ■ Relationships ■ Communications	■ The business value that would be lost by forcing a one-solution answer—we will accept some redundancy with strong justification. ■ Important, pending decisions or events that could impact this decision and timing, including ones that may be known only to the top executives on the Board.

Table 11-4 shows excerpts from the gap assessment and what needs to be changed.

Table 11-4 Gap Assessment Excerpts

Gap Assessment for Outcome Narrative 1

- Technology requirements are identified independently, and evaluated through all stages prior to funding without a way to see overlapping efforts.
- Very few funds are provided during software implementations to accommodate changes to processes and procedures so teams are motivated to select what will best meet the current processes and not require changes.
- Current funding is primarily decided within each business unit, and rubber-stamped by the Board, so many redundancies slip through.

Gap Assessment for Outcome Narrative 2

- Measures are primarily established for business units and not cross-enterprise...

Table 11-5 shows excerpts from the prioritized action plan.

Table 11-5 Prioritized Action Plan Excerpts

Prioritized Enablers and Actions

Outcome Narrative 1	Priority
1. Include an early step in the technology requirements process to help identify business unit requirements that overlap.	High
2. Move responsibility for the software decisions from the business unit to the Board.	High

Continues

Table 11-5 Prioritized Action Plan Excerpts (Continued)

Prioritized Enablers and Actions

Outcome Narrative 1	Priority
3. Look at implementation funding to identify ways to also fund process and procedure changes when the selected solution will require it.	Medium
4. Communicate these changes broadly, beginning with the top.	Medium

Outcome Narrative 2	
1. Move toward a blended measure model with 50 percent focus on ...	High

Table 11-6 shows excerpts from the progress evaluation and additional actions needed.

Table 11-6 Progress Evaluation Excerpts

Progress Evaluation: Outcome Narrative 1

Situation statement: Two groups independently identified a technology requirement and selected software. They selected different packages—ones that were best suited...

Outcome Narrative Expectations	Actual Results and Practices
Desired Outcome: The top priority is to select one package to avoid duplicate costs—and to find the one that best meets the needs of both groups, as well as other groups who may later need that functionality. An independent team...	Most of the time, the desired outcome happens. However, more than expected, the decision is to select both packages. And in all but one case, the Board chose to approve both even though the independent team made a recommendation for one.
In-scope Roles: Group leaders, Project Funding Board members, independent team members	In most cases, the right people were involved. However, in a few, additional business unit leaders got involved.
Role Actions and Behaviors **Group leaders**: Need to remain open to what is best for the company's current and future needs. Need to put forward...	■ In one situation, a group leader made a verbal commitment to a vendor, perhaps to make that decision more likely.

Role Actions and Behaviors	
Project Funding Board members: Need to assign members to the independent team who are perceived as objective by the...	■ In a couple of situations, group leaders openly expressed concern about the objectivity of the independent team members.
Independent team members: Need to be objective—in appearance and substance. Need to analyze the situation broadly...	■ The Board accepted the team's recommendations about 70 percent of the time, and the reasons for overturns were not always clear.

Additional Actions Needed

■ Review the cases where both packages were selected to understand the reasons and the actual business results after implementation to identify lessons learned.

■ Meet with Board members to better understand the reasons for overturning the team's recommendations and determine whether this means changes are warranted.

■ Explore the concerns about team objectivity to see whether adjustments are needed.

■ Ensure that the group leader who made the verbal commitment is cautioned against doing it again, and that this behavior is recognized as unacceptable.

Work Steps

To create the preceding outputs (for Figure 11-1), follow the steps in Table 11-7. And, visit www.almaden.ibm.com/tangibleculture to download applicable tools and templates.

Table 11-7 Work Steps for Transformation

Identify the Right vs. Right Mindsets

1. Meet with key leaders, and others who understand the transformation vision.
  ◆ Gather their descriptions of how things should work in the future.
  ◆ Gather problem situations that may be challenging in the future.
2. Identify a list of potential future mindsets—those that may be best suited to drive future success.
3. Identify current mindsets that correspond to the desired mindsets.
  ◆ *Note*: This is an iterative process and Steps 2 and 3 may be reversed. Beginning with targeted mindsets can help narrow the effort.
  ◆ Phrase current mindsets positively. Otherwise, you will create a Right vs. Wrong combination, which can cause a problem during reconciliation.

Continues

Table 11-7 Work Steps for Transformation (Continued)

Identify the Associated Business Practices, and Reconcile the Right vs. Rights

---

4. Identify the Business Practices associated with each of the identified mindsets.
   - Do not force a one-for-one match, because there is likely to be a many-for-many relationship between the mindsets and Business Practices.
5. Craft the Right vs. Right mindset pairs into the Right vs. Right template (see the first three rows of Table 11-1).
6. Consider the merits of gathering data prior to the reconciliation session.
   - It is important for participants to fully understand the transformation requirements to determine the "right" answers.
   - This step can bring others into the process and build commitment.
7. Convene the decision makers to reconcile the Right vs. Right mindsets, keeping in mind the associated impact on Business Practices.
8. Identify the end-state mindsets (that is, reconciled Right vs. Right mindsets) and how the Business Practices need to change to support them.
   - It may be appropriate to identify transition and end-state Business Practices to support priorities, limited funding, and so on.

Clarify and Communicate the Charter

---

9. Document the end-state mindset decisions and discussions, along with the Business Practices decisions and discussion, into a charter.
10. Develop a communications plan to be used for this stage and future stages.
    - Incorporate a feedback loop for formal and informal input. It will increase commitment and identify areas that need additional clarification.
11. Communicate the decisions documented in the charter.

Develop, Validate, and Communicate the Outcome Narratives

---

12. Identify problem situations (approximately 20 to 30) that represent likely challenges.
    - Focus on situations where people must collaborate on decisions and action, and where answers are unclear or reasonable people can disagree.
    - Recognize that efforts to increase collaboration and inter- and intra-organizational linkages often increase conflicts (Weiss, Hughes). Do not be surprised if your future state seems a bit bleak at this point—it can bring beneficial innovation if the conflicts are handled well!
13. Use the charter as input to create Outcome Narratives, specifically clarifying the following:
    - Desired outcome
    - In-scope roles
    - Desired behaviors and actions for each role

Develop, Validate, and Communicate the Outcome Narratives

- ◆ Additional considerations that could impact the desired outcome
- ◆ References, including Right vs. Rights, values, and principles

14. Validate the Outcome Narratives, as appropriate.

15. Communicate the Outcome Narratives.

- ◆ Consider a workshop format to enable people to develop, compare, and discuss their answers to the official Outcome Narratives.

Identify and Prioritize the Gaps

16. Identify differences between current handling and the Outcome Narratives.

17. Clarify the gaps, looking for both obvious and subtle aspects.

18. Summarize and prioritize the gaps, being careful to prioritize those applicable to multiple Outcome Narratives.

Build and Launch the Prioritized Action Plan

19. Identify and design actions to address the prioritized gaps.

20. Build an action plan, along with an appropriate timetable for evaluating progress.

21. Implement the actions in the prioritized action plan.

Evaluate Progress and Identify Additional Actions

22. At the identified milestones, gather information on how situations were handled.

23. Compare the actual situations to the Outcome Narratives.

- ◆ Was the desired outcome achieved in the desired timeframe?
- ◆ Did the right people get involved at the right time?
- ◆ Did the people perform the identified actions in the described way?
- ◆ Are there indications of additional Right vs. Right conflicts?
- ◆ Are clarifications needed to some Outcome Narratives?
- ◆ Do Outcome Narratives need to be written for new problem situations?

24. Identify additional actions needed to address ongoing gaps.

25. Identify any new or ongoing Right vs. Rights that need reconciliation and initiate the process.

26. Launch definition of additional Outcome Narratives to address new issues and/or issues that were tabled earlier.

Benefits

In general, *Tangible Culture* gets at the root of what drives a successful transformation: mindsets and Business Practices aligned to the future state. Specifically, *Tangible Culture*

- Provides for sustained change by helping to transform collective mindsets.
- Makes the expectations real and tangible for people through Business Practices and Outcome Narratives.
- Enables the organization to target its transformation efforts and funding toward the initiatives that will bring important benefits most quickly.

Conclusion

Most companies will significantly transform at some point, and addressing likely culture barriers is one key to successful transformation. *Tangible Culture* is especially helpful when current mindsets, and the Business Practices they drive, will not work well in the future. And because major transformations are typically multi-year efforts, it is important to use an approach that provides an objective way to evaluate progress and decide what additional actions are needed.

Let's round out Section II, "The Application," with a "grab bag" of sorts—a number of different circumstances where the concepts can be applied creatively.

References

Charan, R. "Conquering a Culture of Indecision," *Harvard Business Review on Culture and Change*. Boston: Harvard Business School Publishing Corporation, 2001.

Gerstner, L. V. *Who Says Elephants Can't Dance? Inside IBM's Historic Turnaround*. New York: HarperCollins Publishers, 2002.

Hamm, S., and S. E. Ante. "Beyond Blue," *BusinessWeek Online*, www.businessweek.com, April 18, 2005.

IBM, "From reengineering to reinvention: the IBM journey to becoming an On Demand Business," IBM White Paper, 2005.

Palmisano, S. J., P. Hemp, and T. A. Stewart. "Leading Change When Business Is Good." *Harvard Business Review*, December 2004.

Street, S., R. Hossack, S. Lin, N. McGee, P. Lawton, and S. Moulton Reger. "It's time to flex: Create the organizational and cultural agility to do business on demand," IBM Institute for Business Value, 2003, p. 8.

Weiss, J., and J. Hughes. "Want Collaboration? Accept—and Actively Manage—Conflict," *Harvard Business Review*, March 2005, p. 93.

12

Key Decisions and Everyday Business— Extending *Tangible Culture* Into the Operational Parts of Your Business

By Sara Moulton Reger, Sue Blum, Cheryl Grise, Lisa Kreeger, Jeff Kreulen, Doug McDavid, George Pohle, Mary Sue Rogers, Dean Spitzer, Jim Spohrer, Ray Strong, and Jennifer Trelewicz

Chapter Contents

Can Two Rights Make a Wrong?
Insights from IBM's Tangible Culture Approach

204

Overview

This chapter briefly applies Business Practices, Right vs. Right, and Outcome Narratives to several "regular" business settings. You may want to quickly scan the topics and select those most relevant to your current needs, and refer back in the future to address additional ones. Also, visit www.almaden.ibm.com/tangibleculture to download *Tangible Culture* tools and templates.

Introduction

This chapter demonstrates the flexibility of the *Tangible Culture* concepts to various business situations. In each situation, culture is relevant, and there are creative ways to gain the benefits of Business Practices, Right vs. Right, and Outcome Narratives.

Evaluating Strategic Options

Evaluating and selecting strategies is an important senior leader activity. Not all strategies will succeed—nor will they be equally easy to execute. Good ideas are not worth much without good execution, and culture can get in the way.

For example, many regulated companies have found the need to shift their cultures to move into competitive markets, and have found that some strategies seem to "fit" better than others. Other companies have selected a strategy only to find that their organization could not "pull it off" after much money and time had been wasted.

As mentioned earlier, Business Practices are a handy surrogate for the topic of culture. With good alignment, the Business Practices will help propel the strategy. With poor alignment, the Business Practices will fight against strategy and cause execution issues.

Considering current Business Practices during strategy development can drive better strategy decisions and enhance designs and plans for executing the chosen strategy.

Here are some ways to include Business Practices in the strategy process:

1. Identify operational requirements needed to drive the strategy's success. For example:

    ◆ This strategy will require us to make rapid decisions.

    ◆ This strategy will require effective collaboration across the extended enterprise network.

    ◆ This strategy will require us to quickly and effectively consolidate our cross-organizational capabilities to respond to customers.

2. Compare the operational requirements to current Business Practices (see Chapter 6, "The Unseen Hand That Propels Organizational Action—Business Practices") and determine the degree of alignment. For example:

    ◆ We can make fast decisions, but not in cross-unit situations because everyone wants a say.

    ◆ We are fairly good at internal "crisis" collaboration, but we need to be better at it on a daily basis and need to learn to better collaborate with our partners.

    ◆ We have been successful at responding to customers cross-organizationally, but we cannot be sure we can do it as quickly as this strategy will require.

3. Determine the best options for dealing with disconnects. For example:

    ◆ Select the strategic option that best aligns with current Business Practices (as long as important benefits are not lost).

    ◆ Make modifications to the chosen strategy to align it better with existing Business Practices.

    ◆ Identify necessary changes to Business Practices to execute the strategy.

4. Ensure the work plan and timeline include the needed steps to modify the strategy and/or Business Practices. See Chapters 8 through 11 ("Mergers and Acquisitions—Managing the Common Sources of Culture Clash," "Alliances—Finding Ways to Leverage Your Collective Capabilities," "Major Restructuring—Gaining Sustained Value From Your Reorganization," and "Major Transformation—Addressing Your Plan's Hidden Barrier," respectively) for additional insights depending on the nature of the strategy.

5. Ensure the business case reflects the cultural realities and work required.

Careful consideration of strategic options and their alignment with existing Business Practices will help companies to

- Improve their strategy selection decisions.
- Identify needed actions to align the strategy and culture for effectiveness.
- Consciously focus on execution, along with the needed decisions and actions.
- Identify and mitigate culture risks before they become issues.

Building an Entrepreneurial or Start-Up Venture

In the early days of an exciting new venture, there are so many things to do. Everything needs to get going—and fast. Consequently, it is hard to give thought to what will happen down the road. Before you know it, your organization has its own habits, or Business Practices. Some may have been planned, but many have simply "happened."

As a small organization grows, changes are inevitable. Organizations often find themselves at key transition points without having given these transitions much forethought. Examples are growing so large that professional management is needed, going public, and sale of the venture. For separate corporate "skunk works" ventures, a key transition is often the reintegration into the host company.

Along with transition comes risk. For instance:

- Customers, speed of execution, and business value may be lost as the organization focuses internally to make needed changes that have not been planned beforehand.
- Employees may perceive the required changes negatively, which may impact their motivation and productivity and lead to retention issues.
- Some beneficial options may not be available to the company because it simply is not ready for them.

Simply letting Business Practices "happen" or evolve on their own is risky because it can lead to issues and bigger changes later. Instead, we offer a few suggestions:

1. Consider the end state, or a long-term future state, for your venture.

   ◆ Do you want to grow and eventually engage professional management, or keep the business small so that the current management team can run it?

   ◆ When and how do you plan to exit the business?

   ◆ Do you plan to go public or sell the business?

   ◆ Will the venture be integrated back into the owning organization?

2. Target and adopt the Business Practices that will best enable the end state and cause the fewest changes at likely transition points. Table 12-1 includes some questions to ask.

Table 12-1   Business Practices Questions

If you plan to go public	■ What Business Practices are best aligned with the financial and operating discipline needed when you go public?
	■ How do those Business Practices compare to what you have today?
	■ What can you do to move closer to that needed discipline?
	■ When and how should you make these moves?
If you plan to sell the business to another company	■ What are some likely acquirers?
	■ Which one(s) fits best with your current Business Practices?
	■ Where are your current Business Practices most different from theirs?
	■ What risks do you run if your Business Practices have not changed by the time of acquisition?
	■ What actions should you take, and when, to morph your Business Practices to make the transition easier?

Continues

Table 12-1   Business Practices Questions (Continued)

If the venture is tethered to another organization (for example, a corporation providing funds and/or management)	■ How integrated does this venture need to be with the owning organization—now and in the future? ■ What Business Practices does the owning organization expect? ■ What Business Practice could you adopt to make both organizations comfortable interacting with each other?

3. Use the Right vs. Right approach (see Chapter 5, "The Good Thing That Can Cause Big Trouble—Right vs. Right") to work through any difficult options that surface. See Table 12-2 for examples.

Table 12-2   Example Right vs. Rights

	100%	99–51%	50/50	51–99%	100%	
Focusing on current requirements is most important.						We need to balance current requirements and the longer term.
We should focus on an exit strategy that optimizes the owners' financial returns.						We need good owner returns, and must take care of the employees who have helped to build this company.
We should make the needed changes using current employees to motivate and give them new challenges.						We should hire consultants or employees from companies similar to our target acquirer to help us change.

4. Develop Outcome Narratives to clarify and communicate the desired changes (see Chapter 4, "How to Get to the Right Place the Right Way—Outcome Narratives").

Note that these decisions may lead the organization to restructure and/or transform. If so, consult Chapters 10 and 11.

A planned approach to likely transition points will result in the following:

- Best possible business value for your IPO or sale
- Retention of the key talent needed to continue providing value
- Reduction in the organizational "trauma" and loss of productivity associated with significant changes during key transition points

Testing a Vision or Future-State Definition

Many companies roll out changes before they are ready—before the vision is really clear. When this happens, delays, inconsistencies, rework, and frustration result—even though the clarifications could have been easy to make earlier in the process.

Outcome Narratives can help because they target problems—an often neglected area in visioning. If a project team can develop answers to the vision's inherent difficulties, the vision is ready. If the team *cannot* develop answers, it is risky and wasteful to deploy the vision out to many people who will need to handle those problems real time. Here are some steps:

1. When you think your vision is clear, yet before it is communicated broadly, identify some problem situations that are likely to occur.
2. Convene an effort to create Outcome Narratives for the problem situations (see Chapter 4). Here are some approaches:
   - Ask individuals to draft Outcome Narrative answers, and then hold a facilitated discussion of similarities and differences.
   - Send the Outcome Narrative format with problem situations listed and ask individuals to submit their thoughts, and then compile and evaluate the responses.
3. Evaluate agreement and disagreement. Disagreements may be due to the following:
   - Unreconciled Right vs. Rights—conflicting options assumed by different members of the project team.

Can Two Rights Make a Wrong?
Insights from IBM's Tangible Culture Approach

210

    ◆ Resistance to the implications and desire to avoid difficult changes.

4. Determine answers to handle the surfaced issues.

    ◆ Note that it is unwise to deploy with unreconciled Right vs. Rights. If the project team cannot agree, it is not likely that many more people will find agreeing easier!

5. Use the Outcome Narrative information for communications.

Project visions can cause many issues when rolled out before ready. Using the Outcome Narrative format can help to

- Gauge the readiness of the vision for rollout.
- Identify specific issues that need to be resolved.
- Provide information for communicating additional details about the vision.

Selecting and Implementing Best Practices

Many companies seek to implement best practices: practices that bring value to others. Although our term *Business Practices* and best practices share an obvious commonality—the word *practices*—they are more different than it may appear. Best practices often refer to what a company uses to achieve a particular business objective (for example, processes, procedures, approaches, systems). Business Practices refer to *how* people do and use these things—subtleties that are less likely to be included in the specific best practices.

Best practices are only "best" in a context that enables them to work effectively—and context includes the Business Practices that tell people how to execute the work. In fact, "best practices" can be "worst practices" in an environment not well suited to them. Pascale and Sternin call best practices a "foreign import," and then go on to say "they suffer a dismal replication rate." Ouch!

When considering best practices from other companies, be sure to think about your own Business Practices and how they will support or collide with them. Here are some ideas:

1. Identify best practices and associated Business Practices (see Chapter 6). For instance, ask the following:

- How closely must the associated processes be followed for success?
- How and where should employees be given latitude?
- What operating decisions are we likely to encounter? How are they best made?

2. Compare the associated Business Practices to your current Business Practices and your expected outcomes:

- What aspects of this best practice will support your objectives (for example, cost reduction, cycle-time reduction, and quality improvements)?
- How well suited is your environment to the associated Business Practices?
- Where disconnects exist, how significant are they?

3. Explore the implementation options:

- Implement some/all of the best practices as is because there is good alignment with the associated Business Practices.
- Modify some/all of the best practices, perhaps with help from experts, to conform most readily to your current Business Practices. (Although this approach may impact some benefits, it will address some key risks and help speed the implementation.)
- Implement some/all of the best practices, and design an effort to adopt the associated Business Practices. (Recognize that changing Business Practices may require many of the steps identified in Chapter 11.)
- Abandon the effort.

4. Capture the learnings for future best practices efforts.

Thoughtful, deliberate decisions and plans are necessary to benefit from best practices because they have been designed for another company. It is important to know how well they "fit" to know what benefit they can drive. Companies that probe on the associated Business Practices, and other elements of the context, will

212

Can Two Rights Make a Wrong?
Insights from IBM's Tangible Culture Approach

- Make better decisions on the front end, before investments are made.
- Set realistic expectations of the benefits that can be achieved.
- Develop thorough work plans and understand the effort required to implement the best practices effectively.

Selecting and Implementing Technology

Many steps are needed for successful technology implementation—both software and hardware—and many are not about the technology itself. For instance, business processes often need to be tailored, roles and responsibilities may need revision, operational measures may require updates, and employees need to be prepared to perform work in a new way.

Companies have options in selecting technologies, and many base these decisions on cost. Looking at technology cost alone, however, can lead to more challenging implementation and an expensive end state. Why? Some technologies "fit" a company less well than others and will require more changes to get everything to work together.

Asking questions about Business Practices (see Chapter 6) can enhance the decision and implementation process. For instance:

1. Ask about the inherent or assumed Business Practices underlying the technology.

   - Does the technology require employees to have certain authorities to make decisions or take action?
   - Does it allow managers their preferred level of review?
   - Does it assume employees will input data on a specific frequency?
   - Does it enable the company's preferences and requirements (for example, ability to work across organizational boundaries, rapidly launch internal "experiments," or specify domain dependent attributes)?

2. Identify where the technology is installed and working well.

   - What Business Practices do these companies use that help the technology to work well?

- How do these Business Practices compare to yours?
- Do these differences imply that you need to alter your Business Practices or the technology to get good alignment and an effective implementation?
- Will the technology require leading technical expertise and adaptability?

3. Select the technology best suited to your current Business Practices, unless you need certain capabilities and are willing to undergo a bigger transition to get them.

   - What specific tradeoffs you are making? Are they one time or ongoing?
   - If Business Practices need to change, which ones? What needs to be done to plan and execute these Business Practice changes on the same schedule?

4. Clarify new expectations through Outcome Narratives (see Chapter 4).

   - Use Outcome Narratives to communicate expectations and as job aids.
   - Use Outcome Narratives for a gap assessment if Business Practices need to change (see Chapter 11).

Due diligence about associated Business Practices can help companies make effective technology decisions. The preceding steps help companies to

- Choose technology solutions that can be implemented most quickly and easily.
- Avoid some key implementation risks.
- Avoid many misalignments in "fit" that can lead to long-term productivity issues and more costly post-implementation operating environments.

214

Can Two Rights Make a Wrong?
Insights from IBM's Tangible Culture Approach

Measuring Performance

Measurement is vital, and there is much published on the topic. Supposedly "what gets measured gets done," yet many companies are disappointed with their results—they are not seeing the focus and changes they want. Some of the issues are found in the context in which the measures are used. This context is vast and includes communications, incentives, rewards and recognition, leadership style, subtle and implicit prioritizations and other messages, vertical and horizontal alignment—and Business Practices.

Some of the Business Practices surrounding organizational performance measures include the following:

- How the measures are used to manage the business (for example, monitor, justify, predict) and employee performance
- How the measures are identified and defined, and targets established
- How often the measures are used and modified
- How consequences (that is, rewards and corrections) are matched to them

Consider how the Business Practices in Table 12-3 might impact performance and motivation.

Table 12-3 Performance Measurement Business Practices

Business Practices for Company A	Business Practices for Company B
Individual measures are created in January, reviewed informally in July, and then measured formally in the annual review process in December, often with little monitoring or feedback in-between.	Managers and employees discuss their individual and collective measures and results monthly, and seek ways to help each other achieve the goals.
Everyone holding the same job has the same individual performance measures.	Each employee's measures begin from a common set for the job, then are customized to reflect specific assignments, career objectives, and so on.
After the individual measures are submitted for the year, they are set—with changes occurring only for extremely unusual circumstances.	Individual measures are initially set in January, but are reviewed frequently and revised by the manager and employee as business conditions warrant.

These are just the "tip of the iceberg." Multiply these kinds of effects across the organizational, group/team, individual, process, and operational measures needed to run a business, and you can see how significant and far-reaching the differences may be.

We'll take this notion one step further to crossing national boundaries where measures can be interpreted differently, leading to divergent responses. For instance, a target for a certain percentage of college hires may be interpreted as guidance in one country, and a no-exceptions policy in another, depending on local Business Practices. These kinds of misunderstandings can aggravate cross-boundary relationships and impact results.

Here are some suggestions for enhancing measurement results:

1. Identify some key measurement Business Practices (see Chapter 6).
   - Who is involved in setting measures and targets? Who is not involved and why?
   - How are priorities included and communicated in the measurement process? How are new focus areas included?
   - How are measures integrated into "regular" work? How are the measures integrated with other relevant enablers (for example, incentives, rewards, recognition)?
   - How closely are employees expected to focus on their official measures?
   - How are problems (for example, performance shortfalls) addressed?

2. Assess how well your Business Practices reinforce your business priorities.

3. Identify changes to improve performance and motivation. For example:
   - Consider changing the people who are involved in setting measures and targets (for example, including lower-level employees to build commitment).
   - Identify your business priorities and find additional ways to reinforce them (for example, special communications or recognition).
   - Identify ways to integrate measures into "regular" work (for example, standing topics on meeting agendas, "how are we doing?" checkpoints).

4. Consider whether Right vs. Right (see Chapter 5) could help you with options:

   ◆ Should measures focus on the company or business unit results, or a combination?

   ◆ Should performance evaluations for bonuses be based on team or individual performance, or a combination?

   ◆ Should we focus only on objective measurements, or are subjective ones acceptable for some areas?

5. Consider whether Outcome Narratives (see Chapter 4) are needed to surface gaps, or communicate your expectations.

   ◆ Recognize that Outcome Narratives can clarify behaviors you want and identify if you inadvertently motivated something undesirable.

Tangible Culture concepts applied to measures can

- Ensure that Business Practices and measures are working together to support and drive priorities.
- Identify ways to systemically reinforce your priorities.
- Pinpoint areas where changes may help drive better results from your measures.

Hiring Practices (and the Flip Side, Job Search)

Selecting the best applicant from internal and external job candidates is important. Knowledge and skills are obvious areas to probe, and many companies focus there and leave "fit" up to chance. However, "fit" is often just as important to an applicant's success—and sometimes even more so.

When companies want change, they often hire experienced people—all of whom come with expertise and habits (that is, Business Practices). "Fit" can be especially challenging when the new hire is a leader. Both the company and individual may need to change—and, if so, discomfort is likely along the way.

In an extended enterprise, global business world, selecting the "right" person is critical. Which candidate will work best with our alliance partners? Which candidate understands the local market and will properly balance that with the needs of the enterprise?

Business Practices can help a company to communicate its culture. They are also a way for candidates to probe and further understand the organization.

Here are some suggestions for the hiring process:

1. Identify factors that have led to previous new hires' successes and failures.

   ◆ Which Business Practices (see Chapter 6) were most difficult for new employees to understand and perform? Which were easiest to understand and perform?

   ◆ Were any Business Practices surprising to new hires after they started?

   ◆ Were any Business Practices frustrating to new hires? If so, which ones?

   ◆ What extended enterprise and global Business Practices will the candidate need to understand and handle?

2. Identify an approach to communicate, and/or explore, important Business Practices during the interview. Table 12-4 shows some examples.

Table 12-4   Incorporating Business Practices into Interviews

Communication Approach	Probing Approach
We prefer consensus decisions.	When confronted with a decision, how do you prefer to make it?
Our managers prefer "no surprises" so it is best to communicate even suspected issues early.	Tell me about a problem you handled in the past. What actions did you take and whom did you involve?
Whenever possible, we adapt to the local market requirements rather than what is easiest for us at headquarters.	When faced with different expectations between leaders in headquarters and the field, what would you do?

3. Consider using Outcome Narratives (see Chapter 4) to probe on the applicant's natural instincts and how well they connect with your expectations. For instance:

   ♦ "As the Accountant, you've been asked to book a transaction, yet you have questions. You've requested and received additional information, but it is confusing and vague. You've consulted the Financial Analyst, and she supports the person making the request, saying that it is confusing but proper given authority levels. You still aren't comfortable. What would you do?"

   ♦ After hearing the answer, it may be appropriate to show him or her the Outcome Narrative and ask: How does this compare with your previous experiences? How comfortable would you be with this expectation?

Finally, be cognizant that new employees will adopt the Business Practices of the existing workforce. When demand is up, people may cut corners to get the work done, which erodes quality (Oliva and Sterman) and may even establish some new, less effective Business Practices. These are times to reinforce your expectations—and perhaps to support your current workforce with contractors, paid overtime, extra vacation banks, and so forth. This is even more important if you are trying to change the culture at the same time!

Because the hiring process is a two-way street, here are some ideas for job applicants to better understand the company and its culture:

1. Research the company's stated values and priorities.
2. Develop some questions to better understand those values and priorities, and the associated Business Practices:

   ♦ I read that one of your values is Respect for the Individual. What are some ways that employees incorporate this value into their daily work?

   ♦ When you cannot do them all, which tends to win: cost, quality or schedule?

   ♦ How do you prefer to make decisions?

   ♦ When confronted with a difficulty, should I work it through myself, seek help from co-workers, or escalate to my manager?

3. Consider the questions you have identified and think through your own preferences and working style before the interview. It will help you to evaluate what you are hearing and how comfortable you will be in that environment.

An effective two-way discussion is important during the hiring process to help the company and candidate ensure a good "fit"—which is essential for a good long-term relationship. Business Practices and Outcome Narratives can be help in several ways:

- The lens of Business Practices can help both interviewer and candidate identify questions to ask and information to provide to better understand each other.

- Business Practices enable the discussion to go beyond knowledge and skills into how well the candidate will "fit" with the business' expectations.

- Outcome Narratives can help the interviewer objectively evaluate a candidate's answers against what is expected.

Operating Globally

Today, few companies operate only within their own country. Even small ventures have websites that enable transactions all over the globe. For many, this means knowing how to navigate import and export laws and shipping requirements. For others, extensive business operations need to be conducted daily with those residing in other countries.

Operating globally means language and time zone complexities, exchange rate and regulatory variations, and differences in how people work, interact with each other, and perceive situations, just to name a few. The differences must be navigated within the context of business objectives. Think for a moment about the culture differences between companies with these goals:

- We operate domestically, but have suppliers from many countries.

- We operate domestically, but need to enable our customers who are highly influenced by the global market.

- We compete by region and need our marketing, channels and suppliers to reflect the preferences in those global regions.
- We operate with one brand, one voice, and one way of working globally.

These areas are complex now and likely to get more complex according to the GLOBE study. "The increasing connection among countries, and the globalization of corporations, does not mean that cultural differences are disappearing or diminishing. On the contrary, as economic borders come down, cultural barriers could go up, thus presenting new challenges and opportunities in business. When cultures come into contact, they may converge on some aspects, but their idiosyncrasies will likely amplify." (House et al.)

Many books are available on cross-boundary business, so we do not discuss the details in depth. However, *Tangible Culture* is a supplement to these sources for several reasons.

First, Business Practices (see Chapter 6) are certainly relevant. They are shaped by many factors, including local regulatory requirements, business customs, interpersonal norms, and other cultural and national expectations. Companies will see differences in Business Practices as they deal with customers, suppliers, and partners from other countries— as well as internal groups/employees in other parts of the world. For example, discussions may be more or less open based on whether leaders are present; approval schedules may require time for private discussion and debate; and protocols and expectations will determine whether customers deem face-time to be intrusive or necessary. Hofstede, Trompenaars, Hampden-Turner, and Adler are good references on these ideas.

Further, Business Practices considered proper in one country can be violations of proper business conduct—and even the law—in other countries. For instance, suppose a company is nearing a bidding process, and one of its leaders accepts a bidder's invitation to attend a special event (for example, sports game in a private box or special dinner). Other bidders may see it, assume the leader intends to give preferential treatment, and withdraw. Even if the actions were proper and taken with a clear conscience, the process may have been compromised and a violation (for example, against single bid tenders) created. With cross-boundary Business Practices, often the *appearance* of impropriety is too close to *actual* impropriety, and this must be interpreted within the countries' cultural contexts.

Second, Right vs. Right (see Chapter 5) becomes even more interesting across borders because more discussion may be needed to understand why the options are valid, let alone right. "Different cultural orientations and views of the world are not right or wrong—they are just different. It is all too easy to be judgmental and distrust those who give different meaning to their world from the meaning you give to yours. Thus the next step is to respect these differences and accept the right of others to interpret the world in the way they have chosen. Respect is easiest when we recognize that all cultural differences are in ourselves. We don't see the world as it is, only as we are. It is as though we are wearing cultural glasses all the time. And the lenses another person wears are different to yours." (Trompenaars and Woolliams)

Third, Right vs. Right may be needed for new decision areas, especially in large, global enterprises. For instance, it is often more difficult to manage duplicate effort globally. Should the company try to prevent duplication (through costly supervision) or allow duplications and differences between countries (and live with reduced efficiencies)? Is it okay to let each geography build its own assets, which may encourage competition, or should the company attempt to manage its assets globally?

Finally, many companies find that different answers are appropriate in different countries. Sometimes it is due to national culture and peoples' preferences, and sometimes due to regulatory requirements. It is often not possible to develop answers that apply equally well everywhere, and Outcome Narratives (see Chapter 4) can help.

To address these points, here are some actions to take:

1. Educate personnel on the topics of Business Practices and Right vs. Right. Simply understanding these concepts and using the terminology can improve communications.
2. Design opportunities for people to share their views and listen to other views.

- One workshop exercise is to separate people into groups by geography, function, etc., then give them problem situations and ask them to

  - Identify their preferred answers—perhaps using the Outcome Narrative format (for example, desired outcome, in-scope roles, role behaviors and actions).
  - Identify the answer they think the other group prefers.
  - Compare their answers.
  - Discuss similarities, differences, perceptions, and implications.

3. Clarify important expectations using Outcome Narratives.

   - Assign countries or geographies to develop Outcome Narratives—identifying answers that will work well within that country or geography. (Consider whether Outcome Narratives should be written at the global level, then countries or geographies given specific latitudes to modify them.)
   - Provide a forum for sharing similarities and differences and why they are appropriate, which can build better cross-border understanding.

Note that often companies think about global implications during a restructure or transformation effort. If so, Chapters 10 and 11 may be helpful.

Enabling employees to explore global differences through the lenses of Business Practices, Right vs. Right, and Outcome Narratives can help to

- Create better cross-border understanding and give employees terminology and ways to discuss differences and similarities.
- Provide ways to talk more effectively with customers, suppliers, and partners about differences and how to handle them for mutual benefit.
- Enable a company to drive toward global consistency while ensuring local requirements and preferences are adequately addressed.

Conclusion

In most business situations, culture is a consideration—and often an important one. Applying Business Practices, Right vs. Right, and Outcome Narratives can improve outcomes. Our hope is, someday, people will recognize and consider Business Practices as readily as they do business processes today. (Many of us "old timers" remember when business people did not talk about processes—*way* back in the late 1980s!) We also hope Right vs. Right will help people constructively address the conflicts they face, and that Outcome Narratives will help clarify and communicate expectations.

Now let's move on to a few brief demonstrations of *Tangible Culture* in action.

References

Adler, N. J. *International Dimensions of Organizational Behavior*. Cincinnati: South-Western College Pub, 2001.

Earley, P. C., and E. Mosakowski. "Cultural Intelligence," *Harvard Business Review*, October 2004.

Hofstede, G. *Culture's Consequences: Comparing Values, Behaviors, Institutions and Organizations Across Nations*. Thousand Oaks, CA: Sage Publications, 2003.

House, R. J., P. J. Hanges, M. Javidan, P. W. Dorfman, and V. Gupta (Eds). *Culture, Leadership, and Organizations: The GLOBE Study of 62 Societies*. Thousand Oaks, CA: Sage Publications, 2004, p. 5.

Oliva, R., and J. Sterman. "Cutting Corners and Working Overtime: Quality Erosion in the Service Industry," *Management Science*, Vol. 45, No. 7, July 2001, pp. 894–914.

Pascale, R. T., and J. Sternin. "Your Company's Secret Change Agents," *Harvard Business Review*, May 2005, p. 79.

Trompenaars, F., and C. Hampden-Turner. *Riding the Waves of Culture: Understanding Cultural Diversity in Global Business*. New York: McGraw-Hill, 1998.

Trompenaars, F., and P. Woolliams. *Business Across Cultures*. West Sussex, England: Capstone Publishing, 2003, p. 28.

SECTION III

The Projects

This section includes some *Tangible Culture* project examples. As we mentioned in Chapter 1, "Introduction—An Overview of *Tangible Culture*," these concepts are still "proving," but many have gained benefits from applying them. Space does not permit us to share how Right vs. Right was used to resolve a persistent business model debate, how Business Practices and Right vs. Right rectified frustrating terminology differences, or how IBM has integrated *Tangible Culture* into its own acquisition playbook. However, we can share two situations that embody creative uses of the concepts—and remember that Chapters 8 through 11 ("Mergers and Acquisitions—Managing the Common Sources of Culture Clash," "Alliances—Finding Ways to Leverage Your Collective Capabilities," "Major Restructuring—Gaining Sustained Value from Your Reorganization," and "Major Transformation— Addressing Your Plan's Hidden Barrier," respectively) also include our consolidated experiences. The cases are purposefully short and targeted at providing ideas about tailoring the concepts to meet specific needs.

13

The Co-operators—
Using Business Practices
to Clarify Expectations

By Sara Moulton Reger and Len Nanjad

Chapter Contents

Overview

This chapter shows how the concept of Business Practices can supplement other information, such as principles, and help clarify the details of a transformational vision. It also shows how the concepts of Right vs. Right and Outcome Narratives can be used informally as questions to guide deeper and more structured discussions.

Introduction

Companies transform for a variety of reasons. In the following case, you will see an organization respond to a new enterprise mission, vision, and associated business model enabled by Client Relationship Management (CRM). As with any enterprise or project vision, the early stages are pivotal—key decisions need to be made and tradeoffs reconciled. Companies often make the mistake of pushing quickly through this important stage, assuming agreement and full understanding.

This story shows how the team used the *Tangible Culture* concepts to clarify expectations during visioning. It also reinforces the view stated in Chapter 11, "Major Transformation—Addressing Your Plan's Hidden Barrier," that mindset shifts (called "business philosophy" here) are at the core of transformation.

The Company

The Co-operators Group Limited (www.cooperators.ca) is a group of Canadian companies offering insurance and financial services based in Guelph, Ontario. They consist of 31 similarly structured organizations known as member-owners, and together represent a combined membership of 4.5 million Canadians and assets in excess of $6 billion.

The Co-operators products and services include auto, home, farm, commercial, travel, life, and group insurance, as well as wealth management, investment, and real estate management services. They have more than 4,200 staff, more than 430 exclusive agents, and approximately 900 independent brokers distributing products and services through 650 outlets and three call centres.

The Co-operators began during a period of adversity following the depression and World War II. Canadian rural communities were threatened by lack of capital, and when insurance policies were cancelled for nonpayment, families who lost their breadwinners were reduced to poverty. In March 1945, The Co-operators was formed and began by training 16 men to sell life insurance.

Today, The Co-operators is one of Canada's Top 50 Best Employers (for both 2004 and 2005) according to *The Globe and Mail*'s Report on Business. Dennis Deters, Senior Vice President of Member and Corporate Relations and Planning, stated in 2004, "Canadian cooperative pioneers have, through our ownership and management, worked hard to create a culture throughout The Co-operators group of companies that reflects the traditional cooperative values of caring and sharing." (Insurance-Canada.ca). Clearly, molding a cooperative, client culture has been an ongoing priority at The Co-operators.

In March 2002, Kathy Bardswick was named the fourth president and CEO, and she affirmed the recently adopted mission and vision:

> Mission: "Financial security for Canadians and their communities."
> Vision: "We will be the Canadian champion; where Canadians are, with the financial security products and services they need, when they need them, however they wish to buy them; a member of, and contributor to, a strong co-operative community."

CRM could help The Co-operators know more about their clients—through a 360-degree view—and thus serve them better. Specifically, CRM could help The Co-operators respond flexibly to client preferences and their individual needs for financial security—in net, more value, less time, and less complexity for clients. For these reasons, CRM was identified as the vehicle for propelling their mission and vision.

"If we want to truly deliver on our mission of providing 'financial security,' we will only be able to do so by recognizing what security means to our clients, not what we think it means," said Kathy Bardswick. "That in turn is only possible when we intimately understand and anticipate their needs and expectations; a tall order and one that requires us to change what we do and how we do it. Our CRM initiatives are driving this fundamental and widespread change. Let me clarify that CRM is not a project—it is a long-term item on our 'to do' list, and is driven by our never-ending priority to put our clients first. That focus will become our way of life."

Can Two Rights Make a Wrong?
Insights from IBM's Tangible Culture Approach

230

CRM at the Co-operators

For many companies, CRM means a systems implementation. For The Co-operators, it is a client-centric business philosophy. The CRM goals are to realign the organizational structure, business rules, and processes around a client focus, then enable them with technology. The CRM vision reinforces the philosophy of relationships:

> *We will have a set of processes and technology that will enable agencies and employees to establish, retain, and enhance mutually beneficial client relationships. Our ongoing strategy will allow us to deliver superior financial solutions by knowing our clients, responding to their needs and preferences, and recognizing their long-term value.*

"Our CRM program was designed to benefit all stakeholders," said Dan Watchorn, the Vice President of CRM. "First it benefits the clients by ensuring the organization knows who they are, recognizes their value and is able to respond to their needs and preferences. It also benefits our agents by differentiating us in the marketplace, thereby enhancing their ability to increase their revenue. And finally, it benefits the organization by ensuring we target our growth to the right clients, increasing efficiency and bottom-line profitability. This win-win-win scenario is key to helping everyone understand 'Why CRM?' and justifies the investment of time, effort, and money."

CRM began in mid 2003, and Release I began rollout in February 2006. It is impacting nearly 4,000 people—2,000 Co-operators employees and approximately 2,000 independent agents and their staff. Release I will

- Provide new processes for taking claim reports, generating leads, recording client contacts, and handling incoming client requests.
- Specify business rules to standardize service quality, levels, and differentiation.
- Implement a central client information database.
- Implement a desktop client information tool to enable a full listing of each client's products and contact history.
- Enable the changes through organizational and transition strategies.

This release is the foundation for their CRM transformation. It will allow everyone within The Co-operators to have a full understanding of the client and their value to the organization when dealing with that client. To be ready for it, the team has

- Defined a CRM value proposition, including the definition of and vision for CRM, and an articulation of key business value drivers.
- Developed a CRM blueprint and roadmap, including an end-state business model, prioritized initiatives to achieve CRM capabilities, and a business case based on a staged transformation roadmap.
- Established a project infrastructure to support roadmap implementation.
- Specified and integrated the overall designs for CRM.

Beyond Release I, The Co-operators CRM project will entail

- Standardizing sales and marketing business processes.
- Creating additional business rules relevant to the new processes.
- Implementing a contact centre to augment the agent channel for sales and service.
- Implementing sales, marketing and campaign management tools using CRM software.
- Deploying all changes to the rest of the organization.

Figure 13-1 shows some of the complexities of the work. The diagram shows the key CRM components and their relationships to each other and the release schedule.

The overall CRM program is targeted at improving client satisfaction and loyalty, quality of services, and productivity. The metrics include growth in target client acquisition, improved loss ratio, and growth in agency and contact centre sales.

"The executive leadership team at The Co-operators recognize and fully embrace the commitment to process, change management, and organizational alignment required to successfully enable their people to achieve the business benefits detailed by their CRM vision," said Philip Grosch, IBM's BCS Partner. "Their integrated approach is driving business acceptance and a clear focus on results."

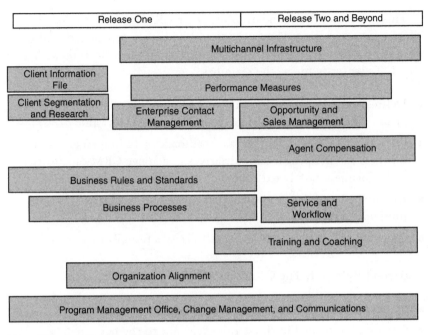

Figure 13-1   Logical diagram of CRM components.

The CRM Culture Challenge

CRM is a new way of doing business for The Co-operators, and they quickly recognized the need to think differently about their business. This meant that senior management needed to support CRM as a top priority, and that the organization and accountabilities needed to be redesigned to align with the new direction.

After senior management was committed to CRM and had begun aligning the needed elements, attention was focused on the independent agents and those who supported them. Let's look at the progressive steps the team used to clarify the CRM vision.

Stakeholder Strategies

One of the first activities was to identify stakeholders, analyze their impacts, and develop strategies for managing the change implications. The team recognized that broad and deep involvement was needed. How else could they change the business philosophy? And how could the organization convincingly communicate a new focus on client relationships without focusing on internal relationships first?

The stakeholder strategies included the following:

- Regular meetings to communicate the CRM vision and its details
- One-on-one meetings with key people to discuss and address needs and concerns
- Involvement from each stakeholder group in creating and evaluating the designs
- Opportunities for feedback on the vision

With the stakeholder strategies underway, work began to clarify the operational vision and help key groups develop ownership of it. From here, we concentrate on two of the stakeholder groups: independent agents and field management. The independent agents are responsible for sales and service activities for insurance clients. Field management is a corporate group that supports the independent agents through coaching and development; performance tracking; and guidance, advice, and consultation on developing their businesses.

CRM Key Focus Areas

Some high-level decisions were made early on. These decisions became key elements of the vision as it unfolded:

- Shift from a product-centric to a client-focused business model.
- Shift from a service orientation to a relationship orientation.
- Extend support channels to help with overflow and expand hours of operation.
- Focus tools and data on knowing clients better and responding more effectively.

You may recognize Right vs. Right in the first two. Certainly product-centric, services orientations are "right" answers, but not here. The communications specifically stated a shift *from* the product-centric, services orientation *to* the client-focused, relationship orientation. Although it may sound obvious, many companies forget the power of communicating what they *do not* want to do. The Co-operators made this shift clear.

Operating Principles

Next, field management envisioned the desired agents of the future. After they had a vision, they would share it with the agents to gauge reactions and gain input. They started by agreeing to the vision's key operating principles:

- Agents need to have a clear contract with The Co-operators.
- Agents have a responsibility to the organization, their clients, and the profession.
- An agency is running and building a business within a business.
- Business profiles include income producers and business builders.

This last principle was a core distinction. Historically, both income producer and business builder profiles were valid. But, were both consistent with their future vision? Here's where Business Practices could help by distinguishing what each profile meant.

Business Practices

For income producer and business builder profiles, high-level Business Practices were identified across an array of CRM business dimensions. Table 13-1 shows excerpts.

A few things may jump out as you review Table 13-1. First, this is a list of Right vs. Right Business Practices. They used the contrasting Business Practices not for reconciliation but rather as a way to examine the differences between the profiles, which led to some pivotal questions. Should both profiles be acceptable as long as individuals produced results? Would the CRM vision necessitate breaking some historical success patterns? The Co-operators made a key decision: They wanted to focus on business builders because it fully embodied their client-focused, relationship orientation.

Table 13-1 Business Practices for Profiles

Business Dimension	Income Producer	Business Builder
Growth mindset	Focused on replacing income	Focused on building a business
Client focus	Focused on providing good service and best price	Focused on building client relationships and providing effective advice
Action orientation	Responds to client requests for information	Proactively seeks a relationship with the client
Client contact practices	Provides client reviews as requested and as an opener for sales activities	Provides annual client reviews, and schedules separate sales appointments
Development mindset	Values individual contributions and strong processes	Values developing people and building strong teams
Risk appetite	May be conservative and risk averse	Is entrepreneurial and willing to take risks
Operating philosophies	Holds values of teamwork, professionalism, ethical behavior, empathy, and honesty	Holds values of teamwork, professionalism, ethical behavior, empathy, and honesty

You may also notice that the values listed in the operating philosophies dimension are exactly the same for both profiles. Clarifying expectations based on values would have provided few (if any) distinguishing characteristics. However, thinking through the Business Practices surfaced a number of differences.

Going Deeper on Business Practices

Until Business Practices are defined at a level where important trade-offs have been considered, they may be hard to put into action, so the team went deeper. For example:

- "Building a business" would include concentrating activities on the highest value client segments and product profitability mix.

- "Building client relationships and providing effective advice" would include educating clients on emerging risks.

- "Proactively seeks a relationship with the client" would include scheduling regular client contacts to understand the client's situation—then, secondarily and typically in a separate meeting, the focus would be on sales.

Now the team could see how priorities would be set, how decisions would be made, how client contacts would be prioritized and handled, and so forth. The team also recognized their vision would require something deeper between field management and the agents—field management needed to become trusted advisors to the agents.

With the Business Practices clarified, support requirements for the new business model were easy to identify. For instance, a client contact role would be needed to manage the proactive client contacts. This role could be a separate job or an activity incorporated into another job. Also, educating and advising clients meant that staff members would need general skills as well as expertise in one or more areas.

The decisions were documented in an Agency of the Future definition. Defining the expectations required Right vs. Right types of discussions of each view and clarifying the elements contained in the Outcome Narrative format (for instance, outcomes, roles, behaviors). In fact, the team found this detail necessary to build the needed understanding.

After the Agency of the Future was developed, communications were provided to stakeholder groups. Feedback was also collected and used to refine the vision and planning for Release I. Here are some of the stakeholders' comments and questions:

- "What will be done to help people with income producer mindsets make the shift? Over what time frame?"

- "We need to stop hiring income producers. Our hiring tools are currently oriented toward sales and service."

- "The agents need training on how to build relationships. We need good question and response techniques. We also need to understand regular reviews from each client's perspective, but set some minimum expectations."

- "We need to rethink our historic definition of business builder because it seems to be changing—and we need to allow for local and regional differences."

- "In this new environment, we need to think about who we put on a pedestal. How important are results versus implementing the actions identified in the Agency of the Future document?"

- "Is the organizational definition too well defined? Shouldn't agencies be given more options and latitude in these areas, or do we want a cookie cutter approach?"

- "Do we really want entrepreneurial risk takers, or do we want people who value our partnership model and are well positioned to operate in our business model?"

- "How do we communicate expectations given this will be a small change for some and a huge change for others?"

Astute comments and questions such as these during pre-rollout communications means that the project sponsors and team have sorted through many decisions at a good level of detail. In fact, this feedback process even identified some misconceptions they needed to dispel before people had taken unintended actions.

Progress To-Date

The Release I rollout just underway at this writing, and already much progress has been made on achieving the new business philosophy for The Co-operators, specifically the following:

- The organization and accountabilities have been redesigned to align with this change in strategic focus.

- The Agency of the Future profile has been communicated broadly, and has been embraced by field management and most employees and agents impacted.

- The business areas are embracing CRM and working actively to determine how they can change their practices and prepare for a client-focused and relationship-oriented environment, even before the new tools and capabilities are implemented.

Of course, this multi-year journey has some challenges ahead. Prioritizing a capability rollout is tricky, and the project team is working to move quickly while not pushing beyond the speed the organization can absorb. This is especially important when a business philosophy is involved—people need time to understand the new ways of thinking and working. To help with the change requirements, and to build capabilities for the future, a series of disciplined change management activities, such as stakeholder management, communications, impact analysis, and benefits realization are being coordinated closely through the program management function.

Lynn Skillen, IBM's Executive Project Manager, commented on the approach. "Shifting the emphasis in the CRM program from being technology-driven to business-driven required very pragmatic, specific activities involving the business area people earlier—and more often. This demanded some innovative approaches through program management and within many of the project initiatives."

How *Tangible Culture* Has Helped

Certainly, the CRM project sponsors and team have done a tremendous job of clarifying their transformation vision, and *Tangible Culture* concepts have been only one small part. However, thinking through Business Practices has helped define the expectations at an actionable level, and has led to effective decisions and meaningful communications.

Perhaps the greatest benefit was the structure it brought to the process. Business Practices, Right vs. Right, and Outcome Narratives enabled the team to focus the discussions by crafting questions from each concept. In fact, before these concepts were incorporated, the discussions bounced around. The concepts enabled the team to nail things down and bring structure to difficult and broad discussions.

"Focusing on improved business practices had two major benefits," said Rick McCombie, Senior Vice President, Direct Distribution. "It made sure the initiatives were business oriented, not technology-driven. It also provided a level of discipline to make sure we met our objective of being a more client-centric organization."

Alasdair Campbell, Vice President, Special Lines, said, "All of the thinking and 'answers' were already there. This process helped us to bring structure and clarity to the discussions to develop a meaningful set of principles and practices. It really helped senior management to sort out their commitment to the direction they would like field management to take nationally."

Conclusion

Business Practices, Right vs. Right, and Outcome Narratives are tools for helping companies clarify their expectations. Here, they were used to dig deeper into a transformation's requirements and pose the questions necessary to clarify expectations. The concepts were combined with a principles approach, which reinforces that *Tangible Culture* does not take anything away—it only adds new capabilities and techniques.

IBM would like to express sincere gratitude to The Co-operators for letting us document parts of their transformation journey in this book.

References

Fanning, C. "Client Relationship Management at The Co-operators," 2005.

Insurance-Canada.ca, www.insurance-canada.ca/humanres/canada/coop-winner-501.php, "The Co-operators Group of Companies a Triple Winner in Workplace Survey."

14

Sales Pipeline— Using Right vs. Right to Differentiate Issues

By Sara Moulton Reger and Kristin von Donop

Chapter Contents

Can Two Rights Make a Wrong?
Insights from IBM's Tangible Culture Approach

242

Overview

This chapter shows you how to use Right vs. Right, along with the underlying concept of Business Practices, to distinguish between different types of issues, specifically execution issues and fundamental business disagreements.

Introduction

Ever had one of those pesky problem areas? You know, the one that you have "fixed" but still is an issue. Or perhaps it is the one that people have resigned themselves to live with because they get a headache just thinking about its complexity?

This case shows how a team used Right vs. Right to clarify the underlying issues in a complex situation. Using the technique, they were able to distinguish between execution issues (where barriers were in the way) and fundamental disconnects (where people did not agree on how the work should be performed and enabled). This understanding helped the team to create an effective path forward knowing the issues they faced.

Collaborate for Growth Initiative

Within IBM, leaders can use several initiatives to launch improvement efforts. One is called "Collaborate for Growth" (CfG) and it was developed to drive transformational change. CfG is an action-learning approach focused on helping IBMers address sticky, cross-organizational issues that impede sustained growth, innovation, and leverage of IBM's collective capabilities.

CfG projects are focused on areas that require collaboration or integration between business units. The IBM Values and Leadership Competencies underpin the process, and are "brought alive" when applied to the challenges. In the end, the targeted business outcomes are achieved through improved business mechanisms (for example, processes, measures, policies), through enhanced cross-organizational understanding and behaviors, and through aligned perspectives and Business Practices.

When a CfG project is launched, people at multiple levels from the relevant organizations are engaged in dialogue and problem solving. CfG projects are structured with one or more sponsors (often senior vice presidents) who are responsible for selecting the project and participants, and for ensuring sustained focus to achieve the needed results. Also, a cross-organizational, cross-geography leadership team—the guiding coalition—is formed from mid-level leaders (often vice presidents and directors) of the business units. The guiding coalition has responsibility to make decisions and guide the work activities. Finally, a series of execution teams are formed to represent specific client sets, functions, and other expertise necessary to the project's success.

A team of consultants is also assigned. Because these projects have "people" written all over them (remember that collaboration is the key focus), the consultants are experts in leadership, organizational development, and change management. Their task is to facilitate dialogue and problem solving, align and orchestrate leadership, and identify ways to sustain the improvements over time.

The Sales Pipeline Project

As you can imagine, sales are an important, ongoing function within IBM. And as we seek to leverage our combined capabilities—the full depth and breadth of IBM globally—the sales process becomes more complex (along with other things).

Frankly, IBMers are old pros at selling discrete products and services. Combining hardware, software, and services into the right capabilities to solve client problems—and doing it quickly—is trickier. For IBM, this means participation from multiple brands and channels—often including external business partners. In this complex sales environment, one worldwide brand executive began asking important questions.

The brand executive wanted to determine ways to improve the consistency and quality of the brand's sales pipeline. This was not simply an issue of better tracking the opportunities, but was a fundamental question of whether people were targeting the right opportunities—and approaching them the right way. Because an effective sales pipeline for this brand requires multiple business units to participate, a CfG project was structured and a guiding coalition assembled.

Can Two Rights Make a Wrong?
Insights from IBM's Tangible Culture Approach

244

To initiate the work, the lead consultants interviewed members of the guiding coalition—a group of 15 executives across several brands, customer sets, and functions within IBM. To broaden the perspectives and better understand the issues, 25 additional stakeholders were interviewed. During the interviews, the consultants began to sense some important underlying disconnects in the answers.

When the consultants compared interview notes, they saw seemingly different opinions on several important topics, from needed skill sets, to how people should be deployed to opportunities, to how sales coordination should be performed. If the consultants' hunches were right and some of the underlying issues were disagreements among the leaders who need to be aligned for success, could Right vs. Right help them clarify the various perspectives? And could exploring these perspectives help them to quickly determine what actions to take to address different root causes?

Choosing the Right vs. Right Technique

After a review of other techniques, the lead consultants chose to use Right vs. Right. To explain the choice, Christopher Nickerson, a Senior Organization Leadership Consultant, explained, "We're working with multiple perspectives across the business—and with seasoned executives with significant experience in their domains. We knew we'd face conflicting views, and that we'd have to help them reconcile the conflicts. Since a goal of this project is to improve IBM's ability to collaborate, we wanted to use a constructive approach. The Right vs. Right approach would be a great way to surface and clarify the competing priorities we saw manifested in the organization."

Applying Right vs. Right

The lead consultants individually poured over the interview notes to identify potential Right vs. Right conflicts in what the executives said—and implied. When they compared notes, many of the same differences showed up on their lists. Aha—they were right—there did appear to be some differences, and they were hearing the same things.

14: Sales Pipeline
Using Right vs. Right to Differentiate Issues

245

The consultants then consolidated their suspected conflicts into 11 pairs of Right vs. Rights. These 11 best embodied the differences reflected in the guiding coalition members' views. Table 14-1 shows an excerpt.

Table 14-1 Suspected Right vs. Rights

The sales representatives for this brand area need only to bring expertise on this portfolio and rely on the client team to help with industry and client business issues.	We need our sales representatives for this brand to be able to represent expertise for the portfolio and also bring an understanding of industry and client issues.
For this area, we need to assign people to specific accounts so they can build long-term relationships and industry knowledge—we need farmers.	For this area, we need to assign people to regions and then concentrate them on accounts where there are immediate opportunities—we need hunters.
To best understand and drive the sales opportunities, our regular reviews of the sales pipeline should be detailed—item by item discussions of the client issues, opportunities, status, and so on.	Our regular reviews are best used to discuss exceptions and concerns—if everything is okay with an opportunity and no one needs help, we should not bother to discuss it.
We should hold our regular sales opportunity reviews across all impacted brands to allow for the greatest degree of collaboration and knowledge sharing.	We need to hold our regular sales opportunity reviews by brand, and schedule cross-brand discussions when there are client opportunities or cross-brand issues.
In general, senior leaders should focus on the metrics and the pipeline, and motivate attention on achieving the business results.	In general, senior leaders should focus on coaching and enabling—finding where there are issues and helping people to drive opportunities and revenue.
Big deals are big deals and they are a priority—this means that we may have to redeploy people to them at times.	We need to support deals of all sizes and not redeploy people who have already been assigned.

Spreadsheets were then created and sent out to the guiding coalition asking them what they believed was best on the Right vs. Right uneven five-point scale. Table 14-2 shows an excerpt from that spreadsheet.

Can Two Rights Make a Wrong?
Insights from IBM's Tangible Culture Approach

246

Table 14-2 Right vs. Right Data Collection Form

	100%	99–51%	50/50	51–99%	100%	
The sales representatives for this brand need only to bring expertise on this portfolio and rely on the client team to help with industry and client business issues.						We need our sales representatives for this brand to be able to represent expertise for the portfolio and also bring an understanding of industry and client issues.

Analyzing the Data Collected

When the results came in, three general categories emerged—and interestingly, the relative numbers were approximately one third of each type of result:

1. One third of the answers showed good agreement between the participants on what was "right" (all of the answers were in two adjacent boxes).
2. The next third showed an emerging answer, yet less agreement and often one or more people who were on the other opposite side of the scale from the rest.
3. The last third showed a complete lack of agreement—in fact they had answers in every box, and approximately the same number in each box!

Now the team had something to work with—and here were their next questions:

- For 1—Where there was general agreement

  - Were the organizations performing the work that way today? In other words, were there barriers that needed to be removed to enable people to do what was best for the clients and the business?

14: **Sales Pipeline**

Using Right vs. Right to Differentiate Issues *247*

- ◆ The consultants dubbed these "execution" issues. People agreed on what to do, but there was some kind of barrier to doing it that way and this is why the issue came up during the interviews.

- ■ For 2—The ones with an emerging answer but some disagreements

  - ◆ Was there a pattern to the differences? For instance, did the different perspectives come from people assigned to certain functions or client sets?

  - ◆ The consultants saw two reasons for these differences. The first was a valid alternate perspective that needed to be considered. For instance, two ways may be appropriate to deal with two different types of clients or projects. The second was that we simply had an execution issue with some minority views, but the majority would prevail. These would require more discussion before the path for resolution would be known.

- ■ For 3—The ones "all over the board"

  - ◆ These were ones where discussion and reconciliation were needed—and where the project could make a real impact. These issues wouldn't be addressed in the regular course of business because they were fundamental disconnects. Even if some actions were taken, they would address only half of the perspectives—at best. Formulating actions without reconciling the disconnects would undoubtedly mean the problems wouldn't be resolved, and the "fix" would have to be revisited in the future.

  - ◆ The consultants knew that the next step with these was to head down the Right vs. Right reconciliation path.

So, with a few short hours of work, the consultants were able to use existing information to cull out a series of potential conflicts. They were also able to gather executive viewpoints (using only 10 or 15 minutes of their time), and use that input to identify different types of issues and ways to handle them. Quickly, three paths of work were launched:

- ■ **Path 1**—The execution teams were convened to discuss the guiding coalition's input, and identify the barriers and ways to address them.

- ■ **Path 2**—The areas with emerging answers yet disagreements were analyzed. During this analysis, a justifiable reason emerged—a difference in handling that was needed between large and smaller clients. The execution teams were chartered to consider the ramifications of having multiple approaches for these different contexts.

- **Path 3**—The guiding coalition was taken through a Right vs. Right reconciliation exercise, and then their decisions were handed off to the execution teams for a Path 1 exercise.

These paths were launched in parallel, which helped to compress the overall timeline. The work is ongoing as of this writing.

Benefits

The team members found several benefits in using Right vs. Right on this project.

First, the technique allowed them to quickly identify appropriate actions and launch different types of work in parallel. Even though they were executing the project rapidly, they were addressing the fundamental issues. Often moving forward quickly means adopting one path for the work, which would have been unsuccessful here.

Second, the technique identified areas for guiding coalition discussion. Executives have limited time, so it is vital to focus their attention to keep them engaged. Frankly, these CfG projects will not work if the guiding coalition members' participation wanes, and Right vs. Right surfaced areas that needed their attention—and they could see it.

Finally, the answers—which showed the three buckets of agreement and disagreement—gave the effort a mandate and call to action. This was especially important because there was a change of sponsor midstream. The new leader could have redirected the effort, but faced with the input collected, he chose to stay the course. The issues would simply not be resolved without collaborative decision making.

Christopher Nickerson explained, "Using this approach, we were able to demystify the topic of culture. We knew that there were underlying cultural issues, and the approach gave us tangible topics to discuss— using the participants' own words. It was a great way to provoke the needed discussion and debate."

Jenna Case-Lee, another Organization Leadership Consultant, added, "It was amazing how quickly the technique helped us pinpoint the real issues. Thinking about their Right vs. Rights helped us to condense the analysis and rapidly launch the real work needed to bring change."

Conclusion

Right vs. Right can be used to understand issues and their source. Many companies jump quickly into creating solutions. If there are unresolved Right vs. Rights, however, it is likely that the issues will continue and someone will have to cover the same territory again. This case demonstrates how a few hours devoted to surfacing and gauging the Right vs. Rights early in the project can push the improvement effort forward quickly, yet ensure that the real issues are being addressed.

The authors of *Tangible Culture* offer sincere thanks to the members of the Sales Pipeline CfG project for allowing us to share their experiences.

Epilogue

So, let's go full circle. Remember how we told you at the outset we did not have a silver bullet? Although we know we have created a better approach, we must admit that it does not solve all culture problems. It expands the toolkit and brings benefits that have been elusive in the past, but it does not make culture a fast or easy topic to address.

Chapter 3, "Traditional Approaches to Culture Transformation—How Others Have Dealt with the Challenge," walked you through pros and cons of traditional approaches to culture change. We feel it is appropriate to give you a candid assessment of our concepts, too.

You have heard the pros already, but let's recap at a high level:

- Business Practices are a good surrogate for the complex topic of culture—one that helps to draw business leaders into the work that needs to be done.

- Right vs. Right is a constructive way to uncover, understand, and reconcile different ways of working and thinking—the kinds of differences that often lead to strife, delays, and lost business value if left to "work out" on their own.

Can Two Rights Make a Wrong?
Insights from IBM's Tangible Culture Approach

252

- Outcome Narratives explain future state expectations, especially how to handle difficult situations that are likely to arise. They are not abstract statements; they are brief, structured stories on how to meet business requirements. For that reason, they surface subtle misalignments that need to be addressed and provide an objective basis for evaluating progress and identifying additional changes that are needed.

Here are the cons in a nutshell—we explain more below:

- Some people do not readily understand the concept of Business Practices.
- Some are reticent to go on a journey until the path is well worn—and this is new and has been described by some as "before its time."
- It requires more leader time and elapsed time than other approaches.
- It requires strong facilitation and writing skills.

Let's start by explaining the cons we believe are short-term issues.

Despite explaining it every way we know how, some people still think "Business Practices" is just a fancy name for business processes, so there is little that is new to be gained. We have whipped out our best evidence to the contrary—including the fact that companies with the same processes do the work differently—still, we have been unsuccessful in convincing some. We hope that this will clear up as more people begin to use the term regularly. Frankly, we understand it; we realized the importance of this concept later, too. However, we long for the day that people readily recognize Business Practices and their powerful impact.

In his June 2005 *Harvard Business Review* article, "The Coming Commoditization of Processes," Tom Davenport wrote about standards and how they are leading to process commoditization—and that this will lead to more and better outsourcing, among other things. In our opinion, this trend will highlight Business Practices: The processes will be the same, but there will be differences between how companies execute them. Taking this notion one step further, after companies achieve world-class capabilities, what differentiates them? We would say that Business Practices are one source of lasting differentiation because they reflect your culture. There is more to explore here, but alas, those who are not cognizant of their Business Practices will not reap the benefits.

Because the concepts are new, some people have not been comfortable going through the process. They cannot see how it will all end, and we cannot provide them with names of 10 other companies in their industry who have done it this way yet. Some have gone on a faith journey with us, and for that we are glad. And we are happy to report that they are benefiting from it. We believe that more will come along in the future.

To round out the near-term cons, we have heard this a few times: "This stuff is before its time." That's a double-edged sword. Clearly, IBM's goal is to be innovative, but we know that the path to business value means doing the right thing at the right time. We hope that you will become an early adopter and that you will help us push the timing a bit.

Now let's move on to the other cons—the ones that may follow this approach over the longer term.

There are no two ways about it: This approach requires more time from your leaders than traditional culture approaches. You are likely to need more than one Right vs. Right reconciliation session, and you will need a quorum of the right leaders to make the decisions stick. Also, these leaders need to agree that the Outcome Narratives represent their desired future. Some leaders recognize this effort as an investment in business results: The more guidance they give, the fewer escalations, personnel issues and other problems they will have to address in the future. And that will give them more time to concentrate on customers, strategies and high-level business decisions. But, candidly, others just have not carved out the time, and it impacted the benefits this approach was able to bring.

And speaking of time, this work takes more time than other approaches. It is best done with a small team—in fact, trying to do the work faster with more people will not be successful. *Tangible Culture* brings a sophisticated solution to a complex area. If there are easier ways to address your issues—by all means, do them! However, if you have tried other approaches, or know that they will not work for your current requirements, you have several months of work to do. But do not forget—you will get benefits along the way.

Finally, this work takes strong writing and facilitation skills. The Right vs. Rights and Outcome Narratives need to be well worded or they may become the focus of the discussions rather than enabling them. Your facilitators need to be objective—and perceived as objective. There is nothing worse than feeling that the facilitator believes your preferred "right" answer is "wrong" during Right vs. Right reconciliation! And the people doing this work need to be comfortable interacting with your business leaders—in some cases, your senior leaders. There is also the need to carefully balance between patience and drive. These are tough decisions and some groups can stew over them, whereas other groups can drive to answers too quickly and neglect some views. There is an art to "enough" discussion—we are still learning it ourselves!

We hope you appreciate our candor. And we hope that it helps you to avoid a few pitfalls. Please visit our Web site (www.almaden.ibm.com/tangibleculture) and tell us what is working—and not working—for you. We want to learn from your experiences. And thank you for giving us this opportunity to share our learnings with you!

APPENDIX

About the Contributors

Michael Armano is a Partner with Essex Partners and is a recognized global leader in the human resources and consulting fields. He has worked as a senior executive in several of the world's most highly regarded professional services, financial services, and technology firms, including as Vice President IBM Global Services, Chief People Officer Mainspring, Director Global Human Resources with the Boston Consulting Group, and Vice President Global Workforce Planning for Fidelity Investments. Michael has completed work toward a Master's degree in Vocational and Psychological Counseling from the University of Massachusetts and holds a Bachelor of Science degree in Education from Suffolk University. During his time at IBM, he co-invented the Business Practices Alignment Method, which is the basis of *Tangible Culture* and filed for patent in 2004.

Barbarajo "BJ" Bliss is a Certified Managing Consultant in the Change & Program Strategy Practice of IBM's Business Consulting Services Group. With 26 years of consulting experience, BJ helps organizations achieve strategic performance objectives by identifying priority barriers and developing robust business transformation strategies. She is recognized within and outside of IBM as a strategic change management thought leader and serves as global expert for IBM's Culture Transformation Community of Interest. BJ holds a Master of Science degree in Communications Management from Simmons College of Boston, Massachusetts, and was the 2001 Beltz Prize recipient. She has authored a senior management seminar that helps develop the skills necessary to effectively respond to the cultural communication challenges associated with M&A implementations. She has been a featured speaker at regional and national professional associations, addressing a variety of topics such as managing the human side of mergers and acquisitions, strategic change management, and transformational leadership.

Jeanette Blomberg manages the Work in Organizational Context group at the IBM Almaden Research Center. Her research focuses on the interplay between people, technology, and organizational practices. Jeanette is also an industry-affiliated Professor of Human Work Science at the Blekinge Institute of Technology in Sweden, where she advises Ph.D. students and organizes a biennial Ph.D. course on Work Practice and Design for students throughout the Nordic countries. Prior to assuming her current position at IBM, Jeanette was Director of Experience Modeling Research at Sapient Corporation, where she helped establish the Experience Modeling practice and managed Sapient's San Francisco Experience Modeling group. Jeanette was also a founding member of the pioneering Work Practice and Technology group at the Xerox Palo Alto Research Center (PARC). Over the years, her research has explored issues in social aspects of technology production and use, ethnographically informed organizational interventions, participatory design, case-based prototyping, and work practice studies. She has published on these topics, given numerous invited talks, and offered workshops in the United States and Europe on the topic of aligning ethnography with product and service design. Jeanette received her Ph.D. in Anthropology from the University of California, Davis, where she taught courses in cultural anthropology and sociolinguistics.

Susan "Sue" Blum is a Managing Consultant with 27 years working experience (15 of which have been as a Consultant) in IBM's Business Consulting Services group. She is the Global Leader for IBM's Culture Transformation Community of Interest. Sue has a particular expertise in pragmatic approaches to embedding change and a passion for ensuring value is elicited from organizational behaviors. Susan has an MBA from Manchester Business School and an MA (Hons) in Psychology from St. Andrews University. She is a Fellow of the Royal Society of Arts and a member of the Association of Management Consultants (UK).

Melissa Cefkin is a Research Staff Member in IBM Research. A member of the Human Systems group with Almaden Services Research, Melissa is a business and design anthropologist with more than 12 years experience in research, management, and consulting. Melissa is a specialist in workplace ethnography with a focus on services research, product and service design and deployment, technology adoption strategies, organizational change management, and training and program development. Prior to joining IBM in 2005, Melissa was a Director of Advanced Research at Sapient Corporation, and previously held a Senior Research Scientist position at the Institute for Research on Learning. A Fulbright award grantee with a Ph.D. in Anthropology from Rice University, Melissa has conducted research globally and designed and taught university courses in cultural anthropology. She is a frequent invited speaker at universities and is a regular contributor to conferences and publication review boards. Currently serving on two member-elected positions for the American Anthropological Association, she is a former member of the Research Committee for the American Society for Training and Development and of the Board of Trustees for the Society for Organizational Learning. Melissa has authored numerous articles, reviews, and book chapters.

Andrew Duncan is a Partner in IBM's Business Consulting Services group. He joined IBM from PwCC, where he led the European Merger Integration practice in Financial Services from 1987 through 2003 from London. He has worked with many large banks and insurers on their merger agendas, including AXA, Aviva, Barclays, Royal Bank of Scotland Group, Abbey National, Irish Life & Permanent, and CIBC. His work focuses on getting the best results from the combination of capabilities and experience from the merger of two businesses—the post-merger integration phases. The creation of one new business following a merger is, in Andrew's view, the largest change program that any company can go through, touching almost everyone in the process. Andrew supports CEOs and Merger Directors through this process.

Andrew was educated at Edinburgh's Heriot Watt University and is a member of the Institute of Chartered Accountants of Scotland. He has spoken at many international conferences on merger integration and on business management in the fund management industry. For 8 years, he authored IBM's annual Investment Management Survey, a review of operational performance in the industry.

Ron Frank is the Partner within IBM Business Consulting Services who leads the Strategy and Change Services practice serving the internal IBM account. His areas of expertise include business and customer strategy, operations strategy, and process redesign and organizational alignment. Ron holds a BA in mathematics from Queens College, City University of New York, and a Ph.D. in Operations Research and Industrial Engineering from the Johns Hopkins University. He has written published articles about leadership and growth, and was an Assistant Professor at Harvard Business School and a director/trustee at Milton Academy, Wordwave, and RadiusPD.

Cheryl Grise is a Partner with IBM's Business Consulting Services group and the Americas Organization Change Strategy Leader. Cheryl has more than 11 years of consulting experience advising the senior management of large corporate organizations. She has expertise in areas including organization strategy and design, change management, and program management. She also has considerable experience in team design and development, process improvement, CRMS visioning and blueprint design, benefits realization, and business transformation. Cheryl has spent the past 4 years working with a multinational entertainment and media company, leading the Business Transformation program to restructure the HR, finance, and IT functions across 86 business units to realize between $130M and $200M in annual labor savings. The effort was led in parallel with a five-wave ERP back-of-house systems implementation and the migration to shared services. Cheryl has an MBA, Information Systems and Management, from the University of Central Florida, a BA, Business Administration, from Richmond College in London, England, and has completed the Information Systems Management Program with General Electric Aerospace. She co-authored and developed the RealProjectTeams methodology to improve project team performance throughout the life cycle of highly complex, global projects.

Anthony Harris is a Managing Consultant with IBM Business Consulting Services group and a Subject Matter Expert in IBM's Culture Transformation Community of Interest for the Asia Pacific Region. He holds a Bachelor of Science degree from Bowling Green State University, Ohio, and has attended Organization Behavior studies at Arizona State University, Tempe. Anthony has more than 20 years of industry and consulting experience concentrating on issues relating to culture and behavioral change, organizational effectiveness, change management, leadership development, strategic planning/alignment, and program management. He has presented at numerous conferences, including the American Society for Training & Development, National Society for Performance and Instruction, Organization Development Network, and University of Colorado School of Business. Anthony is the author of *Step-by-Step Problem-Solving ToolKits* and co-author of *Tools for Valuing Diversity*.

Lisa D. Kreeger is a member of the IBM Almaden Services Research group based in San Jose, California. Lisa's professional and academic expertise is in the development and creation of value through interorganizational services relationships. Her background includes five years in a consulting group focused on building and optimizing business relationships at the senior executive level and more than 10 years in the healthcare industry as a nurse, researcher, and consultant in business and technology strategy. Lisa is currently pursuing a Ph.D. in Leadership and Change from Antioch University. She holds an MBA from Seattle University and Bachelor degrees in Nursing and Psychology from DePaul University.

Jeff Kreulen is the Manager of Operations Technologies at the IBM Almaden Research Center. He holds a Bachelor of Science degree in applied mathematics (computer science) from Carnegie-Mellon University, a Master of Science degree in Electrical Engineering and a Ph.D. in Computer Engineering both from Pennsylvania State University. Since joining IBM in 1992, he has worked on multiprocessor systems design and verification, operating systems, systems management, Web-based service delivery, and integrated text and data analysis. Most recently, Jeff has been leading research and development in services enabling technology efforts for the Almaden Service Research function. He has published in both journals and conference proceedings and holds 10 U.S. patents.

260

Can Two Rights Make a Wrong?
Insights from IBM's Tangible Culture Approach

Eric Lesser is an Associate Partner in IBM's Institute for Business Value, responsible for developing research and thought leadership for IBM's Human Capital Management practice. He has conducted a wide variety of studies and consulted with clients in the knowledge, learning, and human capital areas. He has edited three books: *Creating Value with Knowledge: Insights from the IBM Institute for Business Value* with Larry Prusak (Oxford University Press, 2003), *Knowledge and Communities* with Michael Fontaine and Jason Slusher, and *Knowledge and Social Capital* (both with Butterworth-Heinemann 2000). His articles have appeared in *Sloan Management Review, International Human Resource Information Management Journal, IBM Systems Journal*, and the *Ivey Business Journal*. Eric holds an MBA from the Goizueta School of Business at Emory University (where he was a Robert W. Woodruff fellow) and a Bachelor of Arts in Economics from Brandeis University.

Dave Lubowe is a partner in IBM Business Consulting Services' Strategy & Change practice, and is the Global and Americas Leader for Operations Strategy. Dave has more than 20 years of industry and consulting experience, primarily in operations management. Starting out at Procter & Gamble, Dave had roles of increasing responsibility in manufacturing management and project management, as well as a two-year assignment in finance. Following P&G, Dave set up and managed operations for an electronics start-up, and participated in development of several generations of the product. Then, Dave entered the consulting world, joining Price Waterhouse Consulting. His consulting work has focused on designing, implementing, managing, and continuously improving business processes, including extensive experience with managing outsourcing effectively. Clients have included Applied Materials, Franklin Covey, Union Pacific Railroad, Lam Research, AMD, and Arrow. Dave holds a Bachelor of Science degree in Mechanical Engineering from Princeton University and five U.S. patents.

Michael Lueck is a Managing Consultant in the Organizational Strategy practice within IBM Business Consulting Services. He has led organization transformation, merger integration, and business strategy projects for clients across 11 industries and every business function. Michael received a Bachelor of Science degree from Texas A&M University and an MBA from the University of Chicago Graduate School of Business.

Paul Maglio is Senior Manager of Human Systems Research at the IBM Almaden Research Center, an interdisciplinary group of social, cognitive, and computer scientists focused on supporting the way people work in IBM's Global Services division. In his nine years at IBM Research, Paul has published more than 60 scientific papers and holds 12 patents in areas including human-computer interaction, intelligent agents, Web intermediaries, system management, and autonomic computing. He has a Ph.D. in cognitive science from UCSD, and an SB in Computer Science and Engineering from MIT.

Doug McDavid is an Executive Research Consultant and member of the prestigious IBM Academy of Technology with more than 30 years of experience in bridging the gap between business people and technologists. He has taken leadership roles and performed hands-on modeling and requirements definition on numerous successful engagements in such diverse industries as insurance, public utilities, military, aerospace, telecommunications, manufacturing, travel, and entertainment. He led development of an enterprise database for the world's largest value-added data communications carrier that supports network management, fixed-asset tracking, internal and external order processing, usage-sensitive and fixed monthly billing, and telco bill reconciliation, from a single, integrated database. He has published widely, including two articles in *IBM Systems Journal*: "Business Language Analysis for Object-Oriented Information Systems" (v. 35, no. 2, 1996) and "A Standard for Business Architecture Description" (vol. 38, no. 1, 1999), and was on the editorial board for the *Handbook of Object Technology* from CRC Press and authored a chapter on systems envisioning.

Patrick McDonnell is a Senior Partner and member of the Leadership Team in the Strategy and Change Practice of IBM's Business Consulting Services Business. Pat is Director of IBM's Strategic Leadership Program (SLP), where he assists global and national organizations in transforming their businesses through an innovative integration of strategy, execution, and change and performance management strategies. He worked with the Harvard Business School to develop the SLP as a commercial offering in 2001—it is based on IBM's current internal Strategic Development Process. Pat was the Leader of the Business and Operations Strategy Practice for PwCC and IBM Canada, where he co-authored

IBM's Merger Integration methodology, and was a member of the IBM/PwCC Global Integration Team. He has supported numerous integration projects in multiple industries. Pat has more than 25 years business experience, was a graduate of California State University San Diego, and has numerous Advanced Management Certification Programs from the University of Southern California and the Wharton School of Business.

Len Nanjad is a Senior Consultant in the Organization and Change Strategy practice within IBM Business Consulting Services. Over the past decade, he has worked and advised on organizational change management programs for Customer Relationship Management and technology-driven business transformations. He has served large clients in several industries, including media and entertainment, telecommunications, consumer packaged goods, automotive, and financial services. His focus is on driving high-value change interventions and strategic leadership. Len holds an MBA from the Ivey School of Business, and a Bachelor of Arts degree in Psychology and Economics from the University of Western Ontario, Canada.

Kris Pederson is an expert in large-scale business transformation associated with business process and system integration efforts. She currently holds three leadership positions within IBM Business Consulting Services: (1) Global Organization and Change Strategy Leader, includes oversight of 650 practitioners and 30 partners with competency focus on change management, cultural change, organization design, and change leadership; (2) Global Value Creation Leader, which includes business case development, benchmarking, shareholder value analysis, value pricing; (3) Global Executive of IBM's Global Relationship Partner Program, a team of partners/executives that manage the largest IBM accounts. Kris holds an MBA from Harvard University and a Bachelor of Arts degree in Psychology and Business Administration from UCLA.

George Pohle is a Vice President and Partner in Business Consulting Services. He is the Global Leader of IBM's Institute for Business Value (described below). He has spent 18 years in line leadership and consulting roles and has held senior leadership positions in both start-ups and Fortune 50 organizations. In addition to consulting, he writes and speaks frequently on issues related to corporate strategy and operations management. George holds an MBA from INSEAD (*Institut Europeen d'Administration des Affaires*) in Fontainebleau, France, and a Bachelor of Science degree in Electrical Engineering from Johns Hopkins University.

Mary Sue Rogers is Global Leader for Human Capital Management within IBM Business Consulting Services. Mary Sue is a specialist in the Human Capital Management area, primarily focusing on the transformation of the HR function and the strategically related HR activities. She is a graduate of Oakland University with a degree in Political and Computer Science. She has written and presented numerous articles for organizations such as CARS, HR Technology Conference, Times, HRPS, and a variety of professional HR journals.

Lynn Schuster is an Executive Organization and Leadership Consultant with lead responsibility for most senior executives in IBM Global Services Americas. She is one of the leads for Global Executive and Organization Capability's new Go-To-Market Model "Collaborate for Growth." Lynn is a Graduate of Manhatanville College with Bachelor of Arts in Psychology. Prior to IBM, she was a mergers and acquisitions specialist with more than 25 years experience working in a cross-section of industry both domestic and international. Lynn's areas of expertise include organization growth and change, strategy development and execution, executive integration, leadership and team development, organization design, and results-oriented problem solving for bottom-line impact. She is a published author and speaker on these topics.

Dean Spitzer is a Senior Researcher and Consultant with IBM Corporation. He is an IBM Thought Leader in the area of performance management and measurement and is currently leading groundbreaking research at IBM on business measurement models and on "the socialization of measurement." He has more than 25 years experience in helping individuals and organizations achieve superior performance, and has directed more than 100 successful training and performance-improvement projects. Prior to joining IBM, Dean was a Training/HRD Manager and Internal Consultant with several Fortune 100 companies, Assistant Director of a U.S. government education center, and served as a professor at five universities. He is the author of 6 books and more than 130 chapters and articles on various areas of human performance

improvement, organizational development, and performance management. He has lectured and consulted on five continents. Dean earned his
Ph.D. with honors from the University of Southern California and his
Master of Arts from Northwestern University. He also pursued both
undergraduate and graduate studies at the London School of Economics.

Jim Spohrer is the Director of IBM's Almaden Services Research group,
which focuses on innovation for IBM Global Services. Human sciences,
On Demand Innovation Services (ODIS), deep industry knowledge of
future trends, and service-oriented technology are areas of active explo-
ration. He has also been the CTO of IBM's Venture Capital Relations
Group, where he identified technology trends and worked to establish
win-win relationships between IBM and VC-backed portfolio companies. Previously, Jim directed the IBM Computer Science Foundation
Department, and was Senior Manager and co-strategist for IBM's User
Experience/Human Computer Interaction Research effort. Prior to joining IBM, he was a DEST (Distinguished Engineer, Scientist, and
Technologist) and Program Manager of learning technology projects in
Apple's Advanced Technology Group. Jim received a Bachelor of Science
degree in Physics from MIT and a Ph.D. in Computer Science from Yale
University. He has been a visiting scholar at the University of Rome La
Sapienza and lecturer at major universities across Europe. Jim has published broadly in the areas of speech recognition; empirical studies of
programmers; artificial intelligence; authoring tools; online learning
communities; open source software; intelligent tutoring systems and
student modeling; new paradigms in using computers; implications of
rapid technical change; and the co-evolution of social, business, and
technical systems. Jim is a frequent advisor to the National Science
Foundation, U.S. Department of Education, and others on the implications of rapid technological change to the future of education.

Ray Strong is an IBM Research Staff Member. He received a Ph.D. in
Mathematics from the University of Washington. In more than 30 years
of experience with IBM, Ray has managed projects including Theory of
Programming, Semantic Information Processing, and Distributed
Computing & Information Processing. He has worked in the research
areas of access methods, machine architectures, communication and syn-
chronization, fault-tolerant distributed algorithms, systems management, and service delivery. He was a member of the project that
produced the world's first Relational Database Management System. He

is an author of numerous technical publications and presentations and an inventor of numerous patents, especially in the area of fault-tolerant distributed systems. His recent focus at IBM has been on research strategy for optimal impact on IBM's services business. Ray's strengths include systems architecture, technical project planning and organization, expertise in distributed algorithms and systems, and experience in multi-enterprise interoperation of autonomous database systems.

Jennifer Q. Trelewicz is the Executive Assistant to Nicholas Donofrio, Executive Vice President of Innovation and Technology, in IBM Corporate Headquarters in Armonk, New York. She was previously the Research Relationship Manager for Russia and Eastern Europe and the Manager of the Business Models department in the IBM Almaden Research Center, where she worked with clients, business partners, and academics in Russia and Eastern Europe to develop new tools for analyzing businesses, and to build practical market solutions with IBM technology, services, and solutions. Jennifer holds a Ph.D. in signal processing, which was funded by a NASA Graduate Student Researcher fellowship, and an MNS degree in mathematics. She is a member of the IBM Academy of Technology, a member-at-large of the board of governors of the IEEE Signal Processing Society, and has more than 30 publications in international journals and conference proceedings, 7 issued patents and many more pending.

Kristin von Donop is a Senior Organization Leadership Consultant with IBM's Global Executive and Organization Capability (GEOC), providing leadership and organizational consulting to IBM's Senior Leadership Team members. Kristin has extensive experience in business consulting, executive coaching, leadership team effectiveness, and large-scale organizational change initiatives. She received her Master of Science degree in Industrial and Organizational Psychology from Rensselaer Polytechnic Institute in Troy, New York, and her graduate thesis was on organizational trust. She also holds a Bachelor of Science degree in Business Administration from Northeastern University in Boston, Massachusetts, where she concentrated on international business.

IBM Almaden Services Research (ASR) is the newest function at the IBM Almaden Research Center. Our focus is on innovations that impact IBM Global Services and IBM clients. Our team acts as a catalyst to increase the quantity and quality of Research's interactions with Global

266

Can Two Rights Make a Wrong?
Insights from IBM's Tangible Culture Approach

Services, IBM's largest division. ASR is performing pioneering human systems research in the social, organizational, and behavioral sciences. To work more effectively with clients, ASR is developing deep knowledge of specific industries, providing connections between client needs and the entire IBM Research organization. ASR provides connections and assistance for IBM consultants and specific architectural and technical assistance to IBM outsourcing service providers. In summary, Almaden Services Research is about understanding people in sociotechnical systems, improving service delivery, and linking innovation with business needs. For more information, visit us on the Web at www.almaden.ibm.com/asr.

IBM Business Consulting Services (BCS) is the world's largest consulting organization, a business services partner of unmatched breadth and depth. It employs close to 60,000 professionals in 160 countries, with deep experience and expertise in more than 20 industries. BCS offers a broad set of solutions spanning strategic change, customer relationship management, supply-chain operations, financial management, human capital, IT, and business-process outsourcing. BCS features technology from IBM's Center for Business Optimization and provides Component Business Modeling Technology and access to IBM Research through the On Demand Innovation Services initiative. For more information, visit us on the Web at www.ibm.com/bcs.

The IBM Institute for Business Value (IBV) develops leading-edge thinking and practical insights for senior business executives. It provides senior executives with strategic insights and recommendations that address critical business challenges and capitalize on new opportunities, all with an eye on creating value. Comprised of experienced consultants from around the world, the IBV conducts research and analysis in 17 industries and examines 6 functional disciplines. We work in collaboration with industry experts, leading-edge clients, and our own field practitioners to provide practical recommendations built on a foundation of fundamental research. For more information, visit us on the Web at www.ibm.com/iibv.

IBM On Demand Innovation Services (ODIS). The insights and concepts contained in *Tangible Culture* were created through a collaborative effort between IBM Research and Business Consulting Services. IBM offers this same opportunity to combine world-class research and business consulting expertise to clients. IBM's ODIS brings together members of IBM Research and Business Consulting Services to help clients solve problems and create new business opportunities through a wide array of inventions, tools, technology, and expertise. For more information, visit us on the Web at www.ibm.com/research/odis.

Index

Can Two Rights Make a Wrong?
Insights from IBM's Tangible Culture Approach

270

272

Can Two Rights Make a Wrong?
Insights from IBM's Tangible Culture Approach